Editor: Julie Schnittka
Food Editor: Janaan Cunningham
Associate Food Editors: Coleen Martin, Corinne Willkomm
Senior Recipe Editor: Sue A. Jurack
Recipe Editor: Janet Briggs
Associate Editor: Kristine Krueger
Test Kitchen Assistant: Suzanne Hampton
Art Director: Linda Dzik
Food Photography: Scott Anderson
Food Photography Artist: Stephanie Marchese
Associate Food Photography Artist: Vicky Marie Moseley
Photo Studio Manager: Anne Schimmel
Production: Ellen Lloyd, Claudia Wardius
Publisher: Roy Reiman

Taste of Home Books
©1999 Reiman Publications, LLC
5400 S. 60th St., Greendale WI 53129
International Standard Book Number:
0-89821-267-7
Library of Congress Catalog Card Number:
99-75259

PICTURED ON FRONT COVER. Top to bottom: Rice-Stuffed Tomatoes (p. 215),
Taco Salad (p. 300) and Mini Italian Meat Loaves (p. 26).

PICTURED ON BACK COVER. Top to bottom: Monterey Jack Meatballs (p. 32),
Pizza Loaf (p. 32) and Confetti Meat Loaf (p. 34).

To order additional copies of this book or any other Reiman Publications books,
write *Taste of Home* Books, P.O. Box 990, Greendale WI 53129, call toll-free 1-800/558-1013
to order with a credit card or visit our Web site at **www.reimanpub.com**.

Taste of Home

GROUND BEEF COOKBOOK

TASTY...versatile...economical. These simple words perfectly describe ground beef, an indispensable ingredient in kitchens across the country. It's a meaty mainstay that adds flair and flavor to dishes at any meal without breaking your grocery budget.

This "Ground Beef Cookbook" comes to you from "Taste of Home"—North America's most popular cooking magazine. In this new book, you'll find 445 luscious recipes for ground beef, and each one is a tried-and-true family favorite from a home cook just like you!

There aren't any hard-to-find ingredients in these recipes, so they're easy to make. But the flavors in these guaranteed-to-please dishes go beyond the ordinary!

For instance, you'll find tasty, reliable classics like Grandma's Potpie, Simple Sloppy Joes and Deluxe Chili Con Carne. But you'll also uncover deliciously different dishes, such as Reuben Meat Loaf, Stuffed Artichokes and Meatball Cabbage Rolls, which are bound to become favorites with those who gather at your table.

We've included full-color photos of many dishes, so you can see what they look like before you begin cooking. And to make your time in the kitchen easy and fun, we've explained dozens of cooking techniques in a clear step-by-step format and sprinkled in many handy tips you'll appreciate.

To quickly find the mouth-watering recipes as well as the timely tips in this big book, refer to the three helpful indexes beginning on page 312.

So, turn the page and let the cooking begin! Then round up your hungry clan for some delectable down-home dining.

TABLE OF
CONTENTS

PAGE 10   PAGE 120   PAGE 286

GROUND BEEF BASICS

Well-seasoned and new cooks alike will rely on this chapter's practical pointers for purchasing ground beef... choosing the best type of ground beef for different recipes... refrigerating and freezing...properly cooking ground beef...and more.

DEFROSTING FACTS

For best results, defrost ground beef in the refrigerator and use within 1 to 2 days. (Allow 24 hours for a 1- to 1-1/2-inch-thick package to defrost.)

To catch the juices as ground beef thaws, place the frozen package in a shallow dish.

When time is short, you can quickly thaw frozen ground beef in the microwave. Read your manufacturer's directions for suggested defrosting times and cook immediately after thawing.

Completely defrost ground beef before cooking.

PURCHASING POINTERS

● Ground beef comes from a combination of beef cuts. But it may be used as a generic term to describe ground meat from a specific cut of beef, including chuck, round and sirloin. The label on the meat's package may specify the beef cut from which the product is ground. Certain cuts are more lean than others. See "Degrees of Leanness" (below) for more information.

● Look for ground beef that is bright red, avoiding any with brown or gray patches. For highest quality, purchase before the package's "Sell By" date.

● Ground beef is often sold in large, economy sizes. These packages are a bargain because you can use some of the beef now and freeze some for another use. See the tips under "Refrigerating & Freezing Facts" on the next page.

● The meat package should be tightly sealed and free of tears and feel cold.

● To help keep ground beef cold, make the meat department your last stop while in the store and refrigerate the package as soon as you get home. In warm weather, have your grocer pack all refrigerated items together and, if your ride back home is long, consider keeping a cooler in your trunk.

● One pound of ground beef serves 4.

DEGREES OF LEANNESS

In addition to the cut of beef, the package label usually includes a percentage of lean meat to fat (for example, 80% lean). The higher the percentage, the leaner the meat.

The type of ground beef you use is personal preference, but know that leaner cuts contain less fat and will have a dryer texture when cooked.

We've indicated below the three most typical degrees of leanness and some dishes best suited for each kind. (Photos courtesy of the National Cattlemen's Beef Association)

NOT LESS THAN 73% LEAN
(OFTEN LABELED GROUND BEEF)
Use for recipes in which you drain the fat from the cooked meat, such as chili, soups, sloppy joes and pizza.

NOT LESS THAN 80% LEAN
(OFTEN LABELED GROUND CHUCK)
Use in meat loaves, meatballs and hamburgers.

NOT LESS THAN 85% LEAN
(OFTEN LABELED GROUND ROUND OR SIRLOIN)
Use in casseroles and low-fat recipes.

REFRIGERATING & FREEZING FACTS

• Store ground beef in the coldest part of your refrigerator, which is likely your meat compartment. Use it within 1 to 2 days of purchase.

• Uncooked ground beef can be frozen for 2 weeks in its original packaging. To freeze for a longer period, see "Wrapping Ground Beef for Freezing" (below).

• For highest quality, don't refreeze beef that's been frozen and defrosted.

• Shape uncooked hamburger patties into uniform sizes, separate each with double layers of waxed paper, wrap properly and freeze. That way, you can easily remove as many patties as needed at a time.

• For speedy meal preparation, brown several pounds of ground beef (include chopped onion and minced garlic if you like) and freeze in heavy-duty plastic bags or freezer containers for up to 3 months. Refer to the "Ground Beef Yields" chart (below) to package cooked ground beef in appropriate amounts.

GROUND BEEF YIELDS

Use this chart to package and freeze cooked ground beef in appropriate amounts for a variety of recipes.

UNCOOKED WEIGHT	APPROXIMATE COOKED WEIGHT	COOKED CUP AMOUNT (LOOSELY PACKED)
1 pound	12 ounces	2-1/2 to 3 cups
4 pounds	3 pounds	10 to 12 cups

WRAPPING GROUND BEEF FOR FREEZING

To store uncooked ground beef in the freezer for up to 3 months, we suggest you remove it from its original packaging and wrap it in freezer paper, heavy-duty aluminum foil or plastic freezer bags. This will help prevent the ground beef from becoming dried out and getting freezer burn. For easier stacking and quicker thawing, keep each package flat and uniform in size. If your grocer doesn't carry freezer paper or tape, check your local hardware store.

STEP 1
Place ground beef in the center of the paper. Bring edges of the paper together over the beef.

STEP 2
Fold over several times until the last fold is tight against the beef.

STEP 3
Smooth ends of wrap close to the beef, creasing edges to form triangles.

STEP 4
Turn the package over and tightly fold ends on the bottom. Seal ends with freezer tape; label top of package with the contents and date.

FOOD SAFETY REMINDERS

Thoroughly wash all equipment and your hands with hot soapy water before and after handling uncooked ground beef.

Only thaw ground beef in the refrigerator or microwave. Never thaw it at room temperature.

Never eat raw ground beef.

GENERAL COOKING TIPS

Always cook ground beef until it is medium (160°) and no longer pink. The most accurate way to determine doneness in meat loaves, meatballs and thick patties is with an instant-read thermometer.

When browning ground beef, cook over medium heat and stir often to break apart large pieces. Use a colander to drain fat and blot with crumpled paper towel.

APPETIZERS & SNACKS

These hearty starters
fill the bill when your brood
has a hankering for meaty
munchies. They can be
prepared in a flash
(some can even be
made ahead) for
easy entertaining
or late-night snacking.

BEEF 'N' EGG
POCKETS (P. 21)

MINI CRESCENT BURGERS (P. 12)
PARTY MEATBALLS (P. 12)
VEGGIE NACHOS (P. 15)

MINI CRESCENT BURGERS
(Pictured on page 11)

A friend first brought these snacks to a Sunday school party. The original recipe called for pork sausage, but I substituted ground beef with taste-tempting results.
—Pam Buhr
Mexico, Missouri

1 pound ground beef
1 cup (4 ounces) shredded
 cheddar cheese
1 envelope onion soup mix
3 tubes (8 ounces *each*)
 refrigerated crescent rolls

In a skillet, cook beef over medium heat until no longer pink; drain. Stir in the cheese and soup mix; set aside. Separate crescent dough into triangles; cut each triangle in half lengthwise, forming two triangles. Place 1 tablespoon of the beef mixture along the wide end of each triangle. Roll up; place pointed side down 2 in. apart on ungreased baking sheets. Bake at 375° for 15 minutes or until golden brown. **Yield:** 4 dozen.

TIMELY TIP:
Mini Crescent Burgers can be assembled up to 2 hours in advance. Cover with plastic wrap and refrigerate until ready to bake.

PARTY MEATBALLS
(Pictured on page 11)

These meatballs in a sweet, tangy sauce can be made a day in advance and reheated. We usually serve them at birthday parties.
—Irma Schnuelle
Manitowoc, Wisconsin

3/4 cup evaporated milk
1 envelope onion soup mix
1 tablespoon plus 2
 teaspoons Worcestershire
 sauce, *divided*
2 pounds ground beef
2 cups ketchup
1 cup packed brown sugar

In a large bowl, combine the milk, soup mix and 2 teaspoons Worcestershire sauce. Crumble beef over mixture and mix well. With wet hands, shape into 1-in. balls. Place 1 in. apart in ungreased 15-in. x 10-in. x 1-in. baking pans. Bake, uncovered, at 400° for 12 minutes or until meat is no longer pink. Drain on paper towels. Meanwhile, combine the ketchup, brown sugar and remaining Worcestershire sauce in a large saucepan or Dutch oven. Bring to a boil over medium heat. Cook and stir until thickened. Reduce heat; add meatballs. Simmer until heated through, about 15 minutes. **Yield:** about 5 dozen.

CHEESY PIZZA FONDUE

(Pictured below)

1/2 **pound ground beef**
1 **medium onion, chopped**
2 **cans (15 ounces** *each***) pizza sauce**
1-1/2 **teaspoons dried basil** *or* **oregano**
1/4 **teaspoon garlic powder**
2-1/2 **cups (10 ounces) shredded sharp cheddar cheese**
1 **cup (4 ounces) shredded mozzarella cheese**
Breadsticks

In a heavy saucepan, cook beef and onion over medium heat until meat is no longer pink; drain. Stir in the pizza sauce, basil and garlic powder; mix well. Reduce heat to low. Add cheeses; stir until melted. Transfer to a slow cooker or fondue pot and keep warm over low heat. Serve with breadsticks. **Yield:** about 5 cups.

SERVING SUGGESTION:

In addition to breadsticks, serve Cheesy Pizza Fondue with cubes of French or Italian bread.

While I was growing up, I would sit for hours reading cookbooks from cover to cover. I've carried that love of cooking with me through the years. I found this recipe when we lived in Wisconsin.
—Julie Barwick
Mansfield, Ohio

POPPY SEED SQUARES

(Pictured above)

1 pound ground beef
1-1/2 cups finely chopped fresh
    mushrooms
1 medium onion, finely
    chopped
1 can (10-3/4 ounces)
    condensed cream of celery
    or mushroom soup,
    undiluted
1 tablespoon prepared
    horseradish
1 teaspoon salt
1/2 teaspoon pepper
CRUST:
3 cups all-purpose flour
2 tablespoons poppy seeds
3/4 teaspoon baking powder
3/4 teaspoon salt
1 cup shortening
1/2 cup cold water

In a skillet, cook beef, mushrooms and onion over medium heat until meat is no longer pink. Add the soup, horseradish, salt and pepper; mix well. Remove from the heat; set aside. In a bowl, combine the flour, poppy seeds, baking powder and salt. Cut in shortening until the mixture resembles coarse crumbs. Gradually add water, tossing with a fork until a ball forms. Divide dough in half. Roll out one portion into a 15-in. x 10-in. rectangle; transfer to an ungreased 15-in. x 10-in. x 1-in. baking pan. Spoon meat mixture over dough. Roll out the remaining dough into a 15-in. x 10-in. rectangle; place over filling. Bake at 425° for 25 minutes or until golden brown. Cut into small squares. **Yield:** about 10 dozen.

VEGGIE NACHOS

(Pictured on page 11)

1 pound ground beef
2-1/2 quarts water, *divided*
1 envelope taco seasoning
1 medium bunch broccoli,
  broken into small florets
1 medium head cauliflower,
  broken into small florets
1 package (15-1/2 ounces)
  bite-size tortilla chips
1 can (11 ounces) condensed
  nacho cheese soup,
  undiluted
1/2 cup milk
1/4 cup chopped sweet red
  pepper
1 can (2-1/4 ounces) sliced
  ripe olives, drained

In a skillet, cook beef over medium heat until no longer pink; drain. Add 3/4 cup water and taco seasoning. Simmer for 15 minutes. Meanwhile, in a large saucepan, bring remaining water to a boil. Add broccoli and cauliflower. Cook for 2 minutes; drain. Place chips on a large ovenproof serving platter. Top with beef mixture, broccoli and cauliflower. In a bowl, combine soup, milk and red pepper. Drizzle over vegetables. Sprinkle with olives. Bake at 350° for 10 minutes or until heated through. **Yield:** 12-16 servings.

My family loves traditional nachos, but I was looking to offer something a little different. Now they gobble up this version with ground beef, vegetables and a creamy cheese sauce.
—Merry Holthus
Auburn, Nebraska

MUSHROOM BURGER CUPS

18 slices bread, crusts
  removed
1/4 cup butter *or* margarine,
  softened
1 pound ground beef, cooked
  and drained
1 can (10-3/4 ounces)
  condensed cream of
  mushroom soup, undiluted
1 egg, beaten
1/2 cup shredded cheddar
  cheese
1/4 cup chopped onion
1 teaspoon Worcestershire
  sauce
Salt and pepper to taste

Using a biscuit cutter, cut 2-1/2-in. circles from bread slices. Spread butter over one side of each circle. Press circles, buttered side down, into ungreased miniature muffin cups. In a bowl, combine the remaining ingredients; mix well. Spoon into bread cups. Bake at 350° for 35 minutes or until golden brown. **Yield:** 1-1/2 dozen.

For many years on Christmas Eve, a dear friend would bring these hearty snacks to share with us and our six children. Now our grandchildren nibble on these treats as the adults reminisce about past holidays.
—Lucille Metcalfe
Barrie, Ontario

TIMELY TIP:

You can keep a batch of Mushroom Burger Cups on hand for easy entertaining. After baking them, cool, then freeze in an airtight container for up to 3 months. Reheat frozen cups on a baking sheet at 350° for 20 minutes or until heated through.

RANCH MUSHROOM DIP

2 packages (8 ounces *each*) cream cheese, softened
1 carton (8 ounces) French onion dip
1 envelope ranch salad dressing mix
1 pound ground beef
1/4 cup water
1 envelope taco seasoning
1 large tomato, chopped
2 cups (8 ounces) shredded cheddar cheese
1 medium onion, chopped
1 cup sliced fresh mushrooms
1 can (2-1/4 ounces) sliced ripe olives, drained
Tortilla chips

In a small mixing bowl, combine the first three ingredients; beat until smooth. Spread on a 12-in. or 14-in. serving plate. Refrigerate for 1 hour. In a skillet, cook beef over medium heat until no longer pink; drain. Add water and taco seasoning; cook and stir for 5 minutes. Cool completely. Spread over the cream cheese layer. Refrigerate. Just before serving, sprinkle with tomato, cheese, onion, mushrooms and olives. Serve with chips. **Yield:** about 8 cups.

TIMELY TIP:

When making Ranch Mushroom Dip for a party, prepare the cream cheese base and top with the beef mixture; refrigerate up to 24 hours. Before serving, all you need to do is sprinkle with toppings.

ZUCCHINI PIZZA BITES

4 cups shredded unpeeled zucchini, drained and squeezed dry
1 cup (4 ounces) shredded cheddar cheese, *divided*
1 cup (4 ounces) shredded mozzarella cheese, *divided*
2 eggs, beaten
1 pound ground beef
1 medium onion, chopped
1/4 teaspoon salt
1/4 teaspoon garlic salt
1 can (8 ounces) tomato sauce
2 teaspoons dried oregano
1 medium green pepper, julienned
5 medium fresh mushrooms, sliced
1/3 cup grated Parmesan cheese

In a bowl, combine zucchini, 1/2 cup cheddar cheese, 1/2 cup mozzarella cheese and eggs; mix well. Press onto the bottom and up the sides of a greased 15-in. x 10-in. x 1-in. baking pan. Bake at 400° for 20-25 minutes or until crust is set and lightly browned. Meanwhile, in a skillet, cook beef, onion, salt and garlic salt over medium heat until meat is no longer pink; drain. Stir in tomato sauce and oregano; mix well. Spoon over crust. Sprinkle with the green pepper, mushrooms, Parmesan cheese and remaining cheddar and mozzarella. Bake at 400° for 15 minutes or until golden brown. Let stand 5 minutes before cutting. Cut into 2-in. squares. **Yield:** about 3 dozen.

CHEESE MEATBALLS

3 cups (12 ounces) finely
  shredded cheddar cheese
1 cup biscuit/baking mix
1/2 teaspoon salt
1/4 teaspoon pepper
1/4 teaspoon garlic powder
1 pound lean ground beef

In a large bowl, combine the first five ingredients. Crumble beef over mixture and mix well. Shape into 1-in. balls. Place 2 in. apart in greased 15-in. x 10-in. x 1-in baking pans. Bake at 400° for 12-15 minutes or until the meat is no longer pink. **Yield:** about 4 dozen.

I often rely on these rich, cheesy meatballs for party appetizers. Or serve them alongside a tossed salad for a quick meal in minutes.
—Rachel Frost
Tallula, Illinois

EASY EGG ROLLS

1 pound ground beef, cooked
  and drained
1 package (16 ounces)
  coleslaw mix
2 tablespoons soy sauce
1/2 teaspoon garlic powder
1/4 teaspoon ground ginger
Onion powder to taste
2 packages (16 ounces *each*)
  refrigerated egg roll
  wrappers*
1 tablespoon all-purpose
  flour
Vegetable oil for frying

In a bowl, combine the first six ingredients; mix well. Place a heaping tablespoonful of beef mixture in the center of one egg roll wrapper. Fold bottom corner over filling. Fold sides toward center over filling. In a small bowl, combine flour and enough water to make a paste. Moisten top corner with paste; roll up tightly to seal. Repeat. In an electric skillet, heat 1 in. of oil to 375°. Fry egg rolls for 3-5 minutes or until golden brown. **Yield:** 40 egg rolls. ***Editor's Note:** Fill egg roll wrappers one at a time, keeping the others covered until ready to use.

I've always loved egg rolls, but every recipe I saw seemed too complicated. So I decided to start with a packaged coleslaw mix. Now I can make these yummy treats at a moment's notice.
—Samantha Dunn
Leesville, Louisiana

FILLING AND SHAPING EGG ROLLS

STEP 1
Place a rounded tablespoonful of filling in the center of each egg roll wrapper. Fold bottom corner of wrapper over filling.

STEP 2
Fold sides of wrapper over filling. Using a pastry brush, wet the top corner with a paste of flour and water.

STEP 3
Roll up tightly to seal, forming a tube.

MEXICAN FIESTA PLATTER
(Pictured below)

This recipe proves you don't need to fuss to feed an appetizer to a crowd. With generous layers of beef, rice, corn chips and cheese, it's a nacho lover's dream!
—Ann Nace
Perkasie, Pennsylvania

2-1/2 pounds ground beef
  2 cans (16 ounces *each*) kidney beans, rinsed and drained
  2 cans (15 ounces *each*) tomato sauce
  1 envelope chili seasoning
  1 package (10-1/2 ounces) corn chips
  3 cups hot cooked rice
  2 large onions, chopped
  2 cups (8 ounces) shredded Monterey Jack cheese
  1 medium head iceberg lettuce, shredded
  4 medium tomatoes, chopped

1-1/2 cups chopped ripe olives
Hot pepper sauce, optional

In a Dutch oven or large skillet, cook beef over medium heat until no longer pink; drain. Add beans, tomato sauce and chili seasoning; simmer for 30 minutes, stirring occasionally. On two serving platters with sides, layer the corn chips, rice, onions, meat mixture, cheese, lettuce, tomato and olives. Sprinkle with hot sauce if desired. **Yield:** 20-24 servings.

SOUTHWESTERN BEAN DIP
MEXICAN FIESTA PLATTER

SOUTHWESTERN BEAN DIP

(Pictured below left)

2 pounds ground beef
1 tablespoon dried minced onion
1 can (8 ounces) tomato sauce
1 can (16 ounces) kidney beans, rinsed and drained
1 can (15 ounces) chili beans, rinsed and drained
4 cups (16 ounces) shredded cheddar cheese
Tortilla chips

In a skillet, cook beef over medium heat until no longer pink; drain. Transfer to a bowl; add the onion. Mash with a fork until crumbly; set aside. In a blender or food processor, process the tomato sauce and beans until chunky. Add to beef mixture and mix well. Spoon half into a greased 13-in. x 9-in. x 2-in. baking dish; top with half of the cheese. Repeat layers. Bake, uncovered, at 350° for 30 minutes or until cheese is melted. Serve hot with chips. **Yield:** about 9 cups.

SERVING SUGGESTION:

Instead of serving Southwestern Bean Dip with tortilla chips, spread some onto flour tortillas, roll up and dip into salsa or sour cream.

Just by using different types of beans, you can make this dip as spicy as you like it. My family could eat this as a complete meal.
—Jeanne Shear
Sabetha, Kansas

BARBECUE MEATBALLS

2 eggs
1/2 cup evaporated milk
1 cup dry bread crumbs
1 small onion, chopped
1 teaspoon salt
1/2 teaspoon pepper
2 pounds ground beef
SAUCE:
1-1/2 cups water
2/3 cup packed brown sugar
1/4 cup chili sauce
3 tablespoons vinegar
3 tablespoons soy sauce
2 tablespoons ketchup
1-1/2 teaspoons ground ginger
1/4 teaspoon salt
1/8 teaspoon pepper
Dash Worcestershire sauce

In a large bowl, combine the first six ingredients. Crumble beef over mixture and mix well. With wet hands, shape into 1-in. balls. In a large skillet, brown meatballs in small batches over medium heat, turning often. Remove with a slotted spoon and keep warm; drain. In the same pan, combine sauce ingredients. Bring to a boil over medium heat. Reduce heat; add the meatballs. Simmer, uncovered, for 30 minutes or until sauce is absorbed. **Yield:** 6-1/2 dozen.

I came across this recipe while living abroad many years ago. These meatballs are as finger-licking-good as barbecued ribs but easier to eat.
—Dane Harvill
Mosca, Colorado

I've attended many cooking schools and written cookbooks. But I've found few appetizers that people enjoy as much as this. The recipe came from my cousin.
—Jill Daly
Laramie, Wyoming

HEARTY CHEESE DIP

1 pound ground beef
3/4 cup chopped onion
1/2 cup chopped green pepper
1 garlic clove, minced
1 can (8 ounces) tomato sauce
1/4 cup ketchup
1 teaspoon sugar
2-1/4 teaspoons minced fresh oregano *or* 3/4 teaspoon dried oregano
1/4 teaspoon pepper
1 package (8 ounces) cream cheese, softened
1/3 cup grated Parmesan cheese
Tortilla chips

In a skillet, cook beef, onion, green pepper and garlic over medium heat until meat is no longer pink; drain. Stir in the tomato sauce, ketchup, sugar, oregano and pepper. Bring to a boil. Reduce heat; cover and simmer for 10 minutes. Stir in cheeses. Cook and stir until cheese is melted. Serve hot with chips. **Yield:** 4-1/2 cups.

SERVING SUGGESTION:

For a refreshing change from tortilla chips, offer an assortment of vegetable dippers (like baby carrots, celery sticks and bell pepper strips) with Hearty Cheese Dip.

These roll-ups were served at my baby shower luncheon many years ago. Pineapple, ham and bacon give them a tasty tropical twist.
—Ethel Lenters
Sioux Center, Iowa

HAWAIIAN ROLL-UPS

1/2 cup milk
1 teaspoon prepared mustard
3 drops Worcestershire sauce
1 cup soft bread crumbs
2/3 cup packed brown sugar
1 teaspoon dried minced onion
1 teaspoon salt
1/4 teaspoon pepper
1-1/2 pounds lean ground beef
14 thin slices deli ham
14 bacon strips, halved widthwise
1 can (8 ounces) pineapple tidbits, undrained

In a bowl, combine the first eight ingredients. Crumble beef over the mixture and mix well. Spread beef mixture over ham slices. Roll up, starting with a short side. Cut in half widthwise; wrap a bacon slice around each. Secure with toothpicks. Place in an ungreased 13-in. x 9-in. x 2-in. baking dish. Pour pineapple over roll-ups. Cover and bake at 375° for 30 minutes. Uncover; bake 30 minutes longer or until heated through. **Yield:** 28 roll-ups.

HELPFUL HINT:

Keep this in mind when a recipe calls for a certain number of bacon strips. A 1-pound package of thick-sliced bacon has 12 to 16 strips, thin-sliced bacon has 30 to 35 and regular-sliced bacon has 16 to 20.

Beef 'n' Egg Pockets

(Pictured below and on page 10)

2 cups all-purpose flour
2-1/2 teaspoons baking powder
1 teaspoon salt
2/3 cup shortening
2/3 cup milk
FILLING:
1/2 pound ground beef
1 medium onion, chopped
1 medium tomato, seeded and chopped
1 hard-cooked egg, finely chopped
Salt and pepper to taste

In a bowl, combine the flour, baking powder and salt; cut in shortening until the mixture resembles coarse crumbs. Gradually add milk, tossing with a fork until a ball forms. Cover and refrigerate. Meanwhile, in a skillet, cook beef and onion over medium heat until meat is no longer pink; drain. Add the tomato, egg, salt and pepper; mix well. Roll out pastry into an 18-in. x 9-in. rectangle; cut into 3-in. squares. Place a rounded tablespoonful of the filling in the center of each square. Fold in half, forming triangles; crimp edges to seal. Place on greased baking sheets. Bake at 400° for 15-20 minutes or until golden brown. **Yield:** 1-1/2 dozen.

My mother shared the recipe for these hand-held snacks. They disappear whenever I make them. For added flavor, I sometimes toss in sliced fresh mushrooms or chopped green pepper.
—Kathy Vail Canavoy, Prince Edward Island

MEAT LOAVES & MEATBALLS

With such down-home
flavor, it's no surprise
meat loaves and meatballs
are satisfying standbys
in every kitchen.
This chapter's tried-and-true
recipes enliven those country
classics to create newfound
favorites for your family.

SUNDAY
MEAT LOAF (P. 37)

MEATBALLS WITH PEPPER SAUCE (P. 25)
BROCCOLI MEAT ROLL (P. 24)

MAKING MEAT LOAVES AND MEATBALLS

● When shaping meat loaves and meatballs, handle the mixture as little as possible to keep the final product light in texture. Combine all ingredients except the ground beef. Then crumble the beef over the mixture and mix well.

● The mixture for some meatballs can be very moist. If you're having a hard time shaping them, try wetting your hands.

● To get a jump start on dinner's meat loaf, combine all ingredients except the beef in the morning; refrigerate. Stir in the ground beef just before baking.

● Before baking or broiling meatballs, line the baking pan with greased foil. Bake as directed, then simply toss out the foil. There's no greasy pan to clean.

● The acid from tomato products in some

meat loaves can react with metal baking pans, and the cooked food may lose color and taste bitter. So for best results, use the type of baking dish (glass) or pan (metal) specified in the recipe.

● To accurately determine when a meat loaf is properly cooked, insert an instant-read thermometer in the center of meat loaf near the end of the baking time. When it reads 160°, it's done.

● After baking a meat loaf, drain any fat from the pan and let stand for 5 to 10 minutes before slicing.

● Have cooked meatballs handy for last-minute meals or snacks. After baking, cool, then freeze in a single layer on a baking sheet for about 1 hour. Transfer to a heavy-duty resealable plastic bag and freeze. Remove as many as needed.

BROCCOLI MEAT ROLL

(Pictured on page 23)

Most folks are surprised to see broccoli pieces tucked inside this meat loaf. But this versatile vegetable pairs nicely with the ham and cheese.
—Diane Burling
Pingree, North Dakota

    2 **eggs**
  1/4 cup milk
  1/4 cup ketchup
  3/4 cup soft bread crumbs
1-1/2 teaspoons salt, *divided*
  1/4 teaspoon pepper
  1/4 teaspoon dried oregano
    2 pounds lean ground beef
    1 package (10 ounces) frozen chopped broccoli, thawed and drained
    1 package (2-1/2 ounces) thinly sliced deli ham
    3 slices mozzarella cheese, cut in half diagonally

In a large bowl, combine the eggs, milk, ketchup, bread crumbs, 1/2 teaspoon salt, pepper and oregano. Crumble beef over mixture and mix well. On a piece of heavy-duty aluminum foil, pat beef mixture into a 12-in. x 10-in. rectangle. Cover with broccoli to within 1/2 in. of edges. Sprinkle with remaining salt. Top with ham. Roll up, jelly-roll style, starting with a short side and peeling foil away while rolling. Seal seam and ends. Place in a greased 13-in. x 9-in. x 2-in. baking dish. Bake, uncovered, at 350° for 1-1/4 hours or until meat is no longer pink and a meat thermometer reads 160°; drain. Top with cheese slices. Bake 1 minute longer or until the cheese is melted. **Yield:** 8 servings.

MEAT LOAF DINNER

1 egg
1/2 cup seasoned bread crumbs
1/4 cup chopped onion
1/2 teaspoon seasoned salt
  2 pounds lean ground beef
  4 medium potatoes, quartered
1/2 pound fresh *or* frozen cut green beans
  1 can (14-1/2 ounces) stewed tomatoes

In a large bowl, combine the first four ingredients. Crumble beef over mixture and mix well. Shape into a loaf in a greased roasting pan. Arrange potatoes and green beans around loaf. Pour tomatoes over all. Cover and bake at 350° for 2 hours or until the meat is no longer pink and a meat thermometer reads 160°. **Yield:** 8 servings.

SHAPING MEAT LOAF

STEP 1
In a bowl, combine all meat loaf ingredients except ground beef. Crumble beef over mixture. Using a sturdy spoon or your hands, mix until combined.

STEP 2
Carefully form mixture into a loaf shape or pat into a pan.

MEATBALLS WITH PEPPER SAUCE

(Pictured on page 23)

  1 cup evaporated milk
  1 tablespoon Worcestershire sauce
  1 envelope onion soup mix
  2 pounds ground beef
SAUCE:
1/2 pound fresh mushrooms, sliced
1-1/2 cups ketchup
3/4 cup packed brown sugar
3/4 cup water
1/2 cup chopped green pepper
1/2 cup chopped sweet red pepper
  2 tablespoons chopped onion
  1 tablespoon Worcestershire sauce

In a large bowl, combine the first three ingredients. Crumble beef over mixture and mix well. Shape into 1-in. balls. Place on a greased broiler pan. Broil 4-6 in. from the heat for 5-8 minutes or until browned. In a Dutch oven, combine the sauce ingredients. Bring to a boil. Reduce heat; add meatballs. Simmer, uncovered, for 1 hour or until the meat is no longer pink. **Yield:** 60 meatballs.

When in a hurry, I substitute canned potatoes and green beans for the fresh. I like the fact that I can pop this meat loaf into the oven in the late afternoon and forget about it until dinnertime.
—Florence Dollard
Grand Island,
New York

I've found these colorful meatballs keep well in a slow cooker for a no-fuss meal. We enjoy them served over rice or noodles.
—Julie Neal
Green Bay, Wisconsin

This was one of the first recipes I tried as a new wife many years ago. These single-serving loaves have been a super hit ever since. I like to serve them with pasta or mashed potatoes.
—Ruth Grimm
Rochester, Minnesota

MINI ITALIAN MEAT LOAVES

(Pictured below and on front cover)

1 egg
1 cup milk
1/2 cup seasoned bread crumbs
1 teaspoon salt
1-1/2 pounds lean ground beef
3/4 cup Italian tomato sauce
Shredded Parmesan cheese,
  optional
Hot cooked pasta, optional

In a large bowl, combine the first four ingredients. Crumble beef over mixture and mix well. Shape into six loaves. Place in a greased 13-in. x 9-in. x 2-in. baking dish. Bake, uncovered, at 350° for 30 minutes. Spoon tomato sauce over loaves. Bake 15 minutes longer or until meat is no longer pink and a meat thermometer reads 160°. Sprinkle with Parmesan cheese and serve with pasta if desired. **Yield:** 6 servings.

MEXICALI MEAT LOAF

1/2 cup tomato juice
1 egg
3/4 cup quick-cooking oats
2 teaspoons dried minced onion
1 teaspoon chili powder
1 teaspoon salt
1/4 teaspoon pepper
1-1/2 pounds lean ground beef
3 tablespoons butter *or* margarine
3 tablespoons all-purpose flour
1-1/2 cups milk
8 slices process American cheese
1 can (11 ounces) Mexicorn, drained
2 small green peppers, cut into rings

In a large bowl, combine the first seven ingredients. Crumble beef over mixture and mix well. Pat into a greased 9-in. square baking dish. Bake, uncovered, at 350° for 30 minutes. Meanwhile, in a saucepan, melt the butter. Stir in flour until smooth. Gradually add milk. Bring to a boil; cook and stir for 2 minutes. Reduce heat. Stir in cheese until melted. Add corn. Drain meat loaf; top with corn mixture and pepper rings. Bake 30 minutes longer or until meat is no longer pink and a meat thermometer reads 160°. Let stand 10 minutes before slicing. **Yield:** 6 servings.

My mother made this meat loaf quite often when I was growing up. It's still one of my favorites. I like to take it to church dinners, where it's always met with rave reviews.
—Brenda Stueve
Olpe, Kansas

HELPFUL HINT:

If you don't have a 9-inch square baking pan for Mexicali Meat Loaf, you can use an 11- x 7- x 2-inch pan without adjusting the baking time.

SPAGHETTI MEATBALLS

1 pound lean ground beef
1 envelope spaghetti sauce mix

In a bowl, combine beef and sauce mix. Shape into 1-in. balls. Place in a shallow 2-qt. microwave-safe dish. Cover and microwave on high for 3 minutes. Rotate a quarter turn. Microwave 2 minutes longer or until meat is no longer pink; drain. **Yield:** 30 meatballs. **Editor's Note:** This recipe was tested in a 700-watt microwave.

I've been teaching microwave cooking classes for over 10 years. These meatballs always get people excited about using their microwaves. The recipe is easy enough for kids to prepare on their own.
—Diane Czarnowski
Dewey, Arizona

PERFECT PARTNERS:

Add Spaghetti Meatballs to your favorite spaghetti sauce and serve over noodles with garlic bread and salad. They also make a great snack.

GLAZED BEEF LOAF

2/3 cup milk
2 eggs
3 slices bread, cubed
1-1/2 cups (6 ounces) shredded cheddar cheese
2/3 cup shredded carrot
2/3 cup finely chopped onion
2 teaspoons salt
1/4 teaspoon pepper
2 pounds lean ground beef
1/4 cup packed brown sugar
1/4 cup ketchup
1 tablespoon prepared mustard

In a bowl, combine milk, eggs and bread; let stand for 5 minutes. Add the cheese, carrot, onion, salt and pepper. Crumble beef over mixture and mix well. Shape into a loaf in a greased 13-in. x 9-in. x 2-in. baking dish. Bake, uncovered, at 350° for 1-1/4 hours; drain. Combine brown sugar, ketchup and mustard; spread over meat loaf. Bake 15 minutes longer or until the meat is no longer pink and a meat thermometer reads 160°. **Yield:** 8 servings.

PERFECT PARTNERS:

For a quick dessert to serve after enjoying Glazed Beef Loaf, heat canned peach halves. Place in individual bowls; sprinkle with cinnamon and top with whipped cream.

CHEESE-STUFFED LOAF

1/2 cup ketchup
1 egg
3 tablespoons milk
1/2 cup dry bread crumbs
1/2 teaspoon Italian seasoning
1/2 teaspoon salt
1/4 teaspoon pepper
1 pound lean ground beef
2 cups (8 ounces) shredded mozzarella cheese

In a bowl, combine the first seven ingredients; mix well. Crumble beef over mixture and mix well. On a large piece of heavy-duty foil, pat beef mixture into a 10-in. x 6-in. rectangle. Sprinkle with mozzarella cheese to within 1/2 in. of edges. Roll up, jelly-roll style, starting with a short side and peeling away foil while rolling. Seal seam and ends. Place seam side down in a greased 11-in. x 7-in. x 2-in. baking pan. Bake, uncovered, at 350° for 45 minutes or until meat is no longer pink and a meat thermometer reads 160°. Let stand 10 minutes before slicing. **Yield:** 4 servings.

HELPFUL HINT:

An opened bottle of ketchup can be stored in the refrigerator indefinitely. One 16-ounce bottle yields 1-2/3 cups.

SPICED MEATBALLS

1/2 cup cooked rice
2 tablespoons finely chopped green pepper
1 tablespoon finely chopped onion
1 garlic clove, minced
1 teaspoon salt
1/4 teaspoon celery salt
1 pound lean ground beef
2 cups tomato juice
2 tablespoons sugar
1 tablespoon Worcestershire sauce
4 whole cloves
1/2 teaspoon ground cinnamon

In a bowl, combine the first six ingredients. Crumble beef over mixture and mix well. Shape into 1-1/2-in. balls. In a large skillet, combine the tomato juice, sugar, Worcestershire sauce, cloves and cinnamon. Bring to a boil. Reduce heat; add the meatballs. Cover and simmer for 50 minutes or until the meat is no longer pink, stirring occasionally. Discard the cloves before serving. **Yield:** 16 meatballs.

MAKING MEATBALLS OF EQUAL SIZE

There are two common methods for making meatballs of equal size.

One way is to lightly pat mixture into a 1-inch-thick rectangle. Using a knife, cut the rectangle into the number of meatballs needed for recipe. Gently roll each square into a ball.

Or if you have a 1-1/2- or 1-3/4-inch-diameter scoop, scoop the mixture into equal sized portions. Gently roll each into a ball.

APRICOT MEATBALLS

1 egg
1 cup soft bread crumbs
1/4 cup chopped onion
1 teaspoon salt
1 pound ground beef
1/2 cup apricot preserves
1/4 cup barbecue sauce

In a bowl, combine the first four ingredients. Crumble beef over mixture and mix well. Shape into 1-in. balls. In a skillet, brown meatballs in several batches; drain. Transfer to a greased 2-qt. baking dish. Combine preserves and barbecue sauce; pour over meatballs. Cover and bake at 350° for 30 minutes or until the meat is no longer pink. **Yield:** 38 meatballs.

VEGGIE MEATBALL MEDLEY

(Pictured below)

1 egg
1/4 cup dry bread crumbs
1/2 teaspoon salt
1/4 teaspoon pepper
1 pound ground beef
2 cups frozen stir-fry vegetable blend
1 medium onion, chopped
1 can (10-3/4 ounces) condensed cream of mushroom soup, undiluted
1/4 cup soy sauce
1/4 teaspoon garlic powder
Hot cooked rice

In a large bowl, combine the first four ingredients. Crumble beef over mixture and mix well. Shape into 1-1/2-in. balls. In a large non-stick skillet, cook meatballs, vegetables and onion until meatballs are browned; drain. Stir in the soup, soy sauce and garlic powder. Bring to a boil. Reduce heat; simmer, uncovered, for 20 minutes or until the meat is no longer pink, stirring occasionally. Serve over rice. **Yield:** 4 servings.

SIMPLE SUBSTITUTIONS:

Be creative when making Veggie Meatball Medley.
Use any variety of frozen mixed vegetables your family favors.
Or replace the mushroom soup with cream of broccoli, celery or onion.

CURRY MEAT LOAF

2 eggs
1/2 cup soft bread crumbs
1 envelope Italian salad
   dressing mix
1-1/2 pounds lean ground beef
2 cups crushed seasoned
   stuffing
1/2 cup finely chopped celery
1/2 cup mayonnaise
1/2 cup boiling water
1 teaspoon curry powder
1/2 cup apricot jam

In a bowl, combine the first three ingredients. Crumble beef over the mixture and mix well. On a large piece of heavy-duty foil, pat beef mixture into a 10-in. x 8-in. rectangle. Combine the stuffing mix, celery, mayonnaise, water and curry powder; spoon down center of rectangle. Bring long sides over stuffing mixture, peeling foil away while rolling. Seal edge and ends. Place seam side down in a greased 13-in. x 9-in. x 2-in. baking pan. Bake, uncovered, at 350° for 40 minutes. Meanwhile, in a small saucepan, heat jam; stir to break up pieces of fruit. Spread over the meat loaf. Bake 10 minutes longer or until meat is no longer pink and a meat thermometer reads 160°. **Yield:** 6 servings.

Reach for this recipe when you want to serve something a little more special. This zesty meat loaf has a savory curry stuffing and delicious apricot glaze.
—Bernadette Colvin Houston, Texas

BACON NUT MEATBALLS

10 bacon strips, diced
2 eggs
1/3 cup tomato paste
1-1/2 cups soft bread crumbs
1/3 cup minced fresh parsley
2 tablespoons chopped
   slivered almonds
1 tablespoon dried oregano
1 tablespoon salt
1-1/2 teaspoons pepper
2 pounds ground beef
1 pound fresh mushrooms,
   sliced
1 medium onion, chopped
2 cans (10-3/4 ounces *each*)
   condensed cream of
   mushroom soup, undiluted
1 can (10-1/2 ounces) beef
   consomme

In a large skillet, cook bacon. Remove bacon with a slotted spoon; drain on paper towels. Reserve drippings in skillet. In a large bowl, combine the eggs, tomato paste, crumbs, parsley, almonds, oregano, salt, pepper and bacon. Crumble beef over mixture and mix well. Shape into 1-in. balls. Brown meatballs in drippings. Remove with a slotted spoon. Drain, reserving 1 tablespoon drippings. Saute mushrooms and onion in the drippings. Combine soup and consomme; stir into the mushroom mixture until blended. Return meatballs to pan. Bring to a boil; reduce heat. Simmer, uncovered, for 10 minutes or until meat is no longer pink. **Yield:** 60 meatballs.

Almonds provide the crunchy difference in these irresistible meatballs. Making them a day in advance enhances the flavor even more.
—Sue Downes-Williams Lebanon, New Hampshire

TIMELY TIP:

To quickly chop nuts, place 1 cup of large nut pieces in a food processor. Cover and push the pulse button several times until nuts are the size you prefer.

MONTEREY JACK MEATBALLS

(Pictured at right)

1 egg
1/2 cup milk
1 cup soft bread crumbs
2 tablespoons dried minced onion
1/2 teaspoon salt
1/8 teaspoon pepper
1 pound lean ground beef
1 block (4 ounces) Monterey Jack cheese, cut into 20 cubes
2 tablespoons vegetable oil
1 jar (14 ounces) spaghetti sauce
1/2 cup shredded Monterey Jack cheese

In a bowl, combine the first six ingredients. Crumble beef over mixture and mix well. Divide into 20 portions and shape each portion around a cheese cube. In a large skillet, brown meatballs in oil; drain. Add spaghetti sauce. Bring to a boil. Reduce heat; cover and simmer for 10 minutes or until the meat is no longer pink. Sprinkle with cheese. **Yield:** 20 meatballs.

SERVING SUGGESTIONS:

You can enjoy Monterey Jack Meatballs by themselves. But for an even heartier meal, serve with cooked pasta and salad. Or serve on rolls for a deliciously different sandwich.

PIZZA LOAF

(Pictured at right)

2 eggs
1 cup milk
1 cup butter-flavored cracker crumbs (about 25 crackers)
1 medium onion, chopped
1/2 cup grated Parmesan cheese
1-1/2 teaspoons salt
1 teaspoon minced fresh oregano *or* 1/4 teaspoon dried oregano
2 pounds ground beef
1 cup pizza sauce
1 cup (4 ounces) shredded mozzarella cheese
Sliced fresh mushrooms and green pepper, optional

In a bowl, combine the first seven ingredients. Crumble beef over mixture and mix well. Pat into a greased 8-in. square baking pan. Bake, uncovered, at 350° for 50 minutes or until the meat is no longer pink and a meat thermometer reads 160°; drain. Spread pizza sauce over top. Sprinkle with mozzarella cheese. Bake 10 minutes longer or until the cheese is melted. Meanwhile, if desired, saute mushrooms and green pepper in a skillet. Using two large spatulas, carefully transfer meat loaf to a serving platter. Top with the mushrooms and green pepper. **Yield:** 8 servings.

MONTEREY JACK MEATBALLS
PIZZA LOAF
CONFETTI MEAT LOAF (P. 34)

CONFETTI MEAT LOAF

(Pictured on page 33)

(Pictured on page 33)

Carrot, celery, parsley and peppers give great color to this meat loaf, while the unique addition of apple makes it moist.
—Chris Stewart Underwood, Washington

2 eggs
1 tablespoon cider vinegar
1/3 cup dry bread crumbs
5 bacon strips, cooked and crumbled
1/3 cup grated peeled tart apple
1/3 cup grated carrot
1/3 cup *each* chopped celery, onion, and green and sweet red pepper
3 garlic cloves, minced
3 tablespoons dried parsley flakes
1-1/4 teaspoons salt
1 teaspoon pepper
2 pounds ground beef

In a large bowl, combine the eggs, vinegar, bread crumbs, bacon, apple, vegetables, garlic, parsley, salt and pepper. Crumble beef over the mixture and mix well. Pat into a greased 9-in. x 5-in. x 3-in. loaf pan. Bake, uncovered, at 350° for 1 hour or until meat is no longer pink and a meat thermometer reads 160°; drain. Let stand 10 minutes before slicing. **Yield:** 8 servings.

APPLE MEATBALLS

Since first taking these meatballs to various social events a few years ago, I've shared the recipe many times. Sweet apple jelly provides a nice contrast to the tangy barbecue sauce.
—Kay Townsend Obion, Tennessee

1 egg
2 tablespoons butter *or* margarine, melted
1/4 cup crushed seasoned stuffing
1 envelope onion soup mix
2-1/2 pounds lean ground beef
SAUCE:
2 bottles (18 ounces *each*) barbecue sauce
1 jar (12 ounces) apple jelly
1 can (8 ounces) tomato sauce

In a large bowl, combine the first four ingredients. Crumble beef over mixture and mix well. Shape into 1-in. balls. In a skillet, brown the meatballs; drain. Transfer to a greased 3-qt. baking dish. In a large saucepan, combine the sauce ingredients; bring to a boil. Reduce heat; simmer for 10 minutes. Pour over meatballs. Cover and bake at 325° for 30 minutes or until meat is no longer pink. **Yield:** 72 meatballs.

SERVING SUGGESTION:

Use pretzel sticks instead of toothpicks for serving appetizer meatballs. They taste great and reduce waste and mess.

BEEF ONION LOAF

1 can (8 ounces) tomato sauce, *divided*
1 egg
1 can (2.8 ounces) french-fried onions, *divided*
2 teaspoons dried parsley flakes
1 teaspoon salt
1/2 teaspoon pepper
1/4 teaspoon garlic powder
1-1/2 pounds lean ground beef
1 teaspoon sugar
1 can (15 ounces) sliced carrots, drained
1 can (15 ounces) whole potatoes, drained

In a large bowl, combine 1/2 cup of tomato sauce, egg, 1-1/2 cups onions, parsley, salt, pepper and garlic powder. Crumble beef over mixture and mix well. Shape into a loaf in a greased 11-in. x 7-in. x 2-in. baking dish. Bake, uncovered, at 350° for 45 minutes; drain. Combine sugar and remaining tomato sauce; spread over the meat loaf. Sprinkle with remaining onions. Place carrots and potatoes around loaf. Bake, uncovered, 15 minutes more or until meat is no longer pink and a meat thermometer reads 160°. Let stand 10 minutes before slicing. **Yield:** 6 servings.

When I got married, I made sure to copy this recipe from my mother's files. I've been making it for my own family for over 10 years.
—Sarah Bedia
Lake Jackson, Texas

REUNION MEATBALLS

1/2 cup milk
1 egg
1 medium onion, chopped
3 bacon strips, cooked and crumbled
1/2 cup crushed saltines (about 15 crackers)
2 teaspoons salt
1-1/2 pounds lean ground beef
1/2 pound bulk pork sausage
SAUCE:
1 bottle (14 ounces) ketchup
1-1/4 cups water
1/2 cup vinegar
1/2 cup packed brown sugar
1 medium onion, chopped
1 tablespoon chili powder
1-1/2 teaspoons Worcestershire sauce
Dash salt

In a large bowl, combine the first six ingredients. Crumble beef and sausage over mixture and mix well. Shape into 1-1/2-in. balls. Place in a greased 13-in. x 9-in. x 2-in. baking dish. In a saucepan, combine the sauce ingredients. Bring to a boil; reduce heat. Simmer, uncovered, for 5 minutes. Pour over meatballs. Bake, uncovered, at 350° for 1-1/2 hours or until meat is no longer pink. **Yield:** 40 meatballs.

Whenever we attend a picnic or family get-together, people expect me to bring these saucy meatballs and copies of the recipe. My aunt passed the recipe on to me years ago.
—Toni King
London, Kentucky

TIMELY TIP:

To quickly make saltine cracker crumbs with little mess, place the crackers in a large resealable plastic bag. Close the bag and crush with a rolling pin.

MOCK POT ROAST

With potatoes, carrots, peas and onions, this meat loaf is just like a pot roast. Using ground beef instead of another cut of meat makes it an economical meal.
—Marsha Ransom
South Haven, Michigan

1/2 cup ketchup
2 eggs
1 tablespoon prepared horseradish
1/2 cup quick-cooking oats
1 teaspoon ground mustard
1 teaspoon salt
1/4 teaspoon pepper
2 pounds lean ground beef
1 teaspoon steak sauce
8 medium carrots, halved
8 small red potatoes
16 pearl onions
1 package (10 ounces) frozen peas, thawed

In a large bowl, combine the first seven ingredients. Crumble beef over mixture and mix well. Shape into a loaf in a greased 13-in. x 9-in. x 2-in. baking pan. Brush with steak sauce. Arrange carrots, potatoes and onions around loaf. Cover and bake at 375° for 40 minutes. Add peas. Cover and bake 30 minutes longer. Uncover; baste with pan juices. Bake 5 minutes more or until the meat is no longer pink and a meat thermometer reads 160°. **Yield:** 8 servings.

HELPFUL HINT:

To peel pearl onions, immerse them in boiling water for 3 minutes; drain. Pinch at root ends and they'll slide out of their skins.

NACHO MEATBALLS

One day, I didn't have time to cook spaghetti sauce for my meatballs. So I used canned soup as a substitute. This dish has great cheesy flavor and a little crunch from the french-fried onions.
—June Clark
Clarkrange, Tennessee

2 eggs
1/2 cup ketchup
1 large onion, chopped
2/3 cup crushed saltines (about 20 crackers)
1/2 cup mashed potato flakes
1/2 teaspoon garlic powder
1/4 teaspoon pepper
2 pounds lean ground beef
1 can (11 ounces) condensed nacho cheese soup, undiluted
1 can (10-3/4 ounces) condensed cream of mushroom soup, undiluted
1-1/3 cups water
1 can (2.8 ounces) french-fried onions

In a large bowl, combine the first seven ingredients. Crumble beef over mixture; mix well. Shape into 1-1/2-in. balls. Place in a greased 13-in. x 9-in. x 2-in. baking dish. Bake, uncovered, at 350° for 1 hour, turning once; drain. Combine soups and water; pour over meatballs. Sprinkle with onions. Bake 30 minutes longer or until meat is no longer pink. **Yield:** 30 meatballs.

SUNDAY MEAT LOAF

(Pictured above and on page 22)

1 **cup stewed tomatoes, chopped**	
1 **egg, beaten**	
3/4 **cup quick-cooking oats**	
1 **medium carrot, grated**	
1 **celery rib, diced**	
2 **bacon strips, cooked and crumbled**	
1 **envelope onion soup mix**	
2-1/2 **pounds lean ground beef**	
Ketchup	

In a large bowl, combine the first seven ingredients. Crumble beef over mixture and mix well. Shape into a loaf in a greased 13-in. x 9-in. x 2-in. baking dish. Drizzle with ketchup. Bake, uncovered, at 350° for 1-1/2 hours or until meat is no longer pink and a meat thermometer reads 160°. Using two large spatulas, carefully transfer meat loaf to a serving platter. **Yield:** 10 servings.

HELPFUL HINT:

If you open up a whole package of bacon but don't use it all at once, freeze strips in a single layer on a baking sheet. When frozen, transfer to a large resealable plastic bag. Remove and thaw strips as needed.

I try to make special foods for my family. So I add this and that to recipes to create memorable meals. This meat loaf often appears on our Sunday dinner table.
—Patricia Van Houten
Elkton, Kentucky

These meatballs were brought to an office potluck by one of my co-workers. Water chestnuts give these nicely glazed meatballs a wonderful texture.
—Kim Johnston
East Wenatchee,
Washington

SWEET-AND-SOUR MEATBALLS

1 egg
1/2 cup water
1 cup finely chopped water
   chestnuts
1/2 cup soft bread crumbs
2 tablespoons prepared
   horseradish
1 pound ground beef
SAUCE:
1/4 cup sugar
1 tablespoon cornstarch
1/2 cup water
1/4 cup cider vinegar
1/4 cup soy sauce
1 small onion, finely chopped

In a large bowl, combine the first five ingredients. Crumble beef over mixture and mix well. Shape into 1-in. balls. Place in a greased 15-in. x 10-in. x 1-in. baking pan. Bake, uncovered, at 350° for 25 minutes or until meat is no longer pink. Meanwhile, in a saucepan, combine the first five sauce ingredients until smooth; add onion. Bring to a boil; cook and stir for 2 minutes or until thickened. Drain meatballs; top with sauce. **Yield:** 25 meatballs.

HELPFUL HINT:

If you're going to keep prepared horseradish longer than 1 month after opening, spoon tablespoonfuls onto a waxed paper-lined baking sheet. Freeze until solid; transfer to a heavy-duty resealable plastic bag and freeze for 6 months.

This meat loaf was voted the best main dish in a cooking contest between fire stations in San Bernardino, California. I've used the recipe for years and shared it with many friends.
—Peggy Stevens
Rogue River, Oregon

FIREMEN'S MEAT LOAF

1 package (6 ounces) crushed
   corn bread stuffing mix
2 eggs, beaten
1 can (4 ounces) mushroom
   stems and pieces, drained
2 teaspoons garlic powder
3 pounds lean ground beef
2 cans (4 ounces *each*)
   chopped green chilies
1/4 cup shredded cheddar
   cheese
1/4 cup salsa

In a large bowl, prepare the corn bread stuffing according to package directions. Add eggs, mushrooms and garlic powder. Crumble beef over mixture and mix well. Shape into a loaf in a greased 13-in. x 9-in. x 2-in. baking dish. Bake, uncovered, at 350° for 1-1/4 hours; drain. Top with chilies. Cover and bake 20 minutes longer or until meat is no longer pink and a meat thermometer reads 160°. Sprinkle with cheese and top with salsa. Bake, uncovered, for 5-10 minutes or until cheese is melted. **Yield:** 12 servings.

MEATBALLS WITH SPAETZLE

1 egg
1/4 cup milk
1/4 cup dry bread crumbs
1 tablespoon dried parsley flakes
1/2 teaspoon salt
1/4 teaspoon poultry seasoning
Dash pepper
1 pound ground beef
1 can (10-1/2 ounces) condensed beef broth, undiluted
1 can (4 ounces) mushroom stems and pieces, drained
1 medium onion, chopped
1 tablespoon all-purpose flour
1 teaspoon caraway seeds
1 cup (8 ounces) sour cream

HOMEMADE SPAETZLE:
2 cups all-purpose flour
1 teaspoon salt
2 eggs, lightly beaten
1 cup milk
2 quarts water *or* beef broth

In a bowl, combine the first seven ingredients. Crumble beef over the mixture and mix well. Shape into 1-1/2-in. balls. In a skillet, brown meatballs; drain. Add broth, mushrooms and onion. Bring to a boil. Reduce heat; cover and simmer for 30 minutes. Combine the flour, caraway seeds and sour cream until smooth; stir into meatball mixture. Cook over low heat until heated through and thickened, about 10 minutes. Meanwhile, in a bowl, combine the flour, salt, eggs and milk. Let stand for 5 minutes. In a large saucepan, bring water or broth to a rapid boil. Place spaetzle batter in a colander or spaetzle press. Holding over the boiling liquid, press batter through holes of colander. Cook and stir for 5 minutes or until tender; drain. Serve meatballs and sauce over spaetzle. **Yield:** 4 servings.

This is our children's favorite meal...they've dubbed it a "must make" menu item during college vacations. It never fails to earn compliments and recipe requests.
—Paula Karcavich
Lemont, Illinois

MAKING SPAETZLE

STEP 1
In a bowl, combine spaetzle ingredients; let stand 5 minutes. Transfer to a metal colander with large holes or a spaetzle press.

STEP 2
Hold colander over rapidly boiling water or broth. Press with a wooden spoon until batter comes through holes of colander and drops into broth.

STEP 3
Cook until tender, about 5 minutes; drain. Place spaetzle on serving plates and top with meatballs.

GARDEN'S PLENTY MEATBALLS
(Pictured above)

This is a wonderful dish to take to a potluck dinner…you're certain to come home with an empty dish. My sister shared the recipe with me several years ago.
—Lynn Hook
Picton, Ontario

1 egg
1 cup unsweetened applesauce
1 cup soft bread crumbs
2 teaspoons salt
1/4 teaspoon ground allspice
1/4 teaspoon pepper
2 pounds ground beef
1/2 cup all-purpose flour
3 tablespoons vegetable oil
1 can (28 ounces) diced tomatoes, undrained
1 cup sliced carrots
1 small green pepper, chopped
1 small onion, sliced

In a large bowl, combine the first six ingredients. Crumble beef over mixture and mix well. Shape into 1-1/2-in. balls. Roll in flour. In a large skillet, brown meatballs in oil; drain. Transfer to a greased 3-qt. baking dish. Combine the tomatoes, carrots, pepper and onion. Pour over meatballs. Cover and bake at 350° for 45 minutes or until the meat is no longer pink. **Yield:** 8 servings.

PERFECT PARTNERS:

For a complete meal, serve Garden's Plenty Meatballs over hot cooked rice or pasta.

MEAT LOAF WITH SWEET POTATOES

1 can (8 ounces) tomato
  sauce
1 egg
2 cups crushed butter-
  flavored crackers (about 50
  crackers), *divided*
1/2 cup chopped green pepper
1/4 cup chopped onion
2 teaspoons salt
2 pounds lean ground beef
1 can (23 ounces) cut sweet
  potatoes, drained
1/2 cup molasses
4 bacon strips

In a large bowl, combine the tomato sauce, egg, 1/2 cup of cracker
crumbs, green pepper, onion and
salt. Crumble beef over mixture
and mix well. Shape into a loaf in a
greased 13-in. x 9-in. x 2-in. baking dish. Bake, uncovered, at 350°
for 30 minutes; drain. Combine
sweet potatoes and molasses; roll
potatoes in remaining crumbs. Add
potatoes to the pan; place bacon
strips over meat loaf. Bake 30 minutes longer or until the meat is no
longer pink and a meat thermometer reads 160°. **Yield:** 8 servings.

SIMPLE SUBSTITUTION:

*Instead of a 23-ounce can of sweet potatoes, use four
medium fresh sweet potatoes that have been peeled, cut and cooked.*

STUFFED PEPPER LOAF

1 small green pepper
2 eggs
1/2 cup milk
1/2 cup shredded sharp
  cheddar cheese
1/4 cup ketchup
2 teaspoons Worcestershire
  sauce
1/2 cup dry bread crumbs
1 teaspoon salt
1/4 teaspoon pepper
2 pounds lean ground beef

Remove top and seeds from green
pepper; cut in half lengthwise. In a
large saucepan, cook the pepper
halves in boiling water for 5 minutes or until crisp-tender; set aside.
In a large bowl, beat eggs. Add the
next seven ingredients. Crumble
beef over mixture and mix well.
Stuff pepper halves with some of
the meat mixture. Pat half of the
remaining meat mixture into an
ungreased 9-in. x 5-in. x 3-in. loaf
pan. Arrange pepper halves, stuffed
side down, over meat mixture.
Cover with remaining meat mixture. Bake, uncovered, at 350° for
1 hour. Cover and bake 15-20 minutes longer or until meat is no longer pink and a meat thermometer
reads 160°; drain. Let stand 10 minutes before slicing. **Yield:** 8 servings.

CREAMY HERBED MEATBALLS

1 egg
1/4 cup dry bread crumbs
1/4 cup finely chopped onion
1 tablespoon dried basil
1/2 teaspoon salt
1/2 teaspoon pepper
1 pound ground beef
1 can (10-3/4 ounces) condensed cream of mushroom soup, undiluted
1/2 cup water
2 tablespoons minced fresh parsley

In a large bowl, combine the first six ingredients. Crumble beef over mixture and mix well. Shape into 1-1/2-in. balls. In a large skillet, brown meatballs; drain. Stir in the remaining ingredients. Cover and simmer for 20 minutes or until the meat is no longer pink, stirring occasionally. **Yield:** 16 meatballs.

HEARTY MUSHROOM LOAF

1 can (4 ounces) mushroom stems and pieces
1/4 to 1/3 cup milk
1 egg, beaten
1-1/2 teaspoons Worcestershire sauce
1 teaspoon salt
1/2 teaspoon ground mustard
Dash pepper
1-1/2 pounds lean ground beef
1-1/2 cups soft bread crumbs
2 tablespoons ketchup
1 tablespoon corn syrup

Drain mushrooms, reserving liquid; set mushrooms aside. Add enough milk to mushroom liquid to measure 1/2 cup. In a bowl, combine the mushroom liquid, egg, Worcestershire sauce, salt, mustard, pepper and mushrooms. Crumble beef over the mixture; sprinkle bread crumbs over beef and mix well. Shape into a loaf in a greased 13-in. x 9-in. x 2-in. baking dish. Bake, uncovered, at 350° for 1 hour; drain. Combine ketchup and corn syrup; spoon over loaf. Bake 15 minutes longer or until meat is no longer pink and a meat thermometer reads 160°. **Yield:** 6 servings.

PERFECT PARTNERS:

*Roast some potatoes alongside the Hearty Mushroom Loaf.
Cut the potatoes in half, dot with butter and sprinkle with paprika.*

MEAT LOAF STEW

6 medium potatoes, peeled
6 medium onions, peeled
6 medium carrots, halved
   lengthwise
1/2 cup milk
1 egg
1/2 cup dry bread crumbs
1 tablespoon chopped onion
1/2 teaspoon salt
1/2 teaspoon pepper
1-1/2 pounds lean ground beef
1 can (10-3/4 ounces)
   condensed tomato soup,
   undiluted
1-1/3 cups water
1 tablespoon brown sugar
1/2 teaspoon ground mustard

Place potatoes, whole onions and carrots in a soup kettle or Dutch oven. Cover with water. Bring to a boil; boil for 15 minutes. Meanwhile, in a large bowl, combine milk, egg, bread crumbs, chopped onion, salt and pepper. Crumble beef over mixture and mix well. Shape into a loaf in a large roasting pan. Drain vegetables; arrange around loaf. Combine the soup, water, brown sugar and mustard; pour over meat loaf and vegetables. Cover and bake at 350° for 1-1/2 hours or until meat is no longer pink, a meat thermometer reads 160° and vegetables are tender. **Yield:** 6 servings.

HELPFUL HINT:

Chopped onions can be frozen in a heavy-duty resealable plastic bag or airtight container for up to 3 months. Add them frozen to stews and soup. Or thaw and blot dry before sauteing.

COMPANY MEAT LOAF

3/4 cup V-8 juice
2 eggs
1 medium green pepper,
   finely chopped
1 medium onion, finely
   chopped
2/3 cup quick-cooking oats
2/3 cup chopped celery
2/3 cup sliced stuffed olives
1/2 cup cubed cheddar cheese
1-1/2 teaspoons salt
1 teaspoon garlic powder
1/4 teaspoon cayenne pepper
1 pound lean ground beef
1/2 pound lean ground pork
Ketchup

In a large bowl, combine the first 11 ingredients. Crumble beef and pork over mixture and mix well. Shape into a loaf in a greased 11-in. x 7-in. x 2-in. baking dish. Bake, uncovered, at 350° for 1-1/4 hours or until meat is no longer pink and a meat thermometer reads 160°. Drizzle top of loaf with ketchup. **Yield:** 6 servings.

Cooking vegetables along with this meat loaf makes it a flavorful meal-in-one. I've made this recipe many times since receiving it from a friend years ago.
—Marian Tobin
Underhill, Vermont

The combination of ingredients in this moist, tasty meat loaf is unbeatable. When entertaining, it's nice to be able to visit with my company while dinner's in the oven.
—Donna Biel
La Valle, Wisconsin

MINTED MEATBALLS

4 slices bread
1/2 cup water
1 egg, beaten
1 medium onion, finely chopped
1/2 cup minced fresh parsley
1 garlic clove, minced
2 teaspoons dried mint flakes
1 teaspoon salt
1/8 teaspoon pepper
1 pound ground beef
1 cup all-purpose flour
1/2 cup vegetable oil

Dip bread in water; squeeze out excess moisture. Crumble bread into a large bowl. Add the egg, onion, parsley, garlic, mint, salt and pepper; mix well. Crumble beef over mixture and mix well. Shape into 1-in. balls. Roll in flour. In a large skillet, cook meatballs in oil over medium heat for 15 minutes or until no longer pink. **Yield:** 40 meatballs.

HELPFUL HINT:

If you find you don't often use certain dried herbs (such as dried mint flakes), it's best to refrigerate them after opening. The more airtight the container, the longer they will keep their flavor.

VEGETABLE PINWHEEL ROLL

1 medium onion, chopped
2 tablespoons butter *or* margarine
1 package (10 ounces) frozen mixed vegetables
1 egg
1 tablespoon prepared mustard
2 teaspoons Worcestershire sauce
1 teaspoon salt
1/4 teaspoon pepper
2 pounds lean ground beef
1 cup shredded process American cheese
4 bacon strips, halved

In a skillet, saute onion in butter. Add vegetables. Cover and cook for 5 minutes or until tender; drain and set aside. In a bowl, combine the egg, mustard, Worcestershire sauce, salt and pepper. Crumble beef over mixture and mix well. On a large piece of heavy-duty foil, pat beef mixture into a 16-in. x 10-in. rectangle. Cover with vegetable mixture to within 1 in. of edges. Sprinkle with cheese. Roll up, jelly-roll style, starting with a short side and peeling away foil while rolling. Seal seam and ends. Place seam side down in a greased 13-in. x 9-in. x 2-in. baking dish. Top loaf with bacon strips. Bake, uncovered, at 350° for 1 hour or until meat is no longer pink and a meat thermometer reads 160°; drain. **Yield:** 8 servings.

SIMPLE SUBSTITUTION:

You can easily use whatever vegetable or combination of vegetables your family enjoys in Vegetable Pinwheel Roll.

LASAGNA LOAF

(Pictured above)

1/2 cup tomato juice
2 eggs
3/4 cup dry bread crumbs
2 tablespoons dried parsley
flakes
1 garlic clove, minced
1/2 teaspoon dried oregano
1/2 teaspoon salt
1/2 teaspoon pepper
1 pound lean ground beef
FILLING:
1 carton (15 ounces) ricotta
cheese
1 cup cubed mozzarella
cheese
1/2 cup diced fully cooked ham
1 teaspoon dried parsley
flakes

TOPPING:
2 medium tomatoes, seeded
and diced
4 green onions, chopped
1/4 cup sliced ripe olives

In a large bowl, combine the first eight ingredients. Crumble beef over mixture and mix well. Press into an ungreased 9-in. x 5-in. x 3-in. loaf pan. In a bowl, combine the filling ingredients. Spread over loaf. Bake, uncovered, at 350° for 1 hour. Sprinkle with topping ingredients. Bake 15 minutes longer or until meat is no longer pink and a meat thermometer reads 160°. **Yield:** 4-6 servings.

This recipe is a product of three different recipes and a little imagination. Even the picky eaters in my family enjoy slices of this meat loaf. It tastes like lasagna without the noodles.
—Bobbie Croker Omaha, Nebraska

SWEETHEART MEAT LOAF

2 medium carrots, cut into chunks
2 celery ribs, cut into chunks
1 small green pepper, cut into chunks
1/4 cup chopped onion
2 eggs
2 tablespoons prepared mustard
2 tablespoons ketchup
1 cup crushed saltines (about 30 crackers)
2 pounds ground beef
1 pound ground turkey
Additional ketchup

In a blender or food processor, combine the carrots, celery, green pepper and onion; cover and process until pureed. In a large bowl, combine the eggs, mustard, ketchup, cracker crumbs and vegetable puree. Crumble meat over the mixture and mix well. On a greased broiler pan, pat meat mixture into a heart shape, about 1 in. thick. Cover and bake at 350° for 40 minutes. Uncover; top with additional ketchup. Bake 20 minutes longer or until the meat is no longer pink. **Yield:** 12 servings.

MAKING HEART-SHAPED MEAT LOAF

Gently form meat mixture into a 1-inch-thick heart shape on a greased broiler pan.

MEATBALLS WITH MUSHROOM SAUCE

1/4 cup evaporated milk
1/4 cup dry bread crumbs
1/2 teaspoon salt
1/4 teaspoon pepper
1-1/2 pounds ground beef
SAUCE:
1 can (10-3/4 ounces) condensed cream of mushroom soup, undiluted
2/3 cup evaporated milk
2/3 cup water

In a large bowl, combine the first four ingredients. Crumble beef over mixture and mix well. Shape into 1-1/2-in. balls. In a large oven-proof skillet, brown meatballs; drain. Combine sauce ingredients; pour over meatballs. Bake, uncovered, at 350° for 30 minutes or until meat is no longer pink. **Yield:** 30 meatballs.

HELPFUL HINT:

Leftover evaporated milk should be transferred from the can to another container for storage. If stored in a covered container in the refrigerator, it can be used safely within 3 days.

CRANBERRY MEAT LOAF

3 eggs
1/2 cup beef broth
1-1/2 cups soft bread cubes
1 envelope onion soup mix
3 pounds lean ground beef
SAUCE:
1 can (16 ounces)
  whole-berry cranberry
  sauce
1 can (14 ounces) sauerkraut,
  rinsed, drained and
  chopped
1 bottle (12 ounces) chili
  sauce
1-1/3 cups water
1/2 cup packed brown sugar

In a bowl, combine the first four ingredients. Crumble beef over mixture and mix well. Shape into a loaf in a greased 13-in. x 9-in. x 2-in. baking dish. In a saucepan, combine sauce ingredients. Bring to a boil; reduce heat. Simmer, uncovered, for 5 minutes. Pour over meat loaf. Bake, uncovered, at 350° for 1-1/4 hours or until the meat is no longer pink and a meat thermometer reads 160°. **Yield:** 12 servings.

HELPFUL HINT:

To make canned sauerkraut less salty, place it in a sieve and rinse with cold water. Drain well before using.

AUTUMN MEATBALLS

2 eggs
1 cup dry bread crumbs
1 cup grated peeled tart
  apple
1/4 cup shredded cheddar
  cheese
1 garlic clove, minced
1 teaspoon salt
1/4 teaspoon pepper
1/4 teaspoon ground nutmeg
1 pound lean ground beef
1-3/4 cups tomato juice
3/4 cup ketchup
1/2 cup chopped celery
1/2 teaspoon Worcestershire
  sauce

In a bowl, combine the first eight ingredients. Crumble beef over mixture and mix well. Shape into 1-1/2-in. balls. Place in a greased 2-qt. baking dish. Combine the tomato juice, ketchup, celery and Worcestershire sauce; pour over meatballs. Cover and bake at 350° for 1 hour or until meat is no longer pink. **Yield:** 20 meatballs.

CORNY MEAT ROLL

(Pictured above)

This mild-flavored meat loaf features a fresh corn and parsley filling. It slices nicely into colorful swirls.
—Velma Bonds Worth, West Virginia

1-1/2 **pounds lean ground beef**
    1 **teaspoon salt**
    1/4 **teaspoon pepper**
FILLING:
1-1/2 **cups fresh *or* frozen corn**
    1 **cup soft bread crumbs**
    1 **egg, beaten**
    1/4 **cup minced fresh parsley**
    1/2 **teaspoon salt**
    1/8 **teaspoon pepper**

In a bowl, combine beef, salt and pepper. On a piece of heavy-duty foil, pat beef mixture into a 12-in. x 10-in. rectangle. Combine the filling ingredients. Spoon over beef to within 1 in. of edges. Roll up, jelly-roll style, starting with a short side and peeling foil away while rolling. Seal seam and ends. Place seam side down in a greased 13-in. x 9-in. x 2-in. baking dish. Bake, uncovered, at 350° for 1 hour or until meat is no longer pink and a meat thermometer reads 160°. Using two large spatulas, carefully transfer meat loaf to a serving platter. **Yield:** 6 servings.

MAKING A STUFFED MEAT LOAF

STEP 1
Shape meat mixture into a 12-inch x 10-inch rectangle on a piece of heavy-duty foil. Spoon filling to within 1 inch of edges.

STEP 2
Beginning with a short side, roll up meat mixture, peeling foil away as you roll. Seal seam and edges of roll.

CRISPY MEATBALLS

1 egg
1/4 cup ketchup
1 cup crisp rice cereal
1 tablespoon brown sugar
1 tablespoon finely chopped onion
1 teaspoon salt
1/2 teaspoon ground mustard
1/4 teaspoon pepper
1/8 teaspoon ground nutmeg
1 pound ground beef

In a large bowl, combine the first nine ingredients. Crumble beef over mixture and mix well. Shape into 1-1/2-in. balls and place in a greased 11-in. x 7-in. x 2-in. baking dish. Bake, uncovered, at 400° for 30 minutes or until the meat is no longer pink. **Yield:** 16 meatballs.

SIMPLE SUBSTITUTION:

If a recipe calls for nutmeg and you don't have any on hand, substitute ground ginger or mace.

RIBBON MEAT LOAF

1 egg yolk
1 cup milk
3 slices bread, torn into small pieces
1/4 cup finely chopped onion
1 teaspoon Worcestershire sauce
1/4 teaspoon *each* celery salt, garlic salt, ground mustard, rubbed sage and pepper
1-1/2 pounds lean ground beef
FILLING:
1 cup (4 ounces) shredded cheddar cheese
2 slices bread, torn into small pieces
1 egg white, beaten
1 tablespoon water

In a large bowl, combine the first three ingredients. Let stand for 5 minutes. Add the onion, Worcestershire sauce and seasonings. Crumble beef over mixture and mix well. Pat half into a greased 9-in. x 5-in. x 3-in. loaf pan. Combine filling ingredients; spoon over meat mixture. Pat remaining meat mixture over filling. Bake, uncovered, at 350° for 1-1/2 hours or until meat is no longer pink and a meat thermometer reads 160°; drain. Let stand for 10 minutes before slicing. **Yield:** 6 servings.

HELPFUL HINT:

If you don't own an egg separator, crack an egg into a funnel over a bowl. The yolk will stay in the funnel and the white will pass through.

TERIYAKI MEATBALLS

2 cans (8 ounces *each*) pineapple chunks
1 medium onion, finely chopped
1/4 cup finely chopped sweet yellow pepper
1/4 cup finely chopped sweet red pepper
1/2 cup dry bread crumbs
1/2 teaspoon ground ginger
1/4 teaspoon salt
1 pound lean ground beef
SAUCE:
1/4 cup vegetable oil
1/4 cup soy sauce
3 tablespoons honey
2 tablespoons vinegar
3/4 teaspoon garlic powder
1/2 teaspoon ground ginger

Drain pineapple, reserving 1/4 cup juice (discard remaining juice or save for another use); set pineapple aside. In a bowl, combine the onion, peppers, bread crumbs, ginger, salt and reserved pineapple juice. Crumble beef over mixture and mix well. Shape into 1-in. balls. Place the sauce ingredients in a blender; cover and process for 1 minute. Place 2 tablespoons of sauce in a greased 13-in. x 9-in. x 2-in. baking dish. Add meatballs. Pour remaining sauce over meatballs. Bake, uncovered, at 400° for 20 minutes or until meat is no longer pink. Place one pineapple chunk on each meatball; secure with a toothpick. **Yield:** 42 meatballs.

HELPFUL HINT:

Save the juice from canned pineapple by pouring into ice cube trays and freezing. When solid, transfer the cubes to a freezer bag. When a recipe calls for 1 to 2 tablespoons of pineapple juice, thaw 1 to 2 cubes and use as directed.

FRENCH ONION MEAT LOAF

3 eggs
1 can (10-1/2 ounces) condensed French onion soup, undiluted
1 package (6 ounces) crushed beef-flavored stuffing mix
2 pounds lean ground beef

In a large bowl, combine the eggs, soup and contents of stuffing package; mix well. Crumble beef over mixture and mix well. Shape into a loaf in a greased 13-in. x 9-in. x 2-in. baking pan. Bake, uncovered, at 350° for 1 hour or until meat is no longer pink and a meat thermometer reads 160°. Let stand 10 minutes before slicing. **Yield:** 8 servings.

TIMELY TIP:

If cooking for two, shape the meat mixture for the French Onion Meat Loaf into two smaller loaves instead of one large one. Bake for about 45 minutes or until meat is no longer pink and a meat thermometer reads 160°. Enjoy one loaf and freeze the other to reheat later.

MICROWAVE MEAT LOAF

1/3 cup milk
1 egg, beaten
1 tablespoon ketchup
1 medium onion, chopped
3 tablespoons old-fashioned oats
1 tablespoon minced fresh parsley
1/2 teaspoon *each* salt, dried marjoram and dried thyme
Dash pepper
1-1/2 pounds lean ground beef
1 tablespoon soy sauce
1 tablespoon honey

In a large bowl, combine the first five ingredients. Add seasonings; mix well. Crumble beef over mixture and mix well. Pat into a 9-in. x 5-in. x 3-in. microwave-safe dish. Combine the soy sauce and honey; spread over loaf. Cover and microwave on high for 30 minutes or until meat is no longer pink and a meat thermometer reads 160°, turning dish a quarter turn every 10 minutes; drain. Let stand 5 minutes before slicing. **Yield:** 6 servings. **Editor's Note:** This recipe was tested in a 700-watt microwave.

Because this meat loaf cooks in the microwave, it's easy to prepare after a day's work. My whole family finds each succulent slice tasty and nourishing.
—Suzanne Ritchot
Ste. Anne, Manitoba

SIMPLE SUBSTITUTIONS:

You can easily vary the flavor of Microwave Meat Loaf by replacing the oats with cornmeal or wheat bran. Or if you want to add a little more zing, use chili sauce in place of the ketchup and mustard instead of soy sauce.

REUBEN LOAF

1 egg
1 tablespoon ketchup
2 cups soft bread crumbs
1 teaspoon salt
2 pounds lean ground beef
4 ounces deli pastrami, chopped
1 can (8 ounces) sauerkraut, rinsed and drained
1 cup (4 ounces) shredded Swiss cheese
1/4 cup sour cream
1 tablespoon prepared mustard

In a large bowl, combine the first four ingredients. Crumble beef over the mixture and mix well; set aside. In a bowl, combine pastrami, sauerkraut, cheese, sour cream and mustard. Press a third of the beef mixture into a greased 9-in. x 5-in. x 3-in. loaf pan. Top with half of the pastrami mixture. Repeat layers. Top with remaining beef mixture. Cover and bake at 350° for 1 hour or until meat is no longer pink and a meat thermometer reads 160°; drain. Let stand 10 minutes before slicing. **Yield:** 8 servings.

This meat loaf really captures the wonderful flavor of reuben sandwiches. When my family tires of regular meat loaf, I turn to this recipe from my niece.
—Darlene Loudon
Creston, Iowa

TANGY MEAT LOAF

1 can (8 ounces) crushed pineapple, undrained
4 egg whites, beaten
1/4 cup ketchup
2 cups soft bread crumbs
1 medium onion, chopped
1 teaspoon salt
1/2 teaspoon prepared horseradish
2 pounds lean ground beef
GLAZE:
1/4 cup orange juice
3 tablespoons ketchup

In a large bowl, combine the first seven ingredients. Crumble beef over mixture and mix well. Pat into a greased 9-in. x 5-in. x 3-in. loaf pan. Cover and bake at 350° for 1 hour; drain. Combine glaze ingredients; pour over loaf. Bake, uncovered, 15 minutes longer or until the meat is no longer pink and a meat thermometer reads 160°. **Yield:** 8 servings.

HELPFUL HINT:

To make soft bread crumbs, tear several slices of bread into 1-inch pieces. Place in a food processor or blender; cover and push the pulse button several times. One slice of bread yields about 1/2 cup of crumbs.

TEX-MEX MEAT LOAF

1 can (15 ounces) tomato sauce, *divided*
1/3 cup crushed tortilla chips
1/4 cup chopped onion
2 tablespoons chopped green pepper
1 envelope taco seasoning
1 pound ground beef

In a large bowl, combine 1 cup of tomato sauce, chips, onion, green pepper and taco seasoning. Crumble beef over mixture and mix well. Pat into a greased 9-in. x 5-in. x 3-in. loaf pan. Bake, uncovered, at 350° for 1 hour or until the meat is no longer pink and a meat thermometer reads 160°; drain. Heat the remaining tomato sauce. Slice meat loaf; top with tomato sauce. **Yield:** 4 servings.

SERVING SUGGESTION:

Put leftover slices of Tex-Mex Meat Loaf on flour tortillas; top with cheese, tomatoes, lettuce or any other taco toppings. Roll up and dip in salsa or sour cream.

POTATO-TOPPED CHILI LOAF

(Pictured above)

1 egg
3 tablespoons milk
3/4 cup finely chopped onion
1 can (4 ounces) chopped green chilies
1/3 cup crushed saltines (about 10 crackers)
4-1/2 teaspoons chili powder
3/4 teaspoon salt
1-1/2 pounds lean ground beef
3 cups hot mashed potatoes (prepared with milk and butter)
1 can (11 ounces) Mexicorn, drained
1/4 cup thinly sliced green onions
1/2 to 1 cup shredded Mexican-cheese blend *or* cheddar cheese

In a bowl, combine the first seven ingredients. Crumble beef over the mixture and mix well. Pat into a greased 9-in. square baking dish. Bake, uncovered, at 375° for 30 minutes or until meat is no longer pink and a meat thermometer reads 160°. In a bowl, combine the potatoes, corn and onions; mix well. Spread over meat loaf. Sprinkle with cheese. Broil 6 in. from the heat for 3-5 minutes or until lightly browned. **Yield:** 6 servings.

You'll come to rely on this hearty dish featuring a flavorful meat loaf topped with fluffy mashed potatoes. Add a green salad and you have a complete meal.
—Judy Martinez
Weaverville, California

SLOW COOKER SPECIALTIES

You don't need to
fuss in the kitchen
all day to obtain
"from-scratch" flavor.
Your family will savor every
bite of these slow-cooked
creations…and you'll
appreciate each dish's
fix-and-forget convenience.

EASY-DOES-IT SPAGHETTI (P. 67)

HAMBURGER SUPPER (P. 57)
BEEFY VEGETABLE SOUP (P. 57)

SLOW COOKER SUGGESTIONS

● Browning and draining ground beef before adding to the slow cooker will reduce the amount of fat in the finished dish.

● It's best to follow the cooking temperature and time suggested in each recipe. But generally, figure that 1 hour on high equals about 2 hours on low.

● Avoid lifting the slow cooker's lid, unless a recipe instructs you to. Each time the cover is removed, heat and steam escape, and it can take up to 30 minutes to regain them. Removing the lid too many times may result in longer cooking times.

● To convert a stovetop recipe for use in the slow cooker, you'll likely need to decrease the amount of liquid called for. Read your manufacturer's directions for guidelines on converting conventional recipes to slow cooking.

RECIPE COOKING TIMES

You likely rely on your slow cooker for times when you'll be away from the kitchen all day. But this time-saving tool is also perfect for foods that need less than a full day to cook. Use the guide below to select suitable recipes to fit your daily schedule.

4 TO 6 HOURS

Beef and Barley (page 63)
Beefy Au Gratin Potatoes (page 70)
Colorful Veggie Medley (page 69)
Easy Chow Mein (page 58)
Easy-Does-It Spaghetti (page 67)
Hamburger Supper (page 57)
Hearty Wild Rice (page 63)

No-Bean Chili (page 73)
Pizza in a Pot (page 70)
Poor Man's Steak (page 66)
Slow Cooker Cheese Dip (page 66)
Texas Stew (page 72)
Tomato Hamburger Soup (page 64)
Two-Pot Dinner (page 60)

6 TO 8 HOURS

All-Day Meatballs (page 62)
Chili Mac (page 61)
Creamy Beef and Pasta (page 60)
Enchilada Casserole (page 62)

Ground Beef Stew (page 59)
Hobo Stew (page 66)
Slow 'n' Easy Chili (page 65)
Two-Step Stroganoff (page 65)

8 TO 10 HOURS

Beefy Vegetable Soup (page 57)
Confetti Casserole (page 73)
Meatball Cabbage Rolls (page 68)
Meaty Tomato Soup (page 59)

Savory Winter Soup (page 71)
Slow-Cooked Spaghetti and Meatballs (page 69)
Taco Meat Loaf (page 62)

HAMBURGER SUPPER

(Pictured on page 55)

1 pound ground beef
1/4 cup hot water
3 small potatoes, peeled and diced
1 medium onion, chopped
1 can (15 ounces) peas and carrots, drained
1 can (14-1/2 ounces) diced tomatoes, undrained
1 tablespoon sugar
1/2 teaspoon salt
1/4 teaspoon pepper

Shape beef into four patties. In a skillet, cook patties over medium heat until no longer pink. Transfer to a slow cooker. Add water to skillet and stir to loosen browned bits from pan. Pour into slow cooker. Add the remaining ingredients. Cover and cook on low for 4-6 hours or until potatoes are tender. **Yield:** 4 servings.

SIMPLE SUBSTITUTION:

If you prefer, use 1-1/2 cups frozen mixed vegetables for the canned peas and carrots in the Hamburger Supper recipe.

My mother-in-law shared this recipe with me when my husband and I were first married. Over the past 50 years, I've relied on this meal in one more times than I can count.
—Dolores Hickenbottom Greensburg, Pennsylvania

BEEFY VEGETABLE SOUP

(Pictured on page 55)

1 pound ground beef
1 medium onion, chopped
1 garlic clove, minced
2 cans (8 ounces *each*) tomato sauce
2 cans (16 ounces *each*) kidney beans, rinsed and drained, optional
1 package (10 ounces) frozen corn
1 cup shredded carrots
1 cup chopped green pepper
1 cup chopped sweet red pepper
1 cup chopped fresh tomato
1 tablespoon chili powder
1/2 teaspoon dried basil
1/2 teaspoon salt

1/4 teaspoon pepper
Shredded cheddar cheese, sour cream and tortilla chips, optional

In a skillet, cook beef, onion and the garlic over medium heat until the meat is no longer pink; drain. Transfer to a slow cooker. Add the tomato sauce, beans if desired, vegetables and seasonings; mix well. Cover and cook on low for 8 hours or until thick and bubbly, stirring occasionally. Serve with cheese, sour cream and chips if desired. **Yield:** 8-10 servings (about 2-1/2 quarts).

I adapted this recipe from one I saw in a cookbook in an effort to add more vegetables to our diet. Our two young sons eat this up without hesitation.
—Teresa King Chambersburg, Pennsylvania

TIMELY TIP:

Freeze Beefy Vegetable Soup in serving-size containers for quick, no-fuss lunches.

EASY CHOW MEIN

(Pictured above)

Our daughter welcomed me home from a hospital stay some years ago with this Oriental dish and a copy of the recipe. Now that I'm a widow, I freeze leftovers for fast future meals.
—Kay Bade Mitchell, South Dakota

1 pound ground beef
1 medium onion, chopped
1 bunch celery, sliced
2 cans (14 ounces *each*) Chinese vegetables, drained
2 envelopes brown gravy mix
2 tablespoons soy sauce
Hot cooked rice

In a skillet, cook beef and onion over medium heat until meat is no longer pink; drain. Transfer to a slow cooker. Stir in the celery, Chinese vegetables, gravy mixes and soy sauce. Cover and cook on low for 4 hours or until celery is tender, stirring occasionally. Serve over rice. **Yield:** 8 servings.

HELPFUL HINT:

Purchase celery with crisp, firm and unblemished ribs and fresh green leaves. Refrigerate celery in a plastic bag for up to 2 weeks. Wash and trim the base and leaves just before using.

GROUND BEEF STEW

2 large potatoes, sliced
2 medium carrots, sliced
1 can (15 ounces) peas, drained
3 medium onions, sliced
2 celery ribs, sliced
1-1/2 pounds ground beef, cooked and drained
1 can (10-3/4 ounces) condensed tomato soup, undiluted
1-1/3 cups water

In a slow cooker, layer the first six ingredients in the order listed. Combine soup and water; mix well. Pour over beef. Cover and cook on low for 6-8 hours or until vegetables are tender. **Yield:** 6 servings.

TIMELY TIP:

Bake some corn bread muffins and freeze them alongside serving-size portions of Ground Beef Stew. Pull both packages out of the freezer when you need a quick lunch.

Sinc... it's ... home knowing I have a very delicious meal simmering in the slow cooker. I like to serve generous helpings of this stew with corn bread muffins.
—Mary Jo Walker
Jasper, Tennessee

MEATY TOMATO SOUP

1 can (28 ounces) diced tomatoes, undrained
2 cans (8 ounces *each*) tomato sauce
2 cups water
1/2 pound ground beef, cooked and drained
1/2 pound bulk pork sausage, cooked and drained
2 tablespoons dried minced onion
2 chicken bouillon cubes
3/4 teaspoon garlic salt

3/4 cup uncooked elbow macaroni
Shredded cheddar cheese, optional

In a slow cooker, combine the first eight ingredients; mix well. Cover and cook on low for 8 hours. Add macaroni and mix well. Cover and cook 15 minutes longer or until macaroni is tender. Garnish with cheese if desired. **Yield:** 8-10 servings (2-1/4 quarts).

SIMPLE SUBSTITUTIONS:

If you're out of elbow macaroni, you can use rotini or small shell pasta in Meaty Tomato Soup. For a true Italian twist, replace the pork sausage with Italian sausage.

As an elementary school librarian and church choir director, I've come to rely on— and thoroughly enjoy— slow-cooked meals. A sorority sister shared this recipe with me.
—Ann Bost
Elkhart, Texas

TWO-POT DINNER

1 pound sliced bacon, cut into 2-inch pieces
1 large onion, chopped
1 pound ground beef
1 can (31 ounces) pork and beans
1 can (30 ounces) kidney beans, rinsed and drained
1 can (15 ounces) great northern beans, rinsed and drained
1 cup ketchup
1/3 cup packed brown sugar
3 tablespoons vinegar
1 tablespoon liquid smoke, optional

In a skillet, cook bacon over medium heat until crisp; remove with a slotted spoon to a slow cooker. Reserve 2 tablespoons drippings in the pan. Saute onion in drippings until browned; remove with a slotted spoon to slow cooker. In the same skillet, cook beef until no longer pink; drain and transfer to slow cooker. Add the remaining ingredients; mix well. Cover and cook on low for 4 hours or until heated through. **Yield:** 10 servings.

TIMELY TIP:

When a recipe instructs you to cook diced bacon, cut the bacon with a kitchen shears directly into the skillet. It's faster than chopping with a knife, and there's little mess.

CREAMY BEEF AND PASTA

2 cans (10-3/4 ounces *each*) condensed cream of mushroom soup, undiluted
2 cups (8 ounces) shredded cheddar *or* mozzarella cheese
1 pound ground beef, cooked and drained
2 cups uncooked small pasta
2 cups milk
1/2 to 1 teaspoon onion powder
1/2 to 1 teaspoon salt
1/4 to 1/2 teaspoon pepper

In a slow cooker, combine all ingredients; mix well. Cover and cook on low for 6 hours or until pasta is tender. **Yield:** 4-6 servings.

CHILI MAC

(Pictured below)

1 pound ground beef, cooked and drained
2 cans (15 ounces *each*) hot chili beans, undrained
2 large green peppers, chopped
1 large onion, chopped
4 celery ribs, chopped
1 can (8 ounces) tomato sauce
1 envelope chili seasoning
2 garlic cloves, minced
1 package (7 ounces) elbow macaroni, cooked and drained
Salt and pepper to taste

In a slow cooker, combine the first eight ingredients; mix well. Cover and cook on low for 6 hours or until heated through. Stir in macaroni; mix well. Season with salt and pepper. **Yield:** 12 servings.

PREPARING PEPPERS FOR CHOPPING

Cut peppers in half, starting at stem end. Using a small paring knife, remove stem, seeds and membrane from each half.

This recipe has appeared on my menus once a month for more than 40 years...it's never failed to please. I've also turned it into a soup by adding a can of beef broth.
—Marie Posavec
Berwyn, Illinois

ENCHILADA CASSEROLE

1 pound ground beef
2 cans (10 ounces *each*) enchilada sauce
1 can (10-3/4 ounces) condensed cream of onion soup, undiluted
1/4 teaspoon salt
1 package (8-1/2 ounces) flour tortillas, torn
3 cups (12 ounces) shredded cheddar cheese

In a skillet, cook beef over medium heat until no longer pink; drain. Stir in the enchilada sauce, soup and salt. In a slow cooker, layer a third of the beef mixture, tortillas and cheese. Repeat the layers twice. Cover and cook on low for 6-8 hours or until heated through. **Yield:** 4 servings.

ALL-DAY MEATBALLS

1 cup milk
3/4 cup quick-cooking oats
3 tablespoons finely chopped onion
1-1/2 teaspoons salt
1-1/2 pounds ground beef
1 cup ketchup
1/2 cup water
3 tablespoons vinegar
2 tablespoons sugar

In a bowl, combine the first four ingredients. Crumble beef over the mixture and mix well. Shape into 1-in. balls. Place in a slow cooker. In a bowl, combine the ketchup, water, vinegar and sugar; mix well. Pour over meatballs. Cover and cook on low for 6-8 hours or until the meat is no longer pink. **Yield:** 6 servings.

TACO MEAT LOAF

1 egg
1/2 cup sour cream
1/3 cup salsa
2 to 4 tablespoons taco seasoning
1 cup crushed tortilla chips
1/2 cup shredded cheddar cheese
2 pounds lean ground beef
Optional toppings: sour cream, salsa, shredded cheddar cheese, shredded lettuce, sliced ripe olives

In a large bowl, combine the first six ingredients. Crumble beef over mixture and mix well. Pat into the bottom of a slow cooker. Cover and cook on low for 8 hours or until a meat thermometer reads 160°. Top with sour cream, salsa, cheese, lettuce and olives if desired. **Yield:** 8 servings.

HEARTY WILD RICE

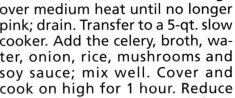

1 pound ground beef
1/2 pound bulk pork sausage
6 celery ribs, diced
2 cans (10-1/2 ounces *each*) condensed beef broth, undiluted
1-1/4 cups water
1 medium onion, chopped
1 cup uncooked wild rice
1 can (4 ounces) mushroom stems and pieces, drained
1/4 cup soy sauce

In a skillet, cook beef and sausage over medium heat until no longer pink; drain. Transfer to a 5-qt. slow cooker. Add the celery, broth, water, onion, rice, mushrooms and soy sauce; mix well. Cover and cook on high for 1 hour. Reduce heat to low; cover and cook for 4 hours or until the rice is tender. **Yield:** 10-12 servings.

SERVING SUGGESTIONS:

Hearty Wild Rice is filling enough to be served as a main course with fresh whole wheat bread and a salad. Or use it as a side dish for any meaty entree.

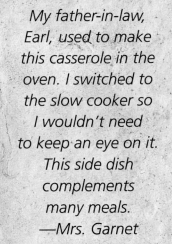

My father-in-law, Earl, used to make this casserole in the oven. I switched to the slow cooker so I wouldn't need to keep an eye on it. This side dish complements many meals.
—Mrs. Garnet Pettigrew Columbia City, Indiana

BEEF AND BARLEY

2 pounds ground beef, cooked and drained
1 can (15 ounces) diced carrots, undrained
1 can (14-1/2 ounces) diced tomatoes, undrained
1 can (10-3/4 ounces) condensed tomato soup, undiluted
2 celery ribs, finely chopped
1/2 cup water
1-1/2 to 2 teaspoons salt
1/2 teaspoon pepper
1/2 teaspoon chili powder
1 teaspoon Worcestershire sauce
1 bay leaf
1 cup quick-cooking barley
2 tablespoons butter *or* margarine
1 cup soft bread crumbs
1 cup (4 ounces) shredded cheddar cheese

In a slow cooker, combine the first 11 ingredients. In a skillet, lightly brown barley in butter. Add to the slow cooker; mix well. Sprinkle with bread crumbs and cheese. Cover and cook on high for 4 hours or until heated through. Discard bay leaf before serving. **Yield:** 8 servings.

I like to double this country-style dish to serve company. I'm not sure where the recipe originated, but I've had it for years.
—Linda Ronk Melbourne, Florida

TOMATO HAMBURGER SOUP

(Pictured above)

1 can (46 ounces) V-8 juice
2 packages (16 ounces *each*) frozen mixed vegetables
1 pound ground beef, cooked and drained
1 can (10-3/4 ounces) condensed cream of mushroom soup, undiluted
2 teaspoons dried minced onion
Salt and pepper to taste

In a 5-qt. slow cooker, combine the first five ingredients; mix well. Cover and cook on high for 4 hours or until heated through. Season with salt and pepper. **Yield:** 12 servings (3 quarts).

SIMPLE SUBSTITUTION:

Vary the flavor of Tomato Hamburger Soup each time you make it by using different blends of frozen mixed vegetables.

As a full-time teacher, I only have time to cook from scratch a few nights each week. This recipe makes a big enough batch to feed my family for 2 nights.
—*Julie Kruger*
St. Cloud, Minnesota

Slow 'n' Easy Chili

1/2 **pound ground beef, cooked and drained**
1/2 **pound bulk pork sausage, cooked and drained**
1 **can (28 ounces) crushed tomatoes**
1 **can (15 ounces) chili beans, undrained**
1 **can (10-3/4 ounces) condensed tomato soup, undiluted**
1 **large onion, chopped**
2 **envelopes chili seasoning**
Shredded cheddar cheese, optional

In a slow cooker, combine the first seven ingredients and mix well. Cover and cook on low for 6-8 hours or until thickened and heated through, stirring occasionally. Garnish with cheese if desired. **Yield:** 6-8 servings.

Serving Suggestion:

For a twist on the traditional, serve steaming spoonfuls of Slow 'n' Easy Chili over hot cooked rice.

What's nice about this recipe is that you can add any extras (like chopped bell peppers or sliced fresh mushrooms) to make it your own specialty. I only get the best reviews when I serve this chili.
—Ginny Puckett Lutz, Florida

Two-Step Stroganoff

2 **pounds ground beef, cooked and drained**
2 **medium onions, chopped**
1 **cup beef consomme**
1 **can (4 ounces) mushroom stems and pieces, drained**
3 **tablespoons tomato paste**
2 **garlic cloves, minced**
1-1/2 **teaspoons salt**
1/4 **teaspoon pepper**
2 **tablespoons all-purpose flour**
3/4 **cup sour cream**
Hot cooked noodles

In a slow cooker, combine the first eight ingredients; mix well. Cover and cook on low for 6 hours. In a small bowl, combine flour and sour cream until smooth; stir into beef mixture. Cover and cook 1 hour longer or until thickened. Serve over noodles. **Yield:** 6 servings.

Helpful Hint:

Beef consomme is a stronger-flavored stock than broth because it has been simmered longer. It is readily available in cans, but regular beef broth can be substituted.

I especially like to use my slow cooker on hot summer days when I want to keep my kitchen cool. I'm always trying new recipes for different functions.
—Roberta Menefee Walcott, New York

HOBO STEW

1-1/2 **pounds ground beef**
  1 **medium onion, diced**
  3 **cans (10-3/4 ounces** *each***) condensed minestrone soup, undiluted**
  2 **cans (15 ounces** *each***) ranch-style beans, undrained**
  1 **can (10 ounces) diced tomatoes and green chilies, undrained**

In a large skillet, cook beef and onion over medium heat until the meat is no longer pink; drain. Transfer to a slow cooker. Add the remaining ingredients. Cover and cook on low for 6 hours or until heated through. **Yield:** 8 servings.

SLOW COOKER CHEESE DIP

  1 **pound ground beef**
1/2 **pound bulk hot pork sausage**
  2 **pounds process American cheese, cubed**
  2 **cans (10 ounces** *each***) diced tomatoes and green chilies, undrained**
Tortilla chips

In a skillet, cook beef and sausage over medium heat until no longer pink; drain. Transfer to a 5-qt. slow cooker. Add cheese and tomatoes; mix well. Cover and cook on low for 4 hours or until the cheese is melted, stirring occasionally. Serve with tortilla chips. **Yield:** 3 quarts.

TIMELY TIP:

If you plan on serving Slow Cooker Cheese Dip at a holiday party or family get-together, make it ahead and freeze it. Then all you need to do is thaw and reheat it.

POOR MAN'S STEAK

  1 **cup crushed saltine crackers (about 30 crackers)**
1/3 **cup water**
Salt and pepper to taste
  2 **pounds ground beef**
1/4 **cup all-purpose flour**
  2 **tablespoons vegetable oil**
  2 **cans (10-3/4 ounces** *each***) condensed cream of mushroom soup, undiluted**
Hot mashed potatoes *or* **noodles**

In a bowl, combine cracker crumbs, water, salt and pepper. Crumble beef over mixture and mix well. Press into an ungreased 9-in. square pan. Cover and refrigerate for at least 3 hours. Cut into 3-in. squares; dredge in flour. In a skillet, cook meat squares in oil until browned on both sides. Transfer to a slow cooker with a slotted spatula or spoon. Add soup. Cover and cook on high for 4 hours or until meat is no longer pink. Serve with mashed potatoes or noodles. **Yield:** 9 servings.

EASY-DOES-IT SPAGHETTI

(Pictured below and on page 54)

2 pounds ground beef, cooked and drained
1 can (46 ounces) tomato juice
1 can (15 ounces) tomato sauce
1 can (8 ounces) mushroom stems and pieces, drained
2 tablespoons dried minced onion
2 teaspoons salt
1 teaspoon garlic powder
1 teaspoon ground mustard
1/2 teaspoon *each* ground allspice, mace and pepper
1 package (7 ounces) spaghetti, broken in half

In a slow cooker, combine beef, tomato juice, tomato sauce, mushrooms and seasonings; mix well. Cover and cook on high for 4 hours. Stir in spaghetti. Cover and cook 1 hour longer or until the spaghetti is tender. **Yield:** 8-10 servings.

SIMPLE SUBSTITUTION:

If you have a little extra preparation time, substitute 1/2 cup chopped onion for the dried minced onion in Easy-Does-It Spaghetti.

This savory spaghetti sauce is a nice change from some of the sweeter store-bought varieties. With fresh bread and a green salad, you have a complete meal.
—Genevieve Hrabe Plainville, Kansas

MEATBALL CABBAGE ROLLS

(Pictured above)

1 large head cabbage, cored
2 cans (one 8 ounces, one 15 ounces) tomato sauce, *divided*
1 small onion, chopped
1/3 cup uncooked long grain rice
2 tablespoons chili powder
Salt and garlic powder to taste
1 pound ground beef

In a Dutch oven, cook cabbage in boiling water only until the outer leaves fall off head, about 3 minutes. Remove cabbage from water and remove as many leaves as will come off easily. Reserve 14-16 large leaves for rolls. Return cabbage to water if more leaves are needed. Remove the thick vein from each leaf. In a bowl, combine 8 oz. of tomato sauce, onion, rice, chili powder, salt and garlic powder. Crumble beef over mixture; mix well. Shape into 2-in. balls. Place one meatball on each cabbage leaf; fold in sides. Starting at an unfolded edge, roll up leaf to completely enclose meatball. Secure with toothpicks. Place in a 5-qt. slow cooker. Pour remaining tomato sauce over cabbage rolls. Cover and cook on low for 8 hours or until meat is no longer pink and cabbage is tender. Discard toothpicks. **Yield:** 4-6 servings.

My mother would often have these cabbage rolls simmering in her slow cooker when my family and I arrived at her house for weekend visits. The mouth-watering meatballs tucked inside make these stand out from any other cabbage rolls I've tried.
—Betty Buckmaster
Muskogee, Oklahoma

SHAPING CABBAGE ROLLS

STEP 1
After the cabbage has been boiled, cut the thick vein from each leaf for easier rolling.

STEP 2
Place one meatball on each cabbage leaf. Fold sides over meatball and roll up. Secure with a toothpick if desired.

COLORFUL VEGGIE MEDLEY

1-1/2 pounds ground beef, cooked and drained
1 package (10 ounces) frozen cut green beans, thawed
1 package (10 ounces) frozen peas, thawed
1 package (6 ounces) frozen pea pods, thawed
1 can (14-1/2 ounces) diced tomatoes, undrained
1-1/2 cups thinly sliced carrots
2 celery ribs, sliced
1 can (8 ounces) sliced water chestnuts, drained
1/2 cup chopped green pepper
3 tablespoons butter *or* margarine
3 tablespoons sugar
3 tablespoons quick-cooking tapioca
1-1/2 teaspoons salt
1/2 teaspoon pepper

In a 5-qt. slow cooker, combine all of the ingredients and mix well. Cover and cook on low for 4 hours or until heated through. **Yield:** 6-8 servings.

TIMELY TIP:

If you don't have time for the Colorful Veggie Medley to simmer in a slow cooker, combine all the ingredients and spoon into a greased 13- x 9- x 2-inch baking pan. Cover and bake at 350° for about 1 hour; uncover for the last few minutes of baking.

SLOW-COOKED SPAGHETTI AND MEATBALLS

3 pounds ground beef
1 cup finely chopped onion, *divided*
1 teaspoon salt
1/2 teaspoon pepper
1 can (46 ounces) tomato juice
1 can (28 ounces) diced tomatoes, drained
1 can (15 ounces) tomato sauce
2 celery ribs, chopped
3 bay leaves
2 garlic cloves, minced

In a bowl, combine the beef, 1/2 cup onion, salt and pepper; mix well. Shape into 1-in. balls. In a large skillet over medium heat, brown meatballs with remaining onion. Transfer to a 5-qt. slow cooker; add the remaining ingredients. Cover and cook on low for 8-10 hours or until heated through, stirring occasionally. Discard bay leaves before serving. **Yield:** 20 servings (about 4-1/2 quarts).

When my freezer or garden is bulging with vegetables, I bring out the slow cooker to make this dish. My mother found the recipe in an area newspaper.
—Kerry Johnson
Decorah, Iowa

I first sampled this spaghetti sauce at my sister-in-law's and had to have the recipe. After all these years, I still think it's about the best I've ever tasted.
—Jackie Grant
Vanderhoof,
British Columbia

BEEFY AU GRATIN POTATOES

1 package (5-1/4 ounces) au gratin *or* cheddar and bacon potatoes
1 can (15-1/4 ounces) whole kernel corn, drained
1 can (10-3/4 ounces) condensed cream of potato soup, undiluted
1 cup water
1 can (4 ounces) chopped green chilies, drained
1 can (4 ounces) mushroom stems and pieces, drained
1 jar (4 ounces) diced pimientos, drained
1 pound ground beef
1 medium onion, chopped

Set potato sauce mix aside. Place potatoes in a slow cooker; top with corn. In a bowl, combine soup, water, chilies, mushrooms, pimientos and reserved sauce mix; mix well. Pour a third of the mixture over corn. In a skillet, cook beef and onion over medium heat until the meat is no longer pink; drain. Transfer to slow cooker. Top with remaining sauce mixture. Do not stir. Cover and cook on low for 4 hours or until potatoes are tender. **Yield:** 4-6 servings.

HELPFUL HINT:

Pimientos are roasted sweet red peppers with the skins removed.
Store unopened jars in a cool dark place for up to 1 year.
Once opened, refrigerate and use within 2 weeks.

PIZZA IN A POT

1-1/2 pounds ground beef
1 medium green pepper, chopped
1 medium onion, chopped
1 can (15 ounces) tomato sauce
1 jar (14 ounces) pizza sauce
2 tablespoons tomato paste
3 cups spiral pasta, cooked and drained
2 packages (3-1/2 ounces *each*) sliced pepperoni

2 cups (8 ounces) shredded mozzarella cheese

In a skillet, cook beef, green pepper and onion over medium heat until meat is no longer pink; drain. Add tomato sauce, pizza sauce and tomato paste; mix well. In a slow cooker, layer pasta, beef mixture, pepperoni and cheese. Cover and cook on low for 3-4 hours or until heated through. **Yield:** 8 servings.

SIMPLE SUBSTITUTION:

If you'd like, substitute 1/2 pound bulk Italian sausage for the pepperoni in Pizza in a Pot. Cook it along with the ground beef, green pepper and onion.

SAVORY WINTER SOUP

(Pictured above)

2 pounds ground beef
3 medium onions, chopped
1 garlic clove, minced
3 cans (10-1/2 ounces *each*)
   condensed beef broth,
   undiluted
1 can (28 ounces) diced
   tomatoes, undrained
3 cups water
1 cup *each* diced carrots and
   celery
1 cup fresh *or* frozen cut
   green beans
1 cup cubed peeled potatoes
2 tablespoons minced fresh
parsley *or* 2 teaspoons
   dried parsley flakes
1 teaspoon dried basil
1/2 teaspoon dried thyme
Salt and pepper to taste

In a skillet, cook beef, onions and garlic over medium heat until the meat is no longer pink; drain. Transfer to a 5-qt. slow cooker. Add the remaining ingredients and mix well. Cover and cook on high for 8 hours or until heated through. **Yield:** 14 servings (3-1/2 quarts).

TIMELY TIP:

To save chopping time, use frozen sliced carrots and cubed hash brown potatoes in Savory Winter Soup.

Even my father, who doesn't particularly like soup, enjoys my full-flavored version of traditional vegetable soup. He asked me to share the recipe with Mom, and I gladly obliged!
—Dana Simmons
Lancaster, Ohio

TEXAS STEW

(Pictured above)

1 can (15-1/2 ounces) hominy, drained
1 can (15-1/4 ounces) whole kernel corn, drained
1 can (15 ounces) sliced carrots, drained
1 can (15 ounces) sliced potatoes, drained
1 can (15 ounces) ranch-style *or* chili beans, undrained
1 can (14-1/2 ounces) diced tomatoes, undrained
1 cup water
1 beef bouillon cube
1/2 teaspoon garlic powder

Chili powder to taste
Dash Worcestershire sauce
Dash hot pepper sauce
1-1/2 pounds ground beef
1 medium onion, chopped

In a slow cooker, combine the first 12 ingredients. In a skillet, cook beef and onion over medium heat until meat is no longer pink; drain. Transfer to the slow cooker; mix well. Cover and cook on high for 4 hours or until heated through. **Yield:** 10-12 servings.

SIMPLE SUBSTITUTION:

If your family doesn't care for hominy, you can use a 15-ounce can of green beans (drained) instead.

I love to experiment with many different types of recipes. But as a mother of young children, I rely on family-friendly ones more and more. Everyone enjoys this stew.
—Kim Balstad
Lewisville, Texas

NO-BEAN CHILI

1-1/2 pounds lean ground beef
1 can (14-1/2 ounces) stewed tomatoes
1 can (8 ounces) tomato sauce
1 small onion, chopped
1 small green pepper, chopped
1 can (4 ounces) chopped green chilies
1/2 cup minced fresh parsley
1 tablespoon chili powder
1 garlic clove, minced
1-1/4 teaspoons salt
1/2 teaspoon paprika
1/4 teaspoon pepper
Hot cooked rice *or* pasta

Crumble the beef into a slow cooker. Add the next 11 ingredients and mix well. Cover and cook on high for 4 hours or until heated through. Serve over rice or pasta. **Yield:** 6 servings.

*I often combine the ingredients for this zesty chili the night before. In the morning, I load up the slow cooker and let it go! It's so easy to prepare.
—Molly Butt
Granville, Ohio*

HELPFUL HINT:

*Thoroughly wash fresh parsley and shake off excess water.
Wrap in paper towels and store in a plastic bag in the refrigerator
for up to 1 week. Chopping parsley is easier if the leaves are thoroughly dry.*

CONFETTI CASSEROLE

1 pound ground beef
1 medium onion, finely chopped
1 teaspoon garlic powder
4 medium potatoes, peeled and quartered
3 medium carrots, cut into 1-inch chunks
1 package (10 ounces) frozen cut green beans
1 package (10 ounces) frozen corn
1 can (14-1/2 ounces) Italian diced tomatoes, undrained

In a skillet, cook beef, onion and garlic powder over medium heat until meat is no longer pink; drain. In a slow cooker, layer potatoes, carrots, beans and corn. Top with beef mixture. Pour tomatoes over the top. Cover and cook on low for 8-10 hours or until the potatoes are tender. **Yield:** 8 servings.

*To create this comforting casserole, I adapted a recipe from the cookbook that came with my first slow cooker. I love to serve this with fresh bread from my bread maker.
—Joy Vincent
Newport,
North Carolina*

HOME-STYLE SALADS & BREADS

Many of these "beefed up"
salads and breads can be
enjoyed as flavorful main
courses. Or take them
along to round out
a family picnic or
potluck buffet.
Either way, leftovers
will be unlikely!

SOMBRERO PASTA
SALAD
(P. 87)

HEARTY SPINACH SALAD (P. 76)
SAUERKRAUT BEEF BUNS (P. 76)

HEARTY SPINACH SALAD
(Pictured on page 75)

Ground beef turns an ordinary spinach salad into a main dish. Minced garlic adds just the right amount of zip. You can easily substitute any type of lettuce for the spinach.
—Rita Goshaw
South Milwaukee,
Wisconsin

1 package (10 ounces) fresh spinach, torn
1 pound ground beef, cooked and drained
2 large tomatoes, cut into wedges
2 cups (8 ounces) shredded sharp cheddar cheese
1/2 cup sliced fresh mushrooms
6 garlic cloves, minced
Salt and pepper to taste
Salad dressing of your choice

In a large salad bowl, toss the spinach, beef, tomatoes, cheese, mushrooms, garlic, salt and pepper. Serve with salad dressing. **Yield:** 14 servings.

HELPFUL HINT:

When putting a garlic clove through a garlic press, there's no need to peel it first. Just pop a clove into the press and squeeze. The garlic gets pushed out, but the skin stays in the press.

SAUERKRAUT BEEF BUNS
(Pictured on page 75)

Our three boys always seemed to be hungry when they were growing up. These golden filled buns were sure to satisfy. Now our grandchildren gobble these up.
—Margaret Kepke
Creston,
British Columbia

1 pound ground beef
1 medium onion, chopped
1 can (27 ounces) sauerkraut, rinsed and drained
4 packages (16 ounces *each*) frozen white dinner roll dough, thawed
Melted butter *or* margarine

In a skillet, cook the beef and onion over medium heat until the meat is no longer pink; drain. Add sauerkraut; mix well. Cool for 15 minutes. Meanwhile, flatten each piece of dough. Top each with a heaping tablespoonful of beef mixture. Fold dough over filling to meet in center; pinch edges to seal. Place seam side down on greased baking sheets. Cover and let rise in a warm place until doubled, about 30 minutes. Bake at 350° for 15-20 minutes or until golden brown. Brush with butter. Serve warm. **Yield:** 4 dozen.

TIMELY TIP:

Leftover Sauerkraut Beef Buns can be frozen. Cool, then wrap individually in heavy-duty foil and place in a large resealable plastic bag. Freeze for up to 3 months. To reheat, bake foil-wrapped buns at 350° for 30 to 35 minutes or until heated through.

BREAKFAST ROLLS

(Pictured above)

1 pound ground beef
1 medium onion, chopped
2 teaspoons beef bouillon
   granules
1/2 teaspoon pepper
1 loaf (1 pound) frozen bread
   dough, thawed
3 slices Swiss cheese, cut into
   strips

In a skillet, cook beef and onion over medium heat until meat is no longer pink; drain. Add bouillon and pepper; mix well. Cool for 15 minutes. On a floured surface, roll out dough into a 12-in. x 8-in. rectangle. Spread beef mixture to within 1/2 in. of short edges and 1 in. of long edges. Roll up, jelly-roll style, starting with a long side; pinch seam to seal. Cut into 12 slices. Place in a greased 13-in. x 9-in. x 2-in. baking pan. Cover and let rise until nearly doubled, about 30 minutes. Bake at 425° for 15-20 minutes or until golden brown. Place two cheese strips over each roll. Bake 5 minutes longer or until the cheese is melted. **Yield:** 12 servings.

As a rancher's wife and member of the Kansas CattleWomen, I'm always on the lookout for ways to serve ground beef. Team these savory rolls with scrambled eggs and fresh fruit for a hearty breakfast.
—Vicki Kelly
Severy, Kansas

SHAPING A BREAD ROLL

STEP 1
Spread beef mixture over dough, leaving space around edges. Beginning with a long side, roll up dough jelly-roll style; pinch seam to seal.

STEP 2
Place meat-stuffed roll seam side down. Cut into 1-inch slices.

While I was up with one of our babies more than 20 years ago, I heard this "secret" family recipe shared on an all-night talk show. None of our 12 children or our growing troop of grandchildren ever pass up this special stuffed bread.
—Elaine Bent
Middleboro,
Massachusetts

STUFFED BREAD BOAT
(Pictured below)

1 loaf (1 pound) Vienna bread, unsliced
1 large onion, chopped
1 medium green pepper, chopped
1 cup chopped fresh spinach
1 medium tomato, chopped
1 pound ground beef
1/2 teaspoon dried oregano
Salt and pepper to taste

Cut a thin slice off the top of bread; set top aside. Hollow out the loaf, leaving a 1/4-in. shell. Dice removed bread and set aside. In a nonstick skillet, saute onion until tender. Add green pepper, spinach and tomato; cook 3-4 minutes longer. Add beef, oregano, salt and pepper; cook until meat is no longer pink. Drain. Stir in diced bread and mix well. Spoon into bread shell; replace top. Wrap tightly in heavy-duty foil. Bake at 400° for 20 minutes or until heated through. Cut into slices. **Yield:** 6-8 servings.

SIMPLE SUBSTITUTIONS:
It's easy to mix and match ingredients in the Stuffed Bread Boat. For instance, add some chopped fresh mushrooms or, for lots of color, use a mix of peppers.

CORN BREAD SALAD

3/4 **pound ground beef**
1-1/2 **cups crumbled corn bread**
1 **can (15 ounces) pinto
   beans, rinsed and drained**
2 **celery ribs, chopped**
1 **large onion, chopped**
4 **medium tomatoes,
   chopped**
TOPPING:
1-1/3 **cups mayonnaise**
2 **teaspoons sugar**
2 **teaspoons vinegar**

In a skillet, cook beef over medium heat until no longer pink; drain and cool slightly. In a large bowl, layer corn bread, beans, celery, onion and tomatoes. In a small bowl, combine the mayonnaise, sugar and vinegar; mix well. Spoon beef over tomato layer. Spread topping over salad (do not toss). **Yield:** 8 servings.

HELPFUL HINT:

When making Corn Bread Salad, you can either use your own homemade corn bread recipe or an 8-1/2-ounce mix. If using a mix, follow package directions. When cool, crumble about half the corn bread to measure 1-1/2 cups for the salad. Crumble and freeze the remaining corn bread for another use, or cut it into squares and serve with soup.

This recipe appeared in our local newspaper years ago. I adapted the recipe to suit our tastes. My husband, Ron, is a great cook, and we've been sharing the kitchen since his retirement.
*—Sherry Edwards
Camden, Arkansas*

FIESTA BISCUIT SQUARES

2 **cups biscuit/baking mix**
2/3 **cup milk**
2 **tablespoons butter *or*
   margarine, melted**
3 **medium tomatoes, sliced**
1/2 **teaspoon garlic salt**
1/4 **teaspoon pepper**
1 **cup (8 ounces) sour cream**
1/2 **cup mayonnaise**
1 **cup (4 ounces) shredded
   cheddar cheese**
1 **medium onion, chopped**
1 **pound ground beef, cooked
   and drained**
1 **cup (4 ounces) shredded
   mozzarella cheese**
Paprika

In a bowl, combine biscuit mix and milk with a fork until the mixture forms a ball. On a floured surface, roll out dough into a 13-in. x 9-in. rectangle. Transfer to a greased 13-in. x 9-in. x 2-in. baking dish; press dough halfway up the sides of dish. Brush with butter. Bake at 325° for 15 minutes. Arrange tomato slices over the crust. Sprinkle with garlic salt and pepper. In a bowl, combine sour cream, mayonnaise, cheddar cheese and onion; spoon over the tomato layer. Top with the beef. Sprinkle with mozzarella cheese and paprika. Bake at 325° for 15-20 minutes longer or until golden brown. Cut into squares. **Yield:** 12 servings.

Life is lively around our house, and time in the kitchen is limited. These biscuit squares topped with ground beef and cheese make a satisfying dinner served with a tossed salad.
*—Mrs. Dale Snow
Cambridge Springs,
Pennsylvania*

PINWHEELS WITH VEGETABLE CREAM SAUCE

2 cups biscuit/baking mix
1 teaspoon paprika
1 cup (8 ounces) sour cream
1 egg
1 small onion, finely chopped
1/4 cup minced fresh parsley
1 tablespoon prepared mustard
1 teaspoon prepared horseradish
1 teaspoon salt
1/4 teaspoon pepper
1 pound lean ground beef
SAUCE:
2 tablespoons butter *or* margarine
2 tablespoons all-purpose flour
1-1/4 cups milk
1 package (10 ounces) frozen peas and carrots, thawed
1/2 teaspoon salt
1/4 teaspoon pepper

In a bowl, combine biscuit mix and paprika. Using a fork, stir in sour cream until mixture forms a ball. On a floured surface, roll out the dough into a 15-in. x 10-in. rectangle. In a bowl, combine egg, onion, parsley, mustard, horseradish, salt and pepper. Crumble beef over mixture and mix well. Spread over dough to within 1 in. of edges. Roll up, jelly-roll style, starting with a long side. Cut into 12 slices. Place in an ungreased 13-in. x 9-in. x 2-in. baking pan. Bake at 400° for 30 minutes or until golden brown. Meanwhile, in a saucepan, melt butter; stir in flour until smooth. Gradually add milk. Bring to a boil; cook and stir for 2 minutes. Reduce heat. Stir in peas and carrots, salt and pepper; heat through. Serve over the pinwheels. **Yield:** 12 servings.

TIMELY TIP:

To make quick work of slicing the Pinwheels with Vegetable Cream Sauce, use an electric knife.

BARBECUED TACO SALAD

1 pound ground beef
1 medium onion, chopped
1 jar (8 ounces) process cheese sauce
1/2 cup barbecue sauce
1 tablespoon chili powder
6 lettuce leaves
3 cups shredded lettuce
3 medium tomatoes, chopped
3 cups corn chips

In a large skillet, cook beef and onion over medium heat until meat is no longer pink; drain. Stir in cheese sauce, barbecue sauce and chili powder. Cook and stir over low heat until cheese is melted. Place each lettuce leaf on a plate. Top with shredded lettuce, beef mixture, tomatoes and corn chips. Serve immediately. **Yield:** 6 servings.

SPICY BEEF SALAD

(Pictured below)

1 pound ground beef
1/3 cup vegetable oil
3 tablespoons lime juice
2 tablespoons soy sauce
2 tablespoons molasses
1 small jalapeno pepper, seeded and minced*
1 garlic clove, minced
3/4 teaspoon ground ginger
6 cups torn salad greens
1 large tomato, cut into wedges
2 green onions, sliced
Jalapeno pepper and lime slices, optional

In a skillet, cook beef over medium heat until no longer pink. Meanwhile, in a small bowl, combine oil, lime juice, soy sauce, molasses, jalapeno, garlic and ginger; mix well. Drain beef; add the oil mixture. Cook, uncovered, over medium heat for 5 minutes or until heated through. On a large platter, layer salad greens, tomato, beef mixture and onions. Garnish with jalapeno and lime slices if desired. **Yield:** 8 servings. ***Editor's Note:** When cutting or seeding hot peppers, use rubber or plastic gloves to protect your hands. Avoid touching your face.

This delicious salad doesn't skimp on ingredients or flavor. I make it often, especially on days when I'm pressed for time. My husband, my mother and I all rate it as a favorite.
—Natercia Yailaian Somerville, Massachusetts

TACO MUFFINS

1 pound ground beef
3/4 cup water
1 envelope taco seasoning
1/4 cup butter *or* margarine, softened
1/4 cup sugar
1 egg
1-3/4 cups all-purpose flour
4 teaspoons baking powder
1/4 teaspoon baking soda
1/4 teaspoon salt
1 cup buttermilk
1 cup salsa
1 cup (4 ounces) shredded cheddar cheese

In a skillet, cook the beef over medium heat until no longer pink; drain. Add water and taco seasoning; simmer, uncovered, for 15 minutes. Cool. In a mixing bowl, cream butter and sugar. Beat in egg. Combine dry ingredients; add to the creamed mixture alternately with buttermilk. Fold in meat mixture. Fill greased muffin cups two-thirds full. Bake at 425° for 12-15 minutes or until golden brown. Carefully remove muffins to a greased 13-in. x 9-in. x 2-in. baking dish. Top each with salsa and cheese. Bake 5 minutes longer or until the cheese is melted. **Yield:** about 16 muffins.

SERVING SUGGESTION:

To serve Taco Muffins as an appetizer, bake in miniature muffin cups, reducing the baking time, and have your guests top their own servings with salsa and cheese.

MEATY GARDEN SALAD

1 pound ground beef
1 garlic clove, minced
1 cup water
1 beef bouillon cube
1 cup instant rice
3 medium unpeeled cucumbers, cubed
4 plum tomatoes, cubed
2 celery ribs, sliced
1/2 cup sliced green onions
1/2 cup diced green pepper
Salt and pepper to taste
Salad dressing of your choice

In a skillet, cook beef and garlic over medium heat until meat is no longer pink; drain and set aside. In a saucepan, bring water and bouillon to a boil. Stir in rice; remove from the heat. Cover and let stand for 5 minutes or until tender. Combine the rice and beef in a large bowl. Cover and refrigerate for 2 hours or until chilled. Add cucumbers, tomatoes, celery, onions, green pepper, salt and pepper; mix well. Serve with salad dressing. **Yield:** 12 servings.

SIMPLE SUBSTITUTION:

For even more fresh flavor, forgo the salad dressing and just squeeze lemon wedges over the top of Meaty Garden Salad.

SIMPLE SUMMER SALAD

1 pound ground beef
3 cups torn lettuce
2 cups (8 ounces) shredded
   cheddar cheese
1 medium tomato, chopped
1 small onion, chopped
4 hard-cooked eggs, chopped
1/2 to 3/4 cup mayonnaise
Salt and pepper to taste

In a skillet, cook beef over medium heat until no longer pink; drain. Cool for 5 minutes. In a large bowl, toss the lettuce, cheese, tomato, onion, eggs and beef. Add mayonnaise, salt and pepper; toss to coat. Serve immediately. **Yield:** 12 servings.

HELPFUL HINT:

It will be easier to chop the hard-cooked eggs for Simple Summer Salad if they're cold.

MUSHROOM BURGER STROMBOLI

1 package (1/4 ounce) active
   dry yeast
2-1/2 cups warm water
   (110° to 115°)
2 tablespoons vegetable oil
2 tablespoons salt
2 teaspoons sugar
7 to 7-1/2 cups all-purpose
   flour
1 pound ground beef
1/4 cup chopped onion
1 can (10-3/4 ounces)
   condensed cream of
   mushroom soup, undiluted
1/2 pound fresh mushrooms,
   chopped
1/2 teaspoon onion salt
1/2 teaspoon seasoned salt
1/8 teaspoon pepper
4 cups (16 ounces) shredded
   mozzarella cheese
Optional toppings: sour cream,
   jalapeno peppers, hot pepper
   sauce

In a mixing bowl, dissolve yeast in water. Add oil, salt, sugar and 2 cups flour; beat until smooth. Add enough remaining flour to form a soft dough. Turn onto a floured surface; knead until smooth and elastic, about 6-8 minutes. Place in a greased bowl, turning once to grease top. Cover and let rise in a warm place until doubled, about 1 hour. Meanwhile, in a skillet, cook beef and onion over medium heat until meat is no longer pink; drain. Add soup, mushrooms and seasonings; set aside. Punch dough down; divide in half. On a floured surface, roll each portion of dough into a 15-in. x 10-in. rectangle. Transfer to greased baking sheets. Spoon the beef mixture lengthwise down half of the rectangles to within 1 in. of edges. Fold dough over filling. Pinch edges to seal. Cut four diagonal slits on top of loaves. Cover and let rise until doubled, about 45 minutes. Bake at 350° for 30-35 minutes or until golden brown. Cut into slices. Serve warm with toppings of your choice. **Yield:** 2 loaves.

CHILI IN BISCUIT BOWLS

(Pictured above)

It's fun to serve a simple chili in edible "bowls" for a casual lunch or evening meal. Cut down on last-minute fuss by making the biscuit bowls in advance and storing in an airtight container.
—Jackie Powell
Jayess, Mississippi

2 cups biscuit/baking mix
2/3 cup milk
1 teaspoon Cajun seasoning, *divided*
1 pound ground beef
1 medium onion, chopped
1 medium green pepper, chopped
2 cans (14-1/2 ounces *each*) chili-seasoned stewed tomatoes
1 can (16 ounces) kidney beans, rinsed and drained
Optional toppings: shredded cheddar cheese, sliced ripe olives, sliced green onions, sour cream

In a bowl, combine the biscuit mix, milk and 1/2 teaspoon Cajun seasoning until a soft dough forms. Knead 4-5 times on a floured surface. Divide dough into six portions. Roll out each into a 6-in. circle. Place six 10-oz. custard cups upside down on a large baking sheet; coat the outside of each with nonstick cook-ing spray. Shape dough circles over custard cups. Bake at 450° for 10-12 minutes or until golden brown. Immediately remove biscuit bowls from cups to wire racks (do not in-vert until cool). Meanwhile, in a skil-let, cook beef, onion and green pepper over medium heat until the meat is no longer pink; drain. Add tomatoes, beans and remaining Ca-jun seasoning. Bring to a boil. Re-duce heat; cover and simmer for 30 minutes or until heated through. Spoon into biscuit bowls. Serve with toppings of your choice. **Yield:** 6 servings.

FORMING BISCUIT BOWLS

Shape dough circles over upside-down 10-ounce custard cups coated with nonstick cooking spray. Bake as directed.

ITALIAN TORTELLINI SALAD

1 pound ground beef
1 envelope Italian salad
  dressing mix
1/4 cup water
1 package (19 ounces) frozen
  cheese tortellini, cooked
  and drained
3 to 4 plum tomatoes,
  chopped
1 medium zucchini, chopped
1 cup (4 ounces) shredded
  mozzarella cheese
2 tablespoons olive *or*
  vegetable oil
2 tablespoons cider *or* red
  wine vinegar

In a skillet, cook beef over medium heat until no longer pink; drain. Add salad dressing mix and water. Bring to a boil. Reduce heat; simmer, uncovered, for 3 minutes. In a large bowl, combine the tortellini, tomatoes, zucchini, cheese and beef mixture. Combine oil and vinegar; pour over salad and toss to coat. Serve immediately or refrigerate for at least 1 hour. **Yield:** 10 servings.

HELPFUL HINT:

Vinegar does not need to be refrigerated, and its shelf life is almost indefinite. The color may change and sediment may appear, but the flavor won't be affected.

This original recipe includes flavors that family and friends love to eat. I usually serve it warm for dinner and chilled for potlucks.
—Kelly Schmitz Mapes
Fort Collins, Colorado

RUSTIC BEEF BREAD

1 cup raisins
1 cup boiling water
2 packages (1/4 ounce *each*)
  active dry yeast
1/2 cup warm water
  (110° to 115°)
1 cup warm milk
  (110° to 115°)
1/3 cup sugar
2 tablespoons shortening
1 tablespoon salt
1 tablespoon molasses
3 cups whole wheat flour
1 cup cooked, drained and
  cooled ground beef (about
  1/3 pound)
3 cups all-purpose flour
Melted butter *or* margarine

In a bowl, soak raisins in boiling water; cool to 110°-115° (do not drain). In a mixing bowl, dissolve yeast in warm water. Add milk, sugar, shortening, salt, molasses and whole wheat flour; beat until smooth. Add beef and raisins. Add enough all-purpose flour to form a soft dough. Turn onto a floured surface; knead until smooth and elastic, about 6-8 minutes. Place in a greased bowl, turning once to grease top. Cover and refrigerate for 1-2 hours; punch dough down. Refrigerate overnight; punch dough down. Divide in half; shape into loaves. Place in two greased 9-in. x 5-in. x 3-in. loaf pans. Cover and let rise in a warm place until doubled, about 1 hour. Bake at 375° for 40-45 minutes, covering loosely with foil during the last 20 minutes. Remove from pans to cool on wire racks. Brush with butter. Store in the refrigerator. **Yield:** 2 loaves.

I've always enjoyed cooking and making dishes out of unusual ingredients. When I brought this slightly sweet bread to a family picnic, they couldn't believe it contained ground beef.
—Margaret Peterson
Forest City, Iowa

ZESTY BURGER PUFFS

1 cup water
1/2 cup butter (no substitutes)
3/4 cup all-purpose flour
1/2 cup cornmeal
1/4 teaspoon salt
4 eggs
FILLING:
1-1/2 pounds ground beef
1/2 cup chopped jalapeno peppers*
1 medium onion, chopped
2 cans (8 ounces *each*) tomato sauce
2 tablespoons lemon juice
1 tablespoon Worcestershire sauce
1-1/2 teaspoons salt
1/2 teaspoon pepper
1/4 teaspoon lemon extract
1/2 cup shredded cheddar cheese

In a saucepan over medium heat, bring water and butter to a boil. Add flour, cornmeal and salt all at once; stir until a smooth ball forms. Remove from the heat; let stand for 5 minutes. Add eggs, one at a time, beating well after each. Cover baking sheets with foil; grease the foil. Drop the batter by rounded tablespoonfuls 3 in. apart onto foil. Bake at 350° for 30-35 minutes or until golden brown. Meanwhile, in a large saucepan, cook beef, jalapenos and onion over medium heat until meat is no longer pink; drain. Add tomato sauce, lemon juice, Worcestershire sauce, salt, pepper and extract. Simmer for 30 minutes. Remove puffs to wire racks; immediately cut a slit in each for steam to escape. To serve, split puffs and remove soft dough. Fill with beef mixture and sprinkle with cheese; replace tops. **Yield:** 16 servings. ***Editor's Note:** When cutting or seeding hot peppers, use rubber or plastic gloves to protect your hands. Avoid touching your face.

TIMELY TIP:

The puffs for Zesty Burger Puffs can be baked a day in advance and refrigerated in an airtight container. To reheat, place on a baking sheet; bake at 325° for 5 to 10 minutes. Split and remove soft dough. Fill with beef mixture and sprinkle with cheese; replace tops.

MAKE-AHEAD MEATBALL SALAD

1 pound ground beef
1/2 cup seasoned bread crumbs
1/2 cup Italian salad dressing
6 cups torn salad greens
1 medium red onion, thinly sliced
1 cup (4 ounces) shredded mozzarella cheese
1 can (2-1/4 ounces) sliced ripe olives, drained
Caesar Italian salad dressing *or* salad dressing of your choice

In a bowl, combine beef and bread crumbs. Shape into 3/4-in. balls. Place in a greased 8-in. square baking pan. Bake at 350° for 15-20 minutes or until meat is no longer pink; drain. Cool for 15-30 minutes. Place Italian salad dressing in a resealable plastic bag; add meatballs. Seal and refrigerate overnight. Drain and discard marinade. On a serving platter or individual plates, arrange greens, onion, cheese and olives. Top with meatballs. Drizzle with dressing. **Yield:** 4 servings.

SOMBRERO PASTA SALAD

(Pictured below and on page 74)

1 package (16 ounces) spiral pasta
1 pound ground beef
3/4 cup water
1 envelope taco seasoning
2 cups (8 ounces) shredded cheddar cheese
1 large green pepper, chopped
1 medium onion, chopped
1 medium tomato, chopped
2 cans (2-1/4 ounces *each*) sliced ripe olives, drained
1 bottle (16 ounces) Catalina *or* Western salad dressing

Cook pasta according to package directions. Meanwhile, in a skillet, cook beef over medium heat until no longer pink; drain. Add water and taco seasoning; simmer, uncovered, for 15 minutes. Rinse pasta in cold water and drain; place in a large bowl. Add beef mixture, cheese, green pepper, onion, tomato and olives; mix well. Add the dressing and toss to coat. Cover and refrigerate for at least 1 hour. **Yield:** 10 servings.

I take this slightly spicy salad to almost every party or picnic I attend. Every time, I come home with lots of compliments, but never any leftovers!
—Patty Ehlen Burlington, Wisconsin

SERVING SUGGESTION:

If you'll be refrigerating Sombrero Pasta Salad for more than 1 hour, reserve 1/2 cup dressing to stir into the salad just before serving.

Our daughter made this recipe for a 4-H food show and won a blue ribbon. It's so simple to prepare, even on hurried, hectic days. We like to eat these squares with sour cream and salsa.
—Tracy Johnson
Canyon, Texas

CHILI CORN BREAD
(Pictured below)

1 cup plus 3 tablespoons cornmeal, *divided*
1 teaspoon salt
1/2 teaspoon baking soda
4 eggs
1 can (14-3/4 ounces) cream-style corn
1 cup milk
2 tablespoons vegetable oil
1 pound ground beef, cooked and drained
2 cups (8 ounces) shredded cheddar cheese
1 can (4 ounces) chopped green chilies
1 medium onion, chopped

Sprinkle a greased 13-in. x 9-in. x 2-in. baking pan with 1 tablespoon of cornmeal; set aside. In a bowl, combine the salt, baking soda and remaining cornmeal. In another bowl, beat eggs; add corn, milk and oil. Stir into dry ingredients just until moistened. Pour half of the batter into prepared pan. Layer with beef, cheese, chilies and onion. Top with remaining batter. Bake at 350° for 45-50 minutes or until golden brown. Let stand for 5 minutes before cutting. **Yield:** 8 servings.

SERVING SUGGESTION:

Chili Corn Bread can be served warm or cold.
Pack some squares for a deliciously different brown-bag lunch.

LAYERED CHALUPA SALAD

3 pounds ground beef
1 can (16 ounces) refried
  beans
1 can (16 ounces) kidney
  beans, rinsed and drained
1/2 cup water
1/4 cup cider vinegar
2 tablespoons garlic salt
1 teaspoon pepper
1 can (8 ounces) tomato
  sauce
1 teaspoon hot pepper sauce
Corn chips
Optional toppings: shredded
  cheddar cheese, shredded
  lettuce, chopped tomatoes,
  finely chopped radishes and
  sweet onion

In a Dutch oven, cook beef over medium heat until no longer pink; drain. Add beans, water, vinegar, garlic salt and pepper. Bring to a boil. Reduce heat; simmer, uncovered, for 30 minutes, stirring occasionally. Meanwhile, in a saucepan, combine tomato sauce and hot sauce; heat through. Place corn chips on a large serving platter; top with beef mixture and toppings of your choice. Drizzle with tomato sauce mixture. **Yield:** 14 servings.

*This favorite is always requested for various family occasions. Although it serves a lot of people, this zippy salad doesn't last long on our dinner table.
—Virginia Zeckser Mode, Illinois*

CHEESEBURGER LOAF

1 pound ground beef
1 small onion, chopped
2/3 cup shredded cheddar
  cheese
1/3 cup shredded mozzarella
  cheese
1/4 cup ketchup
1-1/2 teaspoons salt, *divided*
1/4 teaspoon pepper
1-3/4 cups all-purpose flour
1 tablespoon baking powder
1/4 cup shortening
3/4 cup milk

In a skillet, cook beef over medium heat until no longer pink; drain. Add onion, cheeses, ketchup, 1/2 teaspoon salt and pepper; set aside. In a bowl, combine the flour, baking powder and remaining salt. Cut in shortening until mixture resembles coarse crumbs. Using a fork, stir in milk until mixture forms a ball. On a floured surface, roll out dough into a 15-in. x 10-in. rectangle. Spread meat mixture to within 1 in. of edges. Roll up, jelly-roll style, starting with a long side. Pinch edges to seal. Place seam side down on an ungreased baking sheet. Bake at 425° for 30 minutes or until golden brown. Cut into slices. **Yield:** 1 loaf.

*I received this recipe more than 25 years ago in a chain letter. This stuffed bread travels well to picnics, and leftovers are excellent for lunch.
—Sheila Cormack Vanderhoof, British Columbia*

TIMELY TIP:

Freeze leftovers of Cheeseburger Loaf for up to 3 months in an airtight container. Reheat on a baking sheet at 375° for 20 to 30 minutes or until heated through.

SATISFYING SANDWICHES

Sandwiches are tops for
hearty lunches and casual
dinners. But don't settle
for the ordinary.
This chapter will get
you on a roll, fixing
a savory array of
burgers, pockets, sloppy
joes, subs and more.

DAGWOOD
BURGERS (P. 106)

HAMBURGER HOAGIE (P. 92)
PIZZERIA BURGERS (P. 93)
GUMBO JOES (P. 93)

COOKING GROUND BEEF PATTIES

The chart below indicates approximate cooking times for pan-frying, broiling and grilling beef patties. Keep in mind that these are just guidelines. It's more important that the internal temperature of each patty reaches 160°.

When cooking beef patties, turn them with a spatula. Do not flatten; otherwise, flavorful juices will escape and the burgers will be dry.

COOKING METHOD	THICKNESS	APPROXIMATE COOKING TIME
Pan-frying (over medium heat)	1/2 inch x 4 inches 3/4 inch x 4 inches	10 to 12 minutes 12 to 15 minutes
Broiling (3 to 4 inches from heat)	1/2 inch x 4 inches 3/4 inch x 4 inches	10 to 12 minutes 12 to 14 minutes
Grilling (over medium-hot heat)	1/2 inch x 4 inches 3/4 inch x 4 inches	11 to 13 minutes 13 to 15 minutes

HAMBURGER HOAGIE

(Pictured on page 91)

Why rely on ho-hum lunch meat for a hoagie sandwich when you can fill yours with hot and hearty ground beef? Football Sundays wouldn't be the same without this treat.
—Debbie Guntz
Collegeville,
Pennsylvania

1-1/2 pounds ground beef
1 can (8 ounces) tomato sauce
3 slices process American cheese
1/4 cup chopped onion
2 beef bouillon cubes
1/2 teaspoon garlic powder
1 loaf (1 pound) French *or* Italian bread
Additional process American cheese slices, optional
1 medium green pepper, thinly sliced
1 medium tomato, thinly sliced

In a skillet, cook beef over medium heat until no longer pink; drain. Stir in tomato sauce, cheese, onion, bouillon and garlic powder. Cover and simmer for 10 minutes or until bouillon is dissolved and cheese is melted. Cut the bread in half widthwise and lengthwise. Carefully hollow out top and bottom of loaf, leaving a 1/2-in. shell (discard removed bread or save for another use). Spoon meat mixture into bottom halves of bread. Top with additional cheese if desired, green pepper and tomato. Replace bread tops. Wrap in heavy-duty foil. Bake at 400° for 15-20 minutes or until heated through. Slice and serve warm. **Yield:** 6 servings.

TIMELY TIP:

It's a snap to slice tomatoes if you use a serrated knife. Also, slices will hold their shape better if you slice from stem end to blossom end.

PIZZERIA BURGERS

(Pictured on page 91)

3/4 cup pizza sauce, *divided*
1/4 cup dry bread crumbs
1/4 teaspoon dried oregano
1 teaspoon salt
Dash pepper
1-1/2 pounds ground beef
1/4 pound bulk pork sausage
6 slices mozzarella cheese
6 sandwich rolls, split

In a bowl, combine 1/2 cup pizza sauce, bread crumbs, oregano, salt and pepper. Crumble beef and sausage over mixture; mix well. Shape into six patties. In a skillet, cook patties over medium heat until no longer pink. Top with remaining pizza sauce and the mozzarella cheese. Cover and cook 2 minutes longer or until cheese is melted. Serve on rolls. **Yield:** 6 servings.

SIMPLE SUBSTITUTIONS:

Use bulk Italian sausage and provolone cheese instead of the pork sausage and mozzarella in Pizzeria Burgers.

GUMBO JOES

(Pictured on page 91)

1-1/2 pounds ground beef
1 large onion, chopped
1/4 cup chopped green pepper
1 can (10-3/4 ounces) condensed chicken gumbo soup, undiluted
1/2 cup ketchup
1/4 cup packed brown sugar
3 tablespoons vinegar
1 tablespoon prepared horseradish
1 bay leaf
1 teaspoon salt
1/4 teaspoon pepper
12 sandwich rolls, split

In a large skillet, cook beef, onion and green pepper over medium heat until meat is no longer pink; drain. Stir in soup, ketchup, brown sugar, vinegar, horseradish, bay leaf, salt and pepper. Cover and simmer for 30 minutes. Discard bay leaf. Spoon onto rolls. **Yield:** 12 servings.

PERFECT PARTNERS:

To make Gumbo Joes a complete meal, serve them with baked beans, potato salad, pickles and a gelatin salad.

PEPPER CHEESE PATTIES

(Pictured below)

1 egg
1 can (5 ounces) evaporated milk
1/2 cup crushed butter-flavored crackers (about 15 crackers)
1/2 cup chopped green pepper
1/4 cup chopped onion
1 tablespoon prepared mustard
1 teaspoon salt
1 teaspoon pepper
1-1/2 pounds lean ground beef
1 jar (5 ounces) pimiento *or* American sharp cheese spread, softened

6 hamburger buns, split
Lettuce and tomato slices

In a bowl, combine the first eight ingredients. Crumble beef over the mixture and mix well. On a piece of waxed paper, pat meat mixture into a 12-in. square. Spread with cheese. Roll up jelly-roll style. Cut into 2-in. slices. Place on a greased broiler pan. Broil for 8 minutes on each side or until meat is no longer pink. Serve on buns with lettuce and tomato. **Yield:** 6 servings.

TIMELY TIP:

For easier slicing, first freeze the meat mixture for Pepper Cheese Patties for 20 to 30 minutes. Or prepare it 24 hours in advance and refrigerate.

VEGGIE BEEF BURGERS

1 medium green pepper, finely chopped
1 medium onion, finely chopped
1 celery rib, finely chopped
1 medium carrot, finely chopped
1 tablespoon Worcestershire sauce
1 tablespoon liquid smoke, optional
Salt and pepper to taste
2 pounds ground beef
8 hamburger buns, split
Lettuce leaves and sliced onion, tomatoes and pickles

In a bowl, combine the first five ingredients. Add liquid smoke, salt and pepper if desired. Crumble beef over mixture and mix well. Shape into eight patties. Broil, grill or pan-fry until meat is no longer pink. Serve on buns with lettuce, onion, tomatoes and pickles. **Yield:** 8 servings.

SHAPING HAMBURGER PATTIES

Use a 1/2-cup measuring cup or ice cream scoop to make equal size patties. Gently form each portion into a patty. For moist light-textured burgers, be careful not to overmix or overhandle the meat mixture.

I developed this recipe as a way to get more nutritious vegetables into our diet. Be sure to finely chop the vegetables (I use my food processor) so that they cook thoroughly.
—Dolores Tolson
Oklahoma City, Oklahoma

BACON BURGER PUFFS

16 bacon strips, halved
1-1/2 pounds ground beef
1/2 package (17-1/4 ounces) frozen puff pastry sheets (one sheet), thawed
4 slices mozzarella cheese
4 slices cheddar cheese
1 tablespoon milk
1 envelope au jus sauce mix

In a large skillet, cook bacon over medium heat until crisp. Remove to paper towels. Drain and discard drippings. Shape beef into four patties. In the same skillet, cook patties over medium heat until no longer pink; cool. On a lightly floured surface, roll out puff pastry to half of the original thickness. Cut into four rectangles. Place a slice of mozzarella cheese in the center of each rectangle; top each with four bacon pieces, one beef patty, four more bacon pieces and a slice of cheddar cheese. Wrap pastry around filling. Brush edges with water; seal. Place on a greased baking sheet. Brush with milk. Bake at 425° for 12-15 minutes or until golden brown. Meanwhile, prepare au jus sauce according to package directions. Serve with the burger puffs. **Yield:** 4 servings.

This recipe is the result of my attempt to improve upon a dish I sampled at our local county fair. Friends and family say these are the best burgers they've ever eaten.
—Connie Williams
Starke, Florida

SAUCY HERB HAMBURGERS

1 egg
1/4 cup sour cream
1/4 cup dry bread crumbs
1/4 teaspoon dried parsley
    flakes
1/4 teaspoon dried thyme
1/4 teaspoon salt
Dash pepper
1 pound ground beef
1 cup ketchup
1/4 cup packed brown sugar
2 teaspoons prepared
    mustard
4 hamburger buns, split

In a bowl, combine the first seven ingredients. Crumble beef over mixture and mix well. Shape into four patties. For the barbecue sauce, combine ketchup, brown sugar and mustard in a small bowl. Grill patties, uncovered, over medium-hot heat for 3 minutes on each side. Brush with barbecue sauce. Grill 4-6 minutes longer or until juices run clear, basting and turning several times. Serve on buns. **Yield:** 4 servings.

TIMELY TIP:

It's easy to take Saucy Herb Hamburgers along on a picnic. Make the patties and barbecue sauce early in the morning, store in airtight containers and refrigerate. Transport to the picnic in a cooler filled with ice. Grill hamburgers as directed. Don't forget to pack clean containers for any leftovers.

GRANDMA'S SLOPPY JOES

1 pound ground beef
1 large onion, chopped
1-1/2 cups ketchup
3/4 cup sweet pickle relish
1/2 cup packed brown sugar
8 hamburger buns, split

In a large skillet, cook beef and onion over medium heat until the meat is no longer pink; drain. Stir in the ketchup, relish and brown sugar; mix well. Cover and simmer for 30 minutes or until heated through. Spoon onto buns. **Yield:** 8 servings.

HELPFUL HINT:

To prevent brown sugar from hardening, store it in a resealable plastic bag in a cool dry place. If it does harden, add an apple wedge to the bag until the sugar softens (about 1 to 2 days); discard the apple.

MEATBALL PARTY SUB

(Pictured above)

2 eggs, beaten
1/2 cup dry bread crumbs
1/2 cup grated Romano *or* Parmesan cheese
1/4 cup minced fresh parsley
1 envelope spaghetti sauce mix, *divided*
1/2 teaspoon salt
1-1/2 pounds ground beef
1/2 pound ground pork
1 can (8 ounces) tomato sauce
1/2 cup water
1 loaf (1 pound) French bread

In a bowl, combine the eggs, bread crumbs, cheese, parsley, 2 tablespoons spaghetti sauce mix and salt. Crumble beef and pork over mixture; mix well. Shape into 20-24 meatballs. In a skillet, cook meatballs until no longer pink; drain.

Stir in tomato sauce, water and remaining spaghetti sauce mix. Bring to a boil. Reduce heat; cover and simmer for 25 minutes. Meanwhile, warm the bread. Cut a thin slice off the top; hollow out bottom of loaf, leaving a 3/8-in. shell (discard removed bread or save for another use). Spoon meatballs and sauce into bread shell; replace top. Slice; serve warm. **Yield:** 8 servings.

MAKING A BREAD SHELL

Using a serrated knife, cut a thin slice off the top of the loaf of bread. With a fork, pull out the bread from inside, leaving a 3/8-inch shell.

I've made these meatballs for years to use in this sandwich or to toss into spaghetti sauce. The big sub is a great conversation piece and tasty treat at football parties.
—Colleen Edelsward
Woodinville,
Washington

TERIYAKI BURGERS
(Pictured above)

1-1/2 cups Rice Chex, crushed
1/4 cup finely chopped onion
2 tablespoons soy sauce
1/2 teaspoon dried marjoram
1/4 teaspoon ground ginger
Dash garlic powder
1 pound ground beef
1 can (8 ounces) sliced pineapple, drained
4 sandwich rolls, split

In a bowl, combine the first six ingredients. Crumble beef over mixture and mix well. Shape into four patties. Grill or broil until no longer pink. If desired, grill or broil pineapple rings until lightly browned. Place burgers on roll bottoms. Top with pineapple and roll tops. **Yield:** 4 servings.

SERVING SUGGESTION:

Just before the Teriyaki Burgers have finished cooking, spread a little butter or margarine on the cut side of the rolls and grill or broil them until lightly browned. A toasted roll tastes great topped with any kind of burger!

MEATY PITA POCKETS

3 medium onions, chopped
1/2 cup pine nuts *or* sunflower
    kernels
2 tablespoons vegetable oil
2 pounds ground beef
2 medium tomatoes,
    chopped
1/2 cup chopped green pepper
1/3 cup lemon juice
1/3 cup minced fresh parsley
3 tablespoons cider *or* red
    wine vinegar
1-1/2 teaspoons salt
3/4 teaspoon ground allspice
1/2 teaspoon cayenne pepper
6 pita breads, halved

In a skillet, saute onions and pine nuts in oil until onions are tender and nuts are toasted. Add beef; cook over medium heat until no longer pink. Drain. Stir in tomatoes, green pepper, lemon juice, parsley, vinegar, salt, allspice and cayenne; mix well. Reduce heat; cover and simmer for 30 minutes. Spoon about 1/2 cup meat mixture into each pita half. **Yield:** 6 servings.

HELPFUL HINT:

Store pine nuts in an airtight container in the refrigerator for up to 2 months or freezer for up to 6 months.

Lemon juice gives this meat mixture a Middle Eastern flavor, making it one of my family's favorite meals. The pine nuts or sunflower kernels add a bit of crunch.
—Lauren McMann
Blairsville, Georgia

SIMPLE SLOPPY JOES

2 pounds ground beef
1 large onion, chopped
2 garlic cloves, minced
1 can (8 ounces) tomato
    sauce
1 can (6 ounces) tomato
    paste
1/2 cup ketchup
1/3 cup packed brown sugar
3 tablespoons soy sauce
12 hamburger buns, split and
    toasted

In a skillet, cook beef, onion and garlic over medium heat until meat is no longer pink; drain. Stir in tomato sauce and paste, ketchup, brown sugar and soy sauce; mix well. Bring to a boil. Reduce heat; cover and simmer for 15-20 minutes, stirring occasionally. Spoon about 1/2 cup meat mixture onto each bun. **Yield:** 12 servings.

PERFECT PARTNERS:

Round out a hearty lunch featuring Simple Sloppy Joes with potato or corn chips and carrot sticks.

My mom and I had fun creating this recipe together. My daughter, Jennifer, could eat these sandwiches every day. It's a good thing the recipe makes a big batch!
—Ona Allen
Lancaster, Ohio

REUBEN BURGERS
(Pictured at right)

1 cup soft bread crumbs
2/3 cup Thousand Island salad dressing, *divided*
1 teaspoon salt
1/8 teaspoon pepper
1-1/2 pounds ground beef
8 slices rye bread
1 can (14 ounces) sauerkraut, rinsed and drained
4 ounces sliced Swiss cheese
Butter *or* margarine

In a bowl, combine bread crumbs, 1/3 cup dressing, salt and pepper. Crumble beef over mixture and mix well. Shape into four oval patties, about 1/2 in. thick. Broil or pan-fry until no longer pink. Place each on a slice of bread. Top with sauerkraut, cheese and remaining dressing and bread. Melt butter in a skillet. Cook sandwiches over medium heat until golden brown on each side. **Yield:** 4 servings.

SIMPLE SUBSTITUTION:

Don't have Thousand Island dressing on hand?
Combine 1 cup mayonnaise or salad dressing, 1/4 cup chili sauce,
1 teaspoon prepared horseradish, 1 teaspoon finely chopped onion
and 1/2 teaspoon paprika. Store in the refrigerator.

PEPPY MEATBALL SUBS
(Pictured at right)

1 jar (28 ounces) spaghetti sauce, *divided*
1 egg
1 cup seasoned bread crumbs
1 medium onion, chopped
1/2 cup chopped sweet red pepper
1 garlic clove, minced
1/2 teaspoon Italian seasoning
1/4 teaspoon salt
1/4 teaspoon pepper
1 pound ground beef
6 submarine *or* hoagie buns, split
1 jar (11-1/2 ounces) pepperoncinis, drained and sliced, optional
1 can (2-1/4 ounces) sliced ripe olives, drained, optional
Shredded Parmesan cheese and thinly sliced red onion, optional

In a large bowl, combine 1/2 cup of spaghetti sauce, egg, bread crumbs, onion, red pepper, garlic, Italian seasoning, salt and pepper. Crumble beef over mixture and mix well. Shape into 1-in. balls. Place in a single layer in an ungreased 15-in. x 10-in. x 1-in. baking pan. Bake at 350° for 15-20 minutes or until meat is no longer pink, turning once; drain. Transfer to a large saucepan; add remaining spaghetti sauce. Bring to a boil. Reduce heat; cover and simmer for 15 minutes. Spoon meatballs and sauce onto bun bottoms. Top with pepperoncinis, olives, Parmesan cheese and red onion if desired. Replace bun tops. **Yield:** 6 servings.

REUBEN BURGERS
PEPPY MEATBALL SUBS
MEAT LOAF GYROS (p. 102)

MEAT LOAF GYROS

(Pictured on page 101)

1/4 cup water
1/4 cup finely chopped onion
2 tablespoons minced fresh parsley
2 teaspoons salt
1 teaspoon ground cumin
1 teaspoon dried oregano
3/4 teaspoon pepper
1/4 teaspoon garlic powder
2 pounds lean ground beef
1 large red onion, chopped
1 large tomato, thinly sliced
8 pita breads, halved
1/2 cup plain yogurt

In a large bowl, combine the first eight ingredients. Crumble beef over mixture and mix well. Press into an ungreased 9-in. x 5-in. x 3-in. loaf pan. Bake at 350° for 1-1/4 to 1-1/2 hours or until meat is no longer pink; drain. Let stand for 10 minutes. Cut into thin slices. Place meat loaf, onion and tomato into pita halves; drizzle with yogurt. **Yield:** 8 servings.

SIMPLE SUBSTITUTIONS:

If you're not a fan of yogurt, use creamy cucumber or ranch salad dressing in Meat Loaf Gyros.

STUFFED BARBECUED BURGERS

2 pounds ground beef
1 cup (4 ounces) shredded cheese of your choice
1/3 cup finely chopped green pepper
1/3 cup finely chopped tomato
3 fresh mushrooms, finely chopped
2 green onions, finely chopped
1/2 cup barbecue sauce
1 tablespoon sugar
4 hamburger buns, split

Shape beef into eight patties. In a bowl, combine the cheese, green pepper, tomato, mushrooms and onions. Top half of the patties with vegetable mixture. Cover with remaining patties and firmly press edges to seal. Grill or broil for 3 minutes on each side. Brush with barbecue sauce and sprinkle with sugar. Grill or broil 10-12 minutes longer or until no longer pink, basting and turning occasionally. Serve on buns. **Yield:** 4 servings.

MAKING STUFFED HAMBURGERS

STEP 1
Combine the stuffing ingredients and place an equal amount on each patty.

STEP 2
Place remaining patties over stuffing and firmly press edges to seal.

ORIENTAL PATTIES

1/4 cup soy sauce
2 to 4 tablespoons minced fresh cilantro *or* parsley
1 green onion, chopped
2 garlic cloves, minced
1 teaspoon ground ginger
7 drops hot pepper sauce
Pinch pepper
1 pound ground beef
4 hamburger buns, split

In a bowl, combine the first seven ingredients. Crumble beef over the mixture and mix well. Shape into four patties. Broil or grill until no longer pink. Serve on buns. **Yield:** 4 servings.

HELPFUL HINT:

Freeze leftover minced fresh parsley in a resealable plastic bag. Use it directly from the freezer in any recipe calling for fresh or dried parsley.

I got this recipe from a television cooking show some years ago. I like to mix the burgers together in the morning and refrigerate until dinnertime.
—Patricia Rubsam
Hillsboro, Oregon

BAKED SLOPPY JOES

1 pound ground beef
1/4 cup chopped green pepper
1 tablespoon chopped onion
1 can (8 ounces) tomato sauce
1/2 cup ketchup
2 tablespoons grated Parmesan cheese
3/4 teaspoon garlic powder, *divided*
1/2 teaspoon fennel seed, crushed
1/4 teaspoon dried oregano
3 tablespoons butter *or* margarine, melted
1/2 teaspoon paprika
4 kaiser rolls, split
4 slices mozzarella cheese

In a skillet, cook beef, green pepper and onion over medium heat until meat is no longer pink; drain. Stir in the tomato sauce, ketchup, Parmesan cheese, 1/2 teaspoon of garlic powder, fennel seed and oregano. Bring to a boil. Reduce heat; simmer, uncovered, for 20 minutes. In a bowl, combine butter, paprika and remaining garlic powder; mix well. Brush over cut sides of rolls. Spread meat mixture on roll bottoms; top with mozzarella cheese. Replace roll tops. Wrap each in heavy-duty foil. Place on a baking sheet. Bake at 350° for 15 minutes or until the cheese is melted. **Yield:** 4 servings.

PERFECT PARTNERS:

With a seven-layer salad and french fries, one Baked Sloppy Joe is usually enough for anyone. Brownies or chocolate layer cake top off this casual tasty meal.

When our kids were teenagers, I'd often double this recipe just in case their friends stopped by for dinner unannounced. Leftovers can be reheated and are just as good the second time around.
—Beverly Bahlow
Gray, Tennessee

My sister-in-law fixed this as a spur-of-the-moment lunch one Sunday several years ago. I had her write down the ingredients before she forgot. I've relied on this recipe often ever since.
—Charlotte McDaniel
Williamsville, Illinois

BROILED BEEF 'N' MUSHROOM BREAD

1-1/2 pounds ground beef
1 medium onion, chopped
1 small green pepper, chopped
1 celery rib, chopped
1 garlic clove, minced
1 block (8 ounces) Colby cheese, cut into cubes
1 can (10-3/4 ounces) condensed tomato soup, undiluted
1 jar (6 ounces) sliced mushrooms, drained
1 can (2-1/4 ounces) sliced ripe olives, drained
1/2 teaspoon salt
1/4 teaspoon pepper
1 loaf (1 pound) French bread

In a skillet, cook beef, onion, green pepper, celery and garlic over medium heat until meat is no longer pink and vegetables are tender; drain. Stir in the cheese, soup, mushrooms, olives, salt and pepper; mix well. Simmer, uncovered, for 10-15 minutes or until cheese is melted, stirring occasionally. Meanwhile, cut the bread widthwise into four pieces, then cut each piece lengthwise. Place cut side up on greased baking sheets. Broil 4-5 in. from the heat until lightly toasted. Top with meat mixture. Broil 4 in. from the heat for 2-3 minutes or until edges are browned. **Yield:** 8 servings.

SIMPLE SUBSTITUTION:

If you'd like, use 3/4 cup sliced fresh mushrooms in place of the canned ones when making Broiled Beef 'n' Mushroom Bread.

I love to add this or that to recipes to create my own taste twists. Wild rice is a popular ingredient here in Minnesota. But the only way my kids will touch it is in these burgers.
—Amy Barthelemy
Eagan, Minnesota

WILD RICE BURGERS

1 cup cooked wild rice
1 medium onion, chopped
1/4 cup chopped mushrooms
1/4 cup chopped green pepper
Salt and pepper to taste
1 pound ground beef
6 hamburger buns, split and toasted

In a bowl, combine the rice, onion, mushrooms, green pepper, salt and pepper. Crumble beef over mixture; mix well. Shape into six patties. Grill or broil until no longer pink. Serve on buns. **Yield:** 6 servings.

PERFECT PARTNERS:

Wild Rice Burgers make nice autumn fare when served with acorn squash and apple cider.

WESTERN RANGE SANDWICHES

(Pictured below)

4 bacon strips, diced
1 pound lean ground beef
1 medium onion, chopped
1/2 cup chopped green pepper
2 cans (16 ounces *each*)
    kidney beans, rinsed and
    drained
1 can (8 ounces) tomato
    sauce
2 tablespoons chili powder
1/2 teaspoon salt
1/8 teaspoon pepper
2 cups (8 ounces) shredded
    cheddar cheese
6 English muffins, split and
    toasted

In a large skillet, cook bacon until crisp. Remove to paper towels. Drain, reserving 2 tablespoons of drippings. Cook beef, onion and green pepper in drippings until meat is no longer pink. Add beans, tomato sauce, chili powder, salt, pepper and bacon. Bring to a boil. Reduce heat; add cheese. Cook and stir over low heat until cheese is melted. Spoon onto English muffin halves. **Yield:** 12 servings.

I found this recipe in a cookbook left to me by my mother. Over the past 20 years, it's been a big hit with my family, especially with those who love kidney beans. Using English muffins instead of hamburger buns is a nice change.
—Mauvereen Cannady
Portage, Wisconsin

DAGWOOD BURGERS
(Pictured above and on page 90)

You definitely need a knife and fork to dig into these piled-high burgers. They make a tasty luncheon meal.
—Ruby Berry
Bradenton, Florida

1	**pound ground beef**
1/4	**cup coleslaw salad dressing**
4	**thick slices bread, toasted**
4	**bacon strips, cooked and drained**
4	**slices Swiss cheese**
4	**slices tomato**
4	**slices onion**
8	**slices unpeeled cucumber**
4	**slices dill pickle**
4	**pitted jumbo ripe olives**
1/4	**cup salad dressing of your choice, optional**

Shape beef into four patties. Broil or pan-fry until no longer pink; drain. Spread coleslaw dressing over bread. Top each slice with a beef patty, bacon, cheese, tomato, onion, two cucumber slices, pickle and olive. Secure with a toothpick. Serve with additional salad dressing if desired. **Yield: 4 servings.**

SIMPLE SUBSTITUTIONS:

Vary the flavor of Dagwood Burgers by combining different salad dressings and cheese. For instance, pair Thousand Island with Swiss, ranch with American or creamy Italian with mozzarella.

SURPRISE BURGERS

1 pound ground beef
4 slices pepper Jack *or*
   Monterey Jack cheese
4 slices sweet onion
4 slices green pepper
4 onion rolls, split

Shape beef into eight thin patties. Place a slice of cheese, onion and green pepper on four patties. Top with another patty; press edges to seal. Grill until no longer pink. Serve on rolls. **Yield:** 4 servings.

HELPFUL HINT:

In general, sweet onions have thin, light outer skins and contain a high level of water and sugar. These onions (including Vidalia and Walla Walla) are typically in season from April through August.

Nothing says "Summer!" like hamburgers on the grill. But why settle for the ordinary when you can serve this version that features a surprise filling of cheese, onion and green pepper.
—Debby Murray West Middleton, Indiana

OPEN-FACED PIZZA BURGERS

1-1/2 pounds ground beef
1/4 cup chopped onion
   1 can (15 ounces) pizza sauce
   1 can (4 ounces) mushroom
      stems and pieces, drained
   1 tablespoon sugar
1/2 teaspoon dried oregano
   6 hamburger buns, split and
      toasted
1-1/2 cups (6 ounces) shredded
      mozzarella cheese

In a large skillet, cook beef and onion over medium heat until the meat is no longer pink; drain. Stir in pizza sauce, mushrooms, sugar and oregano; mix well. Spoon onto buns; sprinkle with mozzarella cheese. Place on ungreased baking sheets. Broil 4 in. from the heat for 2 minutes or until the cheese is melted. **Yield:** 12 servings.

TIMELY TIP:

It's easy to freeze Open-Faced Pizza Burgers for quick lunches later. Place the split and toasted buns on a baking sheet. Spoon the meat mixture onto buns; freeze for 1 hour. Transfer to heavy-duty resealable plastic bags or airtight containers. To reheat, thaw, sprinkle with cheese and broil until cheese is melted.

I'm not sure where I first saw this recipe, but I'm glad I did! My family requests these burgers often. A dash of oregano livens up canned pizza sauce.
—Sharon Schwartz Burlington, Wisconsin

BACON-WRAPPED HAMBURGERS

1/2 cup shredded cheddar cheese
1 small onion, chopped
1 egg
2 tablespoons ketchup
1 tablespoon grated Parmesan cheese
1 tablespoon Worcestershire sauce
1/2 teaspoon salt
1/8 teaspoon pepper
1 pound ground beef
6 bacon strips
6 hamburger buns, split

In a bowl, combine the first eight ingredients. Crumble beef over mixture and mix well. Shape into six patties. Wrap a bacon strip around each; secure with a toothpick. Grill until beef is no longer pink. Discard toothpicks. Serve on buns. **Yield:** 6 servings.

TIMELY TIP:

If you prefer, you can bake Bacon-Wrapped Hamburgers in a baking dish at 350° for 25 to 30 minutes or until beef is no longer pink.

LASAGNA IN A BUN

1/2 pound ground beef
1 medium onion, diced
1 can (8 ounces) tomato sauce
1 teaspoon Italian seasoning, *divided*
1/2 teaspoon salt
1 cup (4 ounces) shredded mozzarella cheese, *divided*
1/2 cup ricotta cheese
1 egg white
3 tablespoons grated Parmesan cheese
6 small submarine *or* hoagie buns (8 inches)

In a skillet, cook beef and onion over medium heat until meat is no longer pink; drain. Add tomato sauce, 1/2 teaspoon Italian seasoning and salt. Cook for 5 minutes or until heated through. Meanwhile, combine 1/2 cup mozzarella, ricotta, egg white, Parmesan and remaining Italian seasoning; mix well. Cut a thin slice off the top of each bun. Carefully hollow out bun bottoms, leaving a 1/4-in. shell (discard removed bread or save for another use). Spoon meat mixture into buns; top with the cheese mixture. Sprinkle with remaining mozzarella. Replace bun tops. Wrap each in heavy-duty foil. Place on a baking sheet. Bake at 400° for 25 minutes or until heated through. **Yield:** 6 servings.

LEMON-HERB GYROS

2 pounds ground beef
2 tablespoons minced fresh
  parsley *or* 2 teaspoons
  dried parsley flakes
3 garlic cloves, minced
1/3 cup lemon juice
1/4 cup beef broth
2 tablespoons minced fresh
  oregano *or* 2 teaspoons
  dried oregano
2 beef bouillon cubes
1-1/2 teaspoons minced fresh
  basil *or* 1/2 teaspoon
  dried basil
1 teaspoon salt
1/4 teaspoon pepper
6 pita breads, halved

1 large onion, sliced
1 large tomato, sliced
Ranch salad dressing

In a large skillet, cook beef over medium heat until no longer pink; drain. Add parsley and garlic; cook and stir for 2 minutes. Stir in lemon juice, broth, oregano, bouillon, basil, salt and pepper. Bring to a boil. Reduce heat; simmer, uncovered, for 5 minutes. Spoon about 1/3 cupful into each pita half. Add onion and tomato. Drizzle with salad dressing. **Yield:** 6 servings.

PERFECT PARTNERS:

*Team up Lemon-Herb Gyros and a light pasta
or rice salad for a mouth-watering meal.*

My father developed this recipe as an alternative to traditional gyros, which are made with lamb. This version is easy and made with everyday ingredients that appeal to everyone.
—Gina Mucha
Villa Park, Illinois

ONION LOOSE-MEAT SANDWICHES

1-1/2 pounds ground beef
2 tablespoons all-purpose
  flour
Salt and pepper to taste
1 can (10-1/2 ounces)
  condensed French onion
  soup, undiluted
6 to 8 hamburger buns, split
Sliced cheddar cheese and dill
  pickles, optional

In a skillet, cook beef over medium heat until no longer pink; drain. Stir in the flour, salt and pepper until blended. Gradually add soup. Bring to a boil; cook and stir for 2 minutes or until thickened. Spoon onto buns; top with cheese and pickles if desired. **Yield:** 6-8 servings.

SERVING SUGGESTION:

*For even more onion flavor, add 1/2 cup chopped onion
to the filling of Onion Loose-Meat Sandwiches.*

With French onion soup, these sandwiches don't have the typical flavor of most sloppy joes. My sisters and I rely on this recipe from Mom on days when there's little time to cook.
—Kathy Petrosky
Belle Vernon,
Pennsylvania

SWEET BARBECUE SANDWICHES

2 pounds ground beef
1 medium onion, chopped
1 can (10-3/4 ounces) condensed tomato soup, undiluted
1 can (8 ounces) tomato sauce
2 tablespoons Worcestershire sauce
2 teaspoons molasses
1 teaspoon salt
1 teaspoon ground cinnamon
1 teaspoon ground mustard

1/2 teaspoon chili powder
1/2 teaspoon pepper
1/4 teaspoon ground cloves
10 hamburger buns, split

In a large skillet, cook beef and onion over medium heat until the meat is no longer pink; drain. Stir in the soup, tomato sauce, Worcestershire sauce, molasses and seasonings; mix well. Cover and simmer for 20 minutes. Serve on buns. **Yield:** 10 servings.

TIMELY TIP:

Before measuring molasses, coat the measuring spoon or cup with nonstick cooking spray— the molasses will slide right out with little mess.

GREEN ONION BURGERS

1/4 cup soy sauce
2 tablespoons beef broth
1/4 pound fresh mushrooms, finely chopped
3/4 cup chopped water chestnuts
1/2 cup chopped green onions
2 tablespoons minced fresh gingerroot *or* 2 teaspoons ground ginger
1 tablespoon cornstarch

1/4 teaspoon cayenne pepper
2 pounds lean ground beef
12 hamburger buns, split

In a bowl, combine the first eight ingredients. Crumble beef over the mixture and mix well. Shape into 12 patties. Grill or broil until no longer pink, turning once. Serve on buns. **Yield:** 12 servings.

HELPFUL HINT:

You can find fresh gingerroot in the produce section of your grocery store. If tightly wrapped, it can be refrigerated for 3 weeks or frozen for up to 1 year. Use your garlic press to easily mince peeled fresh gingerroot.

BURGERS WITH GARDEN SAUCE

(Pictured above)

1 large onion, diced
2 medium carrots, diced
1 medium green pepper, diced
2 celery ribs, diced
1 tablespoon minced fresh parsley
1 tablespoon vegetable oil
2 pints cherry tomatoes
1/2 cup ketchup
2 tablespoons brown sugar
2 tablespoons lemon juice
2 tablespoons vinegar
2 tablespoons prepared mustard
1 tablespoon Worcestershire sauce
Salt and pepper to taste
BURGERS:
4 slices bread
1/2 cup water
2 eggs, beaten
1 medium onion, finely chopped
2 teaspoons minced fresh parsley
1 teaspoon salt
1/2 teaspoon pepper
2 pounds ground beef
8 sandwich rolls, split

In a Dutch oven or large saucepan, saute onion, carrots, green pepper, celery and parsley in oil until vegetables are tender. Add tomatoes, ketchup, brown sugar, lemon juice, vinegar, mustard, Worcestershire sauce, salt and pepper. Cover and simmer for 1-1/2 hours. Meanwhile, soak bread in water; squeeze dry and crumble into a bowl. Add the eggs, onion, parsley, salt and pepper. Crumble beef over mixture and mix well. Shape into eight patties. Broil or pan-fry until no longer pink; drain. Add to sauce. Cover and simmer for 30 minutes or until heated through. Serve on rolls. **Yield:** 8 servings.

In western New York State, even the sunniest summer day can quickly turn ugly. So Mom came up with this recipe that conveniently has you cook the burgers indoors.
—Debbie Buchholz
Amherst, New York

I've made this many times when friends and family come over to watch football and basketball games. This sandwich always satisfies the huge appetites we build up cheering for our teams.
—Shelley Banzhaf
Maywood, Nebraska

PEPPERONI STROMBOLI

(Pictured below)

2 loaves (1 pound *each*) frozen bread dough, thawed
2 eggs, beaten
1/3 cup olive *or* vegetable oil
1/2 teaspoon *each* garlic powder, salt and pepper
1/2 teaspoon ground mustard
1/2 teaspoon dried oregano
1 pound ground beef, cooked and drained
1 package (3-1/2 ounces) sliced pepperoni
2 cups (8 ounces) shredded mozzarella cheese
1 cup (4 ounces) shredded cheddar cheese
1 small onion, chopped

Place each loaf of bread dough in a greased bowl, turning once to grease top. Cover and let rise in a warm place until doubled, about 45 minutes. Punch down. Roll each loaf into a 15-in. x 12-in. rectangle. In a bowl, combine eggs, oil and seasonings. Brush over dough to within 1/2 in. of edges; set remaining egg mixture aside. Arrange beef, pepperoni, cheeses and onion on dough to within 1/2 in. of edges. Roll up, jelly-roll style, beginning with a long side. Seal the edges well. Place seam side down on greased baking sheets. Brush with remaining egg mixture. Bake at 375° for 30-35 minutes or until lightly browned. Let stand for 5-10 minutes before cutting. **Yield:** about 16 servings.

EASY OVEN PATTIES

1 egg
1/2 cup soft bread crumbs
1/2 teaspoon salt
1/4 teaspoon pepper
1-1/2 pounds lean ground beef
2 tablespoons prepared mustard
6 slices onion
6 slices process American cheese
3/4 cup condensed tomato soup, undiluted
6 hamburger buns, split

In a bowl, combine the first four ingredients. Crumble beef over mixture and mix well. Shape into six patties. Place in a greased 11-in. x 7-in. x 2-in. baking dish. Spread mustard over each patty. Top with onion and cheese. Pour soup over all. Bake, uncovered, at 350° for 35 minutes or until the meat is no longer pink. Serve on buns. **Yield:** 6 servings.

HELPFUL HINT:

You won't use an entire can of tomato soup in Easy Oven Patties. So freeze the little bit that's left over and add it to the pot next time you make vegetable soup or spaghetti sauce.

In this recipe from my mother-in-law, the toppings are baked along with the hamburger patties. It's so easy even I can make it!
—Dave Almquist
Petersburg, Illinois

BIG-BATCH BURGERS

1-1/2 cups crushed butter-flavored crackers (about 38 crackers)
1 cup applesauce
1 envelope onion soup mix
2 tablespoons Worcestershire sauce
1 tablespoon hot pepper sauce
2-1/2 teaspoons seasoned salt
5 pounds ground beef
20 hamburger buns, split

In a bowl, combine the first six ingredients. Crumble beef over mixture and mix well. Shape into 20 patties. Broil, grill or pan-fry until no longer pink. Serve on buns. **Yield:** 20 servings.

TIMELY TIP:

To save time when entertaining—or to pull out individual patties if cooking for a smaller group—form the Big-Batch Burgers, layer patties between waxed paper, wrap tightly and freeze. Thaw in the refrigerator before cooking.

We had these delicious hamburgers while visiting my aunt's house for a family picnic. Everyone enjoyed them so much we all had to have a copy of the recipe.
—Kay Kendrick
Ruffin, North Carolina

ITALIAN BURGERS

1 medium onion, chopped
1/4 cup Italian salad dressing
1 pound ground beef
4 hamburger buns, split

In a bowl, combine onion and salad dressing. Crumble beef over mixture and mix well. Shape into four patties. Broil, grill or pan-fry until no longer pink. Serve on buns. **Yield:** 4 servings.

TIMELY TIP:

Cooking hamburgers over a very hot fire? Poke a hole in the center of each patty while shaping it. The center will cook faster...and the hole will be gone when the hamburger is done.

CHEESY GARLIC BURGERS

2 pounds ground beef
2 teaspoons garlic powder, *divided*
1 loaf (1 pound) French bread
1/2 cup butter *or* margarine, softened
6 slices provolone cheese
6 slices mozzarella cheese
1 jar (14 ounces) spaghetti sauce, warmed

In a bowl, combine beef and 1 teaspoon garlic powder. Shape into six thin patties. Pan-fry until no longer pink. Meanwhile, cut bread in half lengthwise. Combine butter and remaining garlic powder; spread over cut sides of bread. On the bottom half, layer provolone cheese, beef patties and the mozzarella cheese. Replace bread top. Wrap in a large piece of heavy-duty foil (about 28 in. x 18 in.). Place on a baking sheet. Bake at 375° for 5-10 minutes or until cheese is melted and sandwich is heated through. Cut loaf between each patty. Serve with spaghetti sauce for dipping. **Yield:** 6 servings.

SERVING SUGGESTION:

You can bake Cheesy Garlic Burgers on six hamburger buns instead of on a loaf of French bread.

Texas Cheeseburger

(Pictured above)

1 package (1/4 ounce) active dry yeast
1 cup warm water (110° to 115°)
1 cup quick-cooking oats
1/4 cup butter *or* margarine, softened
1/4 cup instant nonfat dry milk powder
1 egg, *separated*
2 tablespoons sugar
1 teaspoon salt
2-3/4 to 3-1/4 cups all-purpose flour
2 tablespoons sesame seeds

BURGER:
1 egg
3/4 cup ketchup
3/4 cup quick-cooking oats
1 teaspoon salt
1-1/2 pounds ground beef
Lettuce leaves
4 slices process American cheese

In a mixing bowl, dissolve yeast in water. Add oats, butter, milk powder, egg yolk, sugar, salt and 1 cup of flour; beat until smooth. Add enough remaining flour to form a stiff dough. Turn onto a floured surface; knead until smooth and elastic, about 6-8 minutes. Place in a greased bowl, turning once to grease top. Cover and refrigerate for 2-24 hours. Punch dough down and shape into a ball. Press into a greased 9-in. round baking pan. Cover and let rise in a warm place until nearly doubled, about 45 minutes. Brush with egg white; sprinkle with sesame seeds. Bake at 350° for 30 minutes or until golden brown. Remove from pan to a wire rack to cool completely. Meanwhile, combine the first four burger ingredients. Crumble beef over mixture and mix well. On a greased broiler pan, shape meat mixture into an 8-1/2-in. patty. Bake, uncovered, at 350° for 30 minutes or until no longer pink. To serve, split bun in half. Place lettuce, burger and cheese on bottom of bun; replace top. Cut into wedges. **Yield:** 6 servings.

Your family will get a kick out of being served a wedge of this giant burger. To cut down on last-minute preparation, bake the bun ahead and store it in an airtight container. Split the bun in half just before serving.
—Victoria Beckham
Hurst, Texas

We made these sandwiches in my high school home economics class back in the 1960s. Traditional toppings are cleverly tucked inside these plump burgers for a mouthful of wonderful flavor.
—June Croft
Bay Minette, Alabama

STUFFED HALF-POUNDERS
(Pictured below)

2 pounds ground beef
2 eggs, beaten
Salt and pepper to taste
4 slices onion
4 slices tomato
4 teaspoons sweet *or* dill
   pickle relish
4 hamburger buns, split

In a bowl, combine beef, eggs, salt and pepper; mix well. Shape into eight thin patties. Top four patties with onion, tomato and relish. Top with remaining patties and press edges firmly to seal. Broil for 8 minutes on each side or until no longer pink. Serve on buns. **Yield:** 4 servings.

TIMELY TIP:

Before broiling foods, spray the broiler pan with nonstick cooking spray or line it with greased foil. Cleanup will be quick with little mess.

FRANKBURGERS

1 medium onion, chopped
1-1/2 teaspoons chili powder, *divided*
2 tablespoons butter *or* margarine
1 can (10-3/4 ounces) condensed tomato soup, undiluted, *divided*
1 tablespoon brown sugar
1 teaspoon vinegar
1 teaspoon salt
1-1/2 pounds ground beef
6 hot dogs, split lengthwise
12 hot dog buns, split and toasted

In a saucepan, saute the onion and 1/2 teaspoon chili powder in butter until the onion is tender. Add two-thirds of the soup, brown sugar and vinegar. Bring to a boil. Reduce heat; cover and simmer for 30 minutes. Meanwhile, in a bowl, combine salt and the remaining chili powder and soup. Crumble beef over mixture and mix well. Shape into 12 oval patties. Press a hot dog into each patty. Place patties, hot dog side down, on a boiler pan. Broil 6 in. from the heat for 6 minutes. Turn and broil 3-4 minutes longer or until the beef is no longer pink. Serve in buns with the sauce. **Yield:** 12 servings.

MINI BEEF ROLLS

1 pound ground beef
2 cups (8 ounces) shredded cheddar cheese
2 to 4 tablespoons onion soup mix
1 tablespoon mayonnaise
24 miniature dinner rolls, split
1 jar (12 ounces) dill pickle slices

In a skillet, cook beef over medium heat until no longer pink; drain. Add cheese, soup mix and mayonnaise. Cook and stir over low heat until the cheese is melted. Spread 2 tablespoonfuls over roll bottoms. Top each with a pickle slice. Replace roll tops. Wrap in heavy-duty foil and place on baking sheets. Bake at 325° for 30 minutes or until heated through. **Yield:** 2 dozen.

HELPFUL HINT:

If you don't use the entire contents of the onion soup mix when making Mini Beef Rolls, put the remaining mix in a small resealable plastic bag and freeze until the next time you prepare this recipe.

DEVILED ENGLISH MUFFINS

1/3 cup chili sauce
1-1/2 teaspoons ground mustard
1-1/2 teaspoons Worcestershire sauce
1 teaspoon dried minced onion
1 teaspoon salt
Pepper to taste
1 pound ground beef
6 English muffins, split

In a bowl, combine the first six ingredients. Crumble beef over mixture and mix well. Spread meat mixture over muffin halves. Place on an ungreased baking sheet. Broil 4 in. from the heat for 10 minutes or until no longer pink. **Yield:** 6 servings.

SERVING SUGGESTION:

You can also shape the meat mixture for Deviled English Muffins into patties. Broil, grill or pan-fry until no longer pink and serve on hamburger buns.

DAD'S BEST BURGERS

1 package (3 ounces) cream cheese, softened
1 egg
1 medium onion, finely chopped
1/2 cup dry bread crumbs
1-1/2 teaspoons dried parsley flakes
1/2 teaspoon seasoned salt
1/4 teaspoon pepper
1 pound ground beef
1 pound bulk pork sausage
8 hamburger buns, split

In a bowl, combine the first seven ingredients. Crumble beef and sausage over mixture; mix well. Shape into eight patties. Grill, uncovered, over medium-hot heat for 4-6 minutes on each side or until no longer pink. Serve on buns. **Yield:** 8 servings.

SIMPLE SUBSTITUTIONS:

To give Dad's Best Burgers an Italian twist, use seasoned bread crumbs and Italian sausage. Serve with spaghetti or pizza sauce instead of traditional ketchup.

FAMILY-FAVORITE BARBECUES

3 pounds ground beef
3-1/2 cups tomato juice
1-1/2 cups cooked long grain rice
1 tablespoon prepared mustard
2 teaspoons salt
1-1/2 teaspoons chili powder
1 teaspoon pepper
16 hamburger buns, split

In a large saucepan or Dutch oven, cook beef over medium heat until no longer pink; drain. Stir in tomato juice, rice, mustard and seasonings; mix well. Cover and simmer for 25 minutes. Spoon onto buns. **Yield:** 16 servings.

TIMELY TIP:

The filling for Family-Favorite Barbecues can be frozen in an airtight container for up to 3 months.

SMOKED LINKBURGERS

1 tablespoon brown sugar
1 tablespoon lemon juice
1 tablespoon finely chopped onion
1/2 teaspoon salt
Dash pepper
1-1/2 pounds ground beef
1 package (14 ounces) smoked sausage links
8 hot dog *or* hoagie buns, split

In a bowl, combine the first five ingredients. Crumble beef over mixture and mix well. Divide into eight portions and shape each portion around a sausage link. Grill or broil until beef is no longer pink, turning frequently. Serve on buns. **Yield:** 8 servings.

JALAPENO SWISS BURGERS

2 pounds ground beef
4 slices Swiss cheese
1 small onion, thinly sliced
2 to 3 pickled jalapeno peppers, seeded and julienned
4 hamburger buns, split

Shape beef into eight thin patties. Top four patties with cheese, onion and jalapenos. Top with remaining patties; press edges firmly to seal. Grill, uncovered, over medium-hot heat for 8-9 minutes on each side or until no longer pink. Serve on buns. **Yield:** 4 servings.

My Grandma Ackerson served these hearty sloppy joes on her auction lunch wagon. They were also a favorite on the farm at family gatherings. Now I serve them on my farm to her great-grandchildren.
—Velda Larson
Paynesville, Minnesota

We enjoy these sandwiches as a change from plain hamburgers or hot dogs.
—June Burkert
Evans City, Pennsylvania

Mexican culture greatly influences our cuisine, and we eat a lot of spicy foods. In this recipe, the mellow flavor of Swiss cheese cuts the heat of the jalapenos.
—Jeanine Richardson
Floresville, Texas

CLASSIC KETTLE CREATIONS

Looking for delicious
fuss-free fare that is
sure to please your family?
With the irresistible aroma
and flavor of a savory
soup, stew or chili,
your clan will clamor
for seconds...
and thirds!

SOUTH-OF-THE-BORDER SOUP
(P. 156)

BEEF AND BACON CHOWDER (P. 122)
HUNTER'S STEW (P. 125)
GREEN BEAN CHILI (P. 122)

GREEN BEAN CHILI
(Pictured on page 121)

When folks hear this recipe's name, they're certainly skeptical. But after one taste, they're asking for the recipe! This chili is especially nice for those who don't care for kidney beans found in most recipes.
—Barbara Scott
Midland, Texas

1 pound ground beef
1/2 cup chopped green pepper
1/2 cup chopped onion
2 garlic cloves, minced
2 cans (14-1/2 ounces *each*) French-style green beans, drained
1 can (14-1/2 ounces) Mexican stewed tomatoes
1 can (8 ounces) tomato sauce
1/2 cup salsa
1 tablespoon chili powder
1/8 teaspoon crushed red pepper flakes
Salt and pepper to taste

In a large saucepan, cook beef, green pepper, onion and garlic over medium heat until meat is no longer pink; drain. Add the remaining ingredients; bring to a boil. Reduce heat; simmer, uncovered, for 30 minutes or until heated through. **Yield:** 6 servings.

SIMPLE SUBSTITUTION:

If you prefer, you can use 3-1/2 cups frozen French-style green beans for the canned beans in Green Bean Chili. There's no need to thaw the beans before adding them to the soup.

BEEF AND BACON CHOWDER
(Pictured on page 121)

Rave reviews are sure to follow when this creamy chowder appears on the table. Bacon makes it rich and hearty. It's a favorite with my whole family.
—Nancy Schmidt
Center, Colorado

1 pound ground beef
2 cups chopped celery
1/2 cup chopped onion
4 cups milk
3 cups cubed peeled potatoes, cooked
2 cans (10-3/4 ounces *each*) condensed cream of mushroom soup, undiluted
2 cups chopped carrots, cooked
Salt and pepper to taste
12 bacon strips, cooked and crumbled

In a soup kettle or Dutch oven, cook beef, celery and onion over medium heat until the meat is no longer pink and the vegetables are tender; drain. Add the milk, potatoes, soup, carrots, salt and pepper; heat through. Stir in the bacon just before serving. **Yield:** 12 servings (3 quarts).

HEARTY BAKED STEW
(Pictured above)

3 medium potatoes, peeled
   and sliced
3 medium carrots, sliced
3/4 pound lean ground beef
1 can (14-1/2 ounces) diced
   tomatoes, undrained
1/2 cup frozen peas
2 medium onions, sliced
2 tablespoons butter *or*
   margarine
Salt and pepper to taste

In an ovenproof Dutch oven or greased 13-in. x 9-in. x 2-in. baking dish, layer the potatoes and carrots. Crumble beef over carrots. Layer with the tomatoes, peas and onions. Dot with butter. Sprinkle with salt and pepper. Cover and bake at 350° for 1-1/2 hours or until the meat is no longer pink and the vegetables are tender. **Yield:** 6 servings.

TIMELY TIP:

*Make Hearty Baked Stew when you have time.
Cool, cover tightly with foil and freeze.
When you anticipate a busy day, remove the pan from
the freezer and thaw in the refrigerator overnight.
Reheat in the oven or microwave.*

My mother has been making this stew since the 1940s and prepared it for our family many times through the years. It's loaded with vegetables for wonderful flavor and pretty presentation.
—Judith Wood
Fredericktown, Ohio

CHUCK WAGON CHILI

(Pictured below)

1-1/2 **pounds ground beef**
   1 **can (16 ounces) kidney beans, undrained**
   1 **can (10-3/4 ounces) condensed tomato soup, undiluted**
   1 **can (8 ounces) sliced mushrooms, undrained**
   6 **hot dogs, halved and cut into bite-size pieces**
   2 **medium carrots, sliced**
   1 **medium onion, chopped**
   1 **teaspoon salt**
   1 **teaspoon chili powder**
1/4 **teaspoon pepper**

In a large saucepan, cook beef over medium heat until no longer pink; drain. Add the remaining ingredients and bring to a boil. Reduce heat; cover and simmer for 1 hour or until thick and bubbly. **Yield:** 6-8 servings.

FAMILY-FAVORITE SOUP

5-1/2 cups water, *divided*
1 large onion, chopped
1 cup sliced carrots
1 cup cubed potatoes
1/2 cup sliced celery
1/2 teaspoon salt
1/2 teaspoon pepper
1 can (16 ounces) kidney beans, rinsed and drained
1 can (10-3/4 ounces) condensed tomato soup, undiluted
1/2 pound ground beef, cooked and drained
2 tablespoons barbecue sauce
1 teaspoon beef bouillon granules

In a large saucepan, combine 2 cups water, onion, carrots, potatoes, celery, salt and pepper; bring to a boil. Reduce heat; cover and simmer for 15 minutes. Add the remaining ingredients; cover and simmer 30 minutes longer or until vegetables are tender. **Yield:** 6-8 servings.

HELPFUL HINT:

Purchase firm, bright-orange carrots without cracks or dry spots. Store in a plastic bag in the refrigerator for up to 2 weeks. Six medium carrots yields about 3 cups sliced.

This recipe originally called for chili powder. But one day, I found I didn't have any and used barbecue sauce instead. All of our 10 children ask me to make this recipe whenever they come to visit.
—Caye Watson
Sangudo, Alberta

HUNTER'S STEW

(Pictured on page 121)

1 pound lean ground beef
1 medium onion, chopped
3 medium carrots, sliced
3 large potatoes, peeled and sliced
1 package (10 ounces) frozen cut green beans, thawed
1 can (10-3/4 ounces) condensed tomato soup, undiluted
1-1/3 cups water

Crumble beef into an ovenproof Dutch oven or greased 13-in. x 9-in. x 2-in. baking dish. Layer with onion, carrots, potatoes and beans. Combine soup and water; pour over beans. Cover and bake at 375° for 2 hours or until the meat is no longer pink and vegetables are tender. **Yield:** 4 servings.

PERFECT PARTNERS:

Toasted garlic bread or breadsticks will round out a satisfying meal of Hunter's Stew. When the stew is done baking, brush melted butter on bread slices or sticks; sprinkle with Parmesan cheese, dried parsley flakes and garlic powder. Broil until lightly browned.

Since receiving this recipe from a friend years ago, I have appreciated its meal-in-one convenience. While it bakes, I can concentrate on other things I enjoy doing.
—Anne Reynolds
Sprakers, New York

BAKED CHILI

6 bacon strips, diced
1-1/2 pounds ground beef
1 large onion, thinly sliced
1/2 cup chopped green pepper
2 cans (16 ounces *each*) kidney beans, rinsed and drained
1 can (14-1/2 ounces) diced tomatoes, undrained
1 can (6 ounces) tomato paste
4-1/2 teaspoons chili powder
1-1/2 teaspoons salt
1/4 teaspoon dried oregano
1/4 teaspoon ground cumin
1/8 teaspoon rubbed sage

In a large saucepan, cook bacon; remove with a slotted spoon and drain on paper towels. Cook beef, onion and green pepper in drippings over medium heat until meat is no longer pink; drain. Remove from the heat; add the remaining ingredients. Stir in bacon; mix well. Transfer to an ovenproof Dutch oven or greased 13-in. x 9-in. x 2-in. baking dish. Cover and bake at 350° for 45 minutes. Uncover and bake 15 minutes longer or until thick and bubbly. **Yield:** 6-8 servings (about 2 quarts).

TIMELY TIP:

You can easily double the Baked Chili and divide between two 13- x 9- x 2-inch baking pans. Bake one pan as directed. Freeze the other for future use. When ready to use, thaw in the refrigerator overnight. Bake as directed, adding 15-20 minutes to the baking time.

TACO SOUP

2 pounds ground beef
1 medium onion, chopped
2 cans (15 ounces *each*) Italian tomato sauce
1 can (16 ounces) kidney beans, rinsed and drained
1 can (14-1/2 ounces) stewed tomatoes
1 can (12 ounces) whole kernel corn, undrained
Shredded cheddar cheese
Tortilla chips

In a large saucepan, cook beef and onion over medium heat until the meat is no longer pink; drain. Add the tomato sauce, beans, tomatoes and corn; bring to a boil. Reduce heat; simmer, uncovered, for 10 minutes. Garnish with cheese. Serve with tortilla chips. **Yield:** 10 servings (2-1/2 quarts).

OVEN MEATBALL STEW

(Pictured above)

1 egg
1/3 cup milk
1/4 cup cornmeal
2 tablespoons finely chopped onion
2 tablespoons finely chopped green pepper
1-1/2 teaspoons ground mustard
1 teaspoon salt
1 teaspoon chili powder
1 pound lean ground beef
2 to 3 tablespoons olive *or* vegetable oil
1/4 cup all-purpose flour
2-1/2 cups tomato juice
12 pearl onions, peeled
3 medium potatoes, peeled and quartered
6 medium carrots, cut into 3-inch pieces

In a bowl, combine the first eight ingredients. Crumble beef over mixture and mix well. Shape into 12 meatballs. In an ovenproof Dutch oven, brown meatballs in oil. Remove with a slotted spoon and set aside. Whisk flour into drippings until smooth. Gradually whisk in tomato juice; bring to a boil. Cook and stir for 2 minutes or until thickened. Return meatballs to pan. Add vegetables; stir gently. Cover and bake at 350° for 1 hour or until meat is no longer pink and vegetables are tender. **Yield:** 6 servings.

My husband found this recipe almost 30 years ago. He would often prepare it for me and our daughters...now they make it for their own families.
—Madge Harman
Orange Park, Florida

THICKENING A STEW

STEP 1
Remove meatballs after browning, reserving pan drippings. Whisk flour into the drippings until smooth.

STEP 2
Gradually whisk in tomato juice. Bring to a boil. Cook and stir for 2 minutes or until thickened.

FOUR-STAR CHILI

(Pictured above)

This spicy chili features traditional ingredients like ground beef, green peppers and tomatoes, but carrots and white beans make it deliciously different. Serve it over rice for a hearty meal.
—Frank Fenti
Hornell, New York

1-1/2 **pounds ground beef**
   2 **large green peppers, diced**
   1 **medium onion, diced**
   4 **garlic cloves, minced**
   1 **can (28 ounces) crushed tomatoes**
   1 **can (15-1/2 ounces) great northern beans, rinsed and drained**
   1 **can (14-1/2 ounces) chicken broth**
   1 **medium carrot, chopped**
   1 **celery rib, chopped**
   2 **jalapeno peppers, finely chopped***
2-1/2 **teaspoons pepper blend***
   1 **teaspoon paprika**
 1/2 **teaspoon crushed red pepper flakes**
Hot cooked rice

Sour cream
Shredded Colby cheese

In a soup kettle or Dutch oven, cook beef, green peppers, onion and garlic over medium heat until meat is no longer pink; drain. Add the tomatoes, beans, broth, carrot, celery, jalapenos and seasonings; bring to a boil. Reduce heat; cover and simmer for 1-1/2 hours or until thick and bubbly. Serve over rice with sour cream and cheese. **Yield:** 18 servings (4-1/4 quarts). ***Editor's Note:** When cutting or seeding hot peppers, use rubber or plastic gloves to protect your hands. Avoid touching your face. This recipe was tested with McCormick's Hot Shot Black & Red Pepper.

SIMPLE SUBSTITUTION:

As a substitute for the 2-1/2 teaspoons of pepper blend in Four-Star Chili, combine 2 teaspoons coarsely ground black pepper and 1/2 teaspoon cayenne pepper.

HAMBURGER RICE SOUP

1 pound ground beef
1/2 cup chopped onion
3-1/2 quarts water
1 can (28 ounces) diced tomatoes, undrained
1 envelope onion soup mix
3 tablespoons Worcestershire sauce
1 tablespoon salt
1 teaspoon brown sugar
1 teaspoon celery salt
1/8 teaspoon pepper
1/2 cup uncooked long grain rice

In a soup kettle or Dutch oven, cook beef and onion over medium heat until meat is no longer pink; drain. Add the water, tomatoes, soup mix, Worcestershire sauce, salt, brown sugar, celery salt and pepper; bring to a boil. Add rice. Reduce heat; cover and simmer for 20-25 minutes or until rice is tender. **Yield:** 20 servings (5 quarts).

TIMELY TIP:

Hamburger Rice Soup makes a batch big, but it can be frozen in smaller batches or even in individual-serving-size portions.

The aroma of this soup simmering on the stove makes the kitchen smell so good! My family agrees the second helping tastes even better than the first! If there are any leftovers, I pop them in the freezer.
—Jean Fisher Waynesboro, Pennsylvania

CHEESY VEGETABLE SOUP

1-1/2 pounds ground beef
1 medium onion, chopped
4 medium potatoes, peeled and cubed
1 cup chopped carrots
1 cup *each* frozen corn, peas and cut green beans
4 cups water
1 can (46 ounces) V-8 juice
2 pounds process American cheese, cubed

In a soup kettle or Dutch oven, cook beef and onion over medium heat until meat is no longer pink; drain and set aside. Add vegetables and water to the kettle; bring to a boil. Reduce heat; cover and simmer for 15-20 minutes or until vegetables are tender. Add V-8 juice and the beef mixture; heat through. Add cheese; cook and stir until melted. **Yield:** 16 servings (4 quarts).

HELPFUL HINT:

The fastest way to peel potatoes is with a vegetable peeler. Be sure to cut off any eyes or green parts. Prevent diced potatoes from darkening before cooking by keeping them covered with water.

My husband doesn't care much for tomatoes, so I created this recipe that features lots of delicious cheese. We really enjoy steaming bowlfuls on cold winter days with fresh-from-the-oven corn bread.
—Robin Counce Arvada, Colorado

My husband, Steve, actually created the recipe for this meaty chili when he was in high school...he entered a chili cook-off contest and won! I'm usually the one who makes this now, but Steve insists the way he makes it is better!
—Annette Bailey McDonough, Georgia

STEAK AND BEAN CHILI

1 pound ground beef
1/2 pound round steak, cubed
2 cans (16 ounces *each*) kidney beans, rinsed and drained
2 cans (15-1/2 ounces *each*) chili beans, undrained
2 cans (10-3/4 ounces *each*) condensed tomato soup, undiluted
1 to 2 tablespoons chili powder
1 tablespoon onion powder
Salt and pepper to taste
Shredded cheddar cheese, optional

In a large saucepan, cook beef and steak over medium heat until no longer pink; drain. Add the beans, soup and seasonings; bring to a boil. Reduce heat; simmer, uncovered, for 30 minutes or until thick and bubbly. Garnish with cheese if desired. **Yield:** 8 servings (2 quarts).

HELPFUL HINT:

Round steak is one of the least expensive cuts of meat and contains the least marbling. Fresh round steak should have a bright to deep red color and only a small amount of fat on the edge.

SWEET POTATO STEW

Beef broth and herbs pair nicely with the sweet potatoes' subtle sweetness in this hearty stew that's perfect for fall. I'm a happy camper spending my time in the kitchen creating delicious dishes like this.
—Helen Vail Glenside, Pennsylvania

1 can (14-1/2 ounces) beef broth
3/4 pound lean ground beef
2 medium sweet potatoes, peeled and cut into 1/2-inch cubes
1 small onion, finely chopped
1/2 cup V-8 juice
2 teaspoons golden raisins
1 garlic clove, minced
1/2 teaspoon dried thyme
Pinch cayenne pepper

In a large saucepan, bring broth to a boil. Crumble beef into broth. Cover and cook for 3 minutes, stirring occasionally. Add the remaining ingredients; return to a boil. Reduce heat; simmer, uncovered, for 15 minutes or until meat is no longer pink and potatoes are tender. **Yield:** 4 servings.

PEELING A GARLIC CLOVE

To easily peel a garlic clove, place the flat side of a chef's knife on the clove. Firmly press down on the knife blade to separate the skin from the garlic.

CREAM OF HAMBURGER SOUP

1-1/2 cups water
1 cup sliced carrots
1 cup sliced celery
1 cup cubed peeled potatoes
1/4 cup chopped onion
1 pound ground beef, cooked and drained
1 can (10-3/4 ounces) condensed cream of mushroom soup, undiluted
1 can (10-3/4 ounces) condensed cream of potato soup, undiluted
1 tablespoon chili powder
1 teaspoon dried parsley flakes
1/4 teaspoon *each* paprika, garlic salt, seasoned salt and pepper
3 cups milk

In a large saucepan, combine the water, carrots, celery, potatoes and onion; bring to a boil over medium heat. Reduce heat; cover and simmer for 15-20 minutes or until vegetables are tender. Add beef, soups and seasonings; bring to a boil. Reduce heat; cover and simmer for 45 minutes, stirring occasionally. Stir in milk; heat through (do not boil). **Yield:** 10 servings (2-1/4 quarts).

This c[...] gets some spice from chili powder. With meat, potatoes and other vegetables, it's a complete meal. Family and friends agree this soup is really tasty.
—Claudette Renard Green Bay, Wisconsin

DELUXE CHILI CON CARNE

1 pound ground beef
1 medium green pepper, chopped
1 medium onion, chopped
1 garlic clove, minced
1 can (10-3/4 ounces) condensed tomato soup, undiluted
1 can (8 ounces) kidney beans, rinsed and drained
4-1/2 teaspoons chili powder
1 tablespoon Worcestershire sauce
1-1/2 teaspoons salt
1 teaspoon pepper
1/2 pound fresh mushrooms, halved

In a large saucepan, cook beef, green pepper, onion and garlic over medium heat until the meat is no longer pink; drain. Add the soup, beans, chili powder, Worcestershire sauce, salt and pepper; bring to a boil. Reduce heat; cover and simmer for 1 hour or until thick and bubbly. Add mushrooms; cover and simmer 15 minutes longer. **Yield:** 4 servings.

My husband and I are retired with grown children, so it's nice to have a chili recipe that makes a small amount. Mushrooms make this chili stand out from any other varieties I've tried.
—Anne Elsby Chilliwack, British Columbia

SIMPLE SUBSTITUTION:

If you don't have fresh mushrooms on hand, you can use two 4-1/2-ounce cans of whole mushrooms (drained) in Deluxe Chili Con Carne.

Pinto Pepperoni Chili

My husband and I have always loved chili, but our daughters would pick out the kidney beans. When I discovered the girls loved Mexican food, I decided to use pinto beans in my chili instead. They loved every bite!
—Tara Dvorak
Grand Forks, North Dakota

1 pound dry pinto beans
4 cups water
1 medium onion, cut into wedges
1 pound ground beef, cooked and drained
1 large green pepper, chopped
1 large sweet red pepper, chopped
1 package (3-1/2 ounces) sliced pepperoni
1 can (28 ounces) whole tomatoes, undrained
1 can (15 ounces) tomato sauce
1 cup salsa
1 teaspoon chili powder
1 teaspoon salt
1/2 teaspoon pepper

Place the beans in a soup kettle or Dutch oven; add enough water to cover by 2 in. Bring to a boil; boil for 2 minutes. Remove from the heat; cover and let stand for 1 hour. Drain and discard liquid. Add 4 cups water and onion to the beans; bring to a boil. Reduce heat; simmer, uncovered, for 1 hour or until beans are almost tender. Add remaining ingredients. Cook, uncovered, for 3 hours or until thick and bubbly, stirring occasionally. **Yield:** 14 servings (3-1/2 quarts).

Sloppy Joe Stew

This old-fashioned stew has a slightly sweet taste from the addition of canned corn. You can make the stew ahead of time and reheat it for a quick meal later on.
—Clair Long
Destrehan, Louisiana

2 pounds ground beef
1 medium onion, chopped
1 small green pepper, chopped
1-1/2 cups water
1 can (12 ounces) whole kernel corn, undrained
1 can (10-3/4 ounces) condensed tomato soup, undiluted
1/4 cup sugar
1 tablespoon Worcestershire sauce
1 teaspoon hot pepper sauce
Salt and pepper to taste

In a large saucepan, cook beef, onion and green pepper over medium heat until meat is no longer pink; drain. Add the remaining ingredients; bring to a boil. Reduce heat; cover and simmer for 1 hour. **Yield:** 6 servings.

Serving Suggestion:

Serve additional hot pepper sauce on the side for folks who want a little more "kick" to their Sloppy Joe Stew.

MIXED BEAN SOUP

(Pictured above)

1 package (12 ounces) mixed dry beans
2 quarts water
1/2 pound ground beef, cooked and drained
1 can (14-1/2 ounces) diced tomatoes, undrained
1 cup chopped celery
1 tablespoon salt
1 teaspoon dried parsley flakes
2 garlic cloves, minced
1 teaspoon dried thyme
2 bay leaves
Pepper to taste

Place beans in a large saucepan or Dutch oven; add enough water to cover by 2 in. Bring to a boil; boil for 2 minutes. Remove from the heat; cover and let stand for 1 hour. Drain and discard liquid. Add 2 qts. water to the beans; bring to a boil. Cover and simmer for 30 minutes. Add remaining ingredients; bring to a boil. Reduce heat; cover and simmer for 1-1/2 to 2 hours or until beans are tender. Discard bay leaves before serving. **Yield:** 10 servings (2-1/2 quarts).

Guests and family alike praise this soup and always ask for seconds. The nicest thing about it is that any variation of dry beans can be used.
—Arlene Hilman Cawston, British Columbia

RANCH STEW
(Pictured above)

*My husband,
our five children and I
have enjoyed this
easy-to-make stew
for years. We especially
love the dumplings.
Our bachelor
son even makes
it for himself!*
—Margaret Froehling
Wood Dale, Illinois

1 pound ground beef
**1 can (16 ounces) kidney
beans, undrained**
**1 can (15-1/4 ounces) whole
kernel corn, undrained**
**1 can (14-1/2 ounces) diced
tomatoes, undrained**
1 cup biscuit/baking mix
1/3 cup milk

In a large saucepan, cook beef over medium heat until no longer pink; drain. Add the beans, corn and tomatoes; bring to a boil. Reduce heat. In a bowl, combine biscuit mix and milk just until moistened. Drop by tablespoonfuls onto sim-mering stew. Cover and simmer for 12 minutes or until a toothpick inserted in a dumpling comes out clean (do not lift cover while simmering). Serve immediately. **Yield:** 4 servings.

MAKING DUMPLINGS

To make dumplings, combine biscuit mix and milk. With a spoon in each hand, drop batter by tablespoonfuls onto simmering stew.

SAVORY VEGETABLE BEEF SOUP

4 large potatoes, peeled and
    cubed
2 cups water
3 large carrots, sliced
1 large onion, chopped
Salt and pepper to taste
4 cups fresh *or* frozen cut
    green beans
4 cups tomato juice
1-1/2 pounds ground beef,
    cooked and drained
2 cups fresh *or* frozen corn
1 teaspoon Italian seasoning
1/2 teaspoon garlic powder
2 bay leaves

In a large saucepan, combine the potatoes, water, carrots, onion, salt and pepper; bring to a boil. Reduce heat; cover and simmer for 25 minutes or until tender. Add the remaining ingredients. Cover and simmer 30 minutes longer or until heated through, stirring occasionally. Discard bay leaves before serving. **Yield:** 10-12 servings (2-3/4 quarts).

*I developed this recipe as a way to use my homegrown vegetables. My teaching responsibilities keep me busy, but I love cooking for my husband and daughter most of all.
—Leslie Luthe Parkersburg, Illinois*

CHEESY TACO CHILI

1 pound ground beef
1/2 cup chopped onion
1/2 cup chopped green pepper
1 tablespoon minced
    jalapeno pepper*
1 garlic clove, minced
1 can (16 ounces) kidney
    beans, rinsed and drained
2/3 cup cubed process
    American cheese
2 tablespoons salsa
1/8 teaspoon chili powder

In a large saucepan, cook beef, onion, peppers and garlic over medium heat until meat is no longer pink; drain. Add the remaining ingredients. Simmer, uncovered, for 5 minutes or until cheese is melted (do not boil). **Yield:** 5 servings.
*Editor's Note: When cutting or seeding hot peppers, use rubber or plastic gloves to protect your hands. Avoid touching your face.

*This recipe was created out of desperation when everyone was hungry and I only had a few items on hand. Now it's a standby in my kitchen.
—Janet Lammers St. Marys, Ohio*

SERVING SUGGESTION:

For a tasty taco salad, serve Cheesy Taco Chili on a bed of lettuce. Sprinkle with shredded cheese and chopped tomatoes; top with sour cream and French or Russian salad dressing.

SCALLOPED POTATO CHILI
(Pictured at right)

Potatoes are a unique addition to ordinary chili. My mom used to serve this when I was growing up. My husband loves spicy food, so I put the chili powder on the table for him to add more.
—Sherry Hulva Decatur, Illinois

1-1/2 pounds ground beef
3/4 cup chopped onion
1/2 cup chopped green pepper
2 cans (16 ounces *each*) kidney beans, undrained
2 cans (14-1/2 ounces *each*) stewed tomatoes
1 package (5-1/4 ounces) scalloped potatoes
1 can (8 ounces) sliced mushrooms, drained
1 cup water
1 teaspoon salt
3/4 teaspoon chili powder
Shredded Parmesan cheese

In a large saucepan, cook beef, onion and green pepper over medium heat until meat is no longer pink; drain. Stir in the beans, tomatoes, contents of potato package, mushrooms, water, salt and chili powder; bring to a boil. Reduce heat; cover and simmer for 40-45 minutes or until potatoes are tender. Garnish with Parmesan cheese. **Yield:** 10 servings (2-1/2 quarts).

TIMELY TIP:
If you're making Scalloped Potato Chili for a potluck, prepare it at home on the stove, then take it to the gathering in a slow cooker.

ITALIAN WEDDING SOUP
(Pictured at right)

I'm not sure where the name of this soup originated, but my aunt in Pennsylvania shared the recipe with me. Even in our hot Florida climate, this soup always satisfies. Family and friends frequently ask me to prepare it.
—Nancy Ducharme Deltona, Florida

1 egg
3/4 cup grated Parmesan *or* Romano cheese
1/2 cup dry bread crumbs
1 small onion, chopped
3/4 teaspoon salt, *divided*
1-1/4 teaspoons pepper, *divided*
1-1/4 teaspoons garlic powder, *divided*
2 pounds ground beef
2 quarts chicken broth
1/3 cup chopped spinach
1 teaspoon onion powder
1 teaspoon dried parsley flakes
1-1/4 cups cooked medium shell pasta

In a bowl, combine the egg, cheese, bread crumbs, onion, 1/4 teaspoon salt, 1/4 teaspoon pepper and 1/4 teaspoon garlic powder. Crumble beef over mixture and mix well. Shape into 1-in. balls. In a soup kettle or Dutch oven, cook the meatballs until no longer pink; drain. Add the broth, spinach, onion powder, parsley, and remaining salt, pepper and garlic powder; bring to a boil. Reduce heat; simmer, uncovered, for 5 minutes. Stir in pasta; heat through. **Yield:** 12 servings (3 quarts).

SCALLOPED POTATO CHILI
ITALIAN WEDDING SOUP
EASY VEGETABLE SOUP (P. 138)

EASY VEGETABLE SOUP

(Pictured on page 137)

(Pictured on page 137)

We like to eat this tasty soup with tortilla chips. Canned tomatoes and beans and frozen vegetables give you a head start when preparing this recipe.
—Jan Sharp
Blue Springs, Missouri

1 pound ground beef
1 medium onion, chopped
1 can (28 ounces) diced tomatoes, undrained
1 package (16 ounces) frozen vegetable blend of your choice
1 can (16 ounces) kidney beans, undrained
1 can (14-1/2 ounces) beef broth
1 envelope taco seasoning
1 garlic clove, minced
Shredded cheddar cheese, optional

In a large saucepan or Dutch oven, cook beef and onion over medium heat until meat is no longer pink; drain. Add tomatoes, vegetables, beans, broth, taco seasoning and garlic; bring to a boil. Reduce heat; simmer, uncovered, for 10 minutes. Garnish with cheese if desired. **Yield:** 10-12 servings (2-3/4 quarts).

ORIENTAL CHILI

My husband and I have done extensive traveling during our more than 50 years of marriage. As a matter of fact, I came across this recipe during a visit to Japan. The Oriental flavor is a nice change.
—Martha Ann Bernard
New Vienna, Ohio

1-1/2 pounds ground beef
1 medium onion, chopped
1 can (46 ounces) tomato juice
1 can (28 ounces) Chinese mixed vegetables, drained
1 can (14 ounces) bean sprouts, drained
1 tablespoon chili powder
Salt to taste
Shredded Parmesan cheese

In a large saucepan, cook beef and onion over medium heat until the meat is no longer pink; drain. Add tomato juice, vegetables, bean sprouts, chili powder and salt; bring to a boil. Reduce heat; cover and simmer for 1 hour or until thick and bubbly. Garnish with Parmesan cheese. **Yield:** 10 servings (2-1/2 quarts).

PERFECT PARTNERS:

Pair out-of-the-ordinary Oriental Chili with store-bought egg rolls and fortune cookies for a fun casual meal with little fuss. And for extra ease, keep serving-size portions of chili in the freezer to defrost and reheat in a hurry.

COUNTRY CABBAGE SOUP

(Pictured below)

2 pounds ground beef
2 cans (28 ounces *each*) stewed tomatoes
1 medium head cabbage, shredded
2 large onions, chopped
6 celery ribs, chopped
Salt and pepper to taste

In a large saucepan or Dutch oven, cook beef over medium heat until no longer pink; drain. Add the tomatoes, cabbage, onions and celery; bring to a boil. Reduce heat; simmer, uncovered, for 25 minutes or until vegetables are tender. Add salt and pepper. **Yield:** 12-14 servings (3-1/4 quarts).

SIMPLE SUBSTITUTIONS:

Be creative when making Country Cabbage Soup. For instance, stir in some shredded carrots or frozen mixed vegetables. For a more filling soup, add 2 cups of cooked rice or pasta.

My mother-in-law, who is a wonderful cook, has shared many terrific recipes with me, including this one. Beef and tomatoes go nicely with cabbage, onion and celery.
—Vicky Catullo
Youngstown, Ohio

CHOCK-FULL CHILI

1-1/2 pounds ground beef
1 small onion, chopped
2 cans (16 ounces *each*) kidney beans, rinsed and drained
2 cans (15-1/2 ounces *each*) pork and beans
2 cans (14-1/2 ounces *each*) stewed tomatoes
1 can (15-1/2 ounces) lima beans, rinsed and drained
1 can (15-1/4 ounces) whole kernel corn, drained
3 medium carrots, chopped
3 celery ribs, chopped
1 small green pepper, chopped
8 fresh mushrooms, chopped
3 tablespoons chili powder
2 tablespoons vinegar
2 tablespoons Worcestershire sauce
1 tablespoon sugar
1 teaspoon *each* salt, pepper and paprika
1/4 teaspoon cayenne pepper
1/4 teaspoon ground cloves
1 cup medium shell pasta, cooked and drained

In a soup kettle or Dutch oven, cook beef and onion over medium heat until meat is no longer pink; drain. Add vegetables and seasonings; bring to a boil. Reduce heat; simmer, uncovered, for 50 minutes, stirring occasionally. Add the pasta; simmer 10 minutes longer or until heated through. **Yield:** 12 servings (3 quarts).

TIMELY TIP:

After browning the ground beef and onion for Chock-full Chili, transfer to a slow cooker; add remaining ingredients except pasta. Cook on low for about 3 hours; add pasta and heat through.

VEGETABLE MEATBALL STEW

1 can (8 ounces) tomato sauce, *divided*
1 egg
1 medium onion, finely chopped
1/2 cup dry bread crumbs
1/2 teaspoon salt
1/4 teaspoon pepper
1/8 teaspoon ground allspice
1 pound ground beef
3 cups water
3 medium potatoes, peeled and quartered
6 medium carrots, sliced
1 package (10 ounces) frozen peas
1/2 cup chopped green pepper
1 envelope onion soup mix

In a bowl, combine 1/4 cup tomato sauce, egg, onion, bread crumbs, salt, pepper and allspice. Crumble beef over mixture and mix well. Shape into 1-in. balls. In a large saucepan, brown meatballs; drain. Add the water, potatoes, carrots, peas, green pepper, soup mix and remaining tomato sauce; bring to a boil. Reduce heat; cover and simmer for 45 minutes or until meat is no longer pink and vegetables are tender. **Yield:** 8 servings.

GRANDMOTHER'S CHOWDER

1 pound ground beef
1 medium onion, chopped
12 medium potatoes, peeled
and cubed
3 cups water
Salt and pepper to taste
2 cups milk
1 can (15-1/4 ounces) whole
kernel corn, undrained
2 teaspoons dried parsley
flakes
1 cup (8 ounces) sour cream

In a soup kettle or Dutch oven, cook beef and onion over medium heat until the meat is no longer pink; drain. Add the potatoes, water, salt and pepper; bring to a boil. Reduce heat; cover and simmer for 15-20 minutes or until potatoes are tender. Stir in milk, corn and parsley; cook for 5 minutes or until heated through. Add a small amount of hot soup to sour cream. Gradually return all to pan, stirring constantly. Heat through but do not boil. **Yield:** 14 servings (3-1/2 quarts).

Nothing ... to homemade sou..., especially when this is the delicious result! Winter days seem a little warmer when I prepare this savory chowder.
—Dulyse Molnar
Oswego, New York

ZESTY CHEESEBURGER SOUP

2 pounds ground beef
1 medium onion, chopped
Salt, pepper and garlic powder
to taste
1-1/2 cups cubed peeled potatoes
1-1/2 cups water
1 can (15-1/4 ounces) whole
kernel corn, drained
1 can (14-3/4 ounces)
cream-style corn
1 can (11 ounces) condensed
cheddar cheese soup,
undiluted
1 can (10-3/4 ounces)
condensed cream of
asparagus soup, undiluted
1 can (10-3/4 ounces)
condensed cream of
mushroom soup, undiluted

1 can (10 ounces) diced
tomatoes and green chilies
2 cups half-and-half cream

In a soup kettle or Dutch oven, cook beef, onion, salt, pepper and garlic powder over medium heat until meat is no longer pink; drain. Add potatoes and water; bring to a boil. Reduce heat; cover and simmer for 15-20 minutes or until the potatoes are tender. Add the corn, soups and tomatoes; mix well. Bring to a boil. Reduce heat. Stir in cream; heat through but do not boil. **Yield:** 14-16 servings (3-3/4 quarts).

A dear friend shared this recipe with me. Every time I serve it, I'm met with recipe requests. Even my son-in-law, who's a picky eater, can't get enough of this soup!
—Norma Rowe
Winfield, Kansas

SIMPLE SUBSTITUTION:

To cut down on the spiciness of Zesty Cheeseburger Soup, use a 14-1/2-ounce can of plain diced tomatoes instead of diced tomatoes and green chilies.

CREOLE SOUP
(Pictured above)

Special seasonings set this flavorful soup apart from any others I've tried. It makes a nice big batch, so it's perfect when feeding a crowd. Plus, leftovers freeze well.
—Del Mason
Martensville,
Saskatchewan

1 pound ground beef
1 medium onion, finely chopped
2 quarts water
1 can (28 ounces) diced tomatoes, undrained
3 cups shredded cabbage
3 cups cubed peeled potatoes
1 can (15-1/2 ounces) pork and beans
1 can (11-1/8 ounces) condensed Italian tomato soup, undiluted
1 can (4 ounces) mushroom stems and pieces, undrained
1 cup sliced carrots
1 cup chopped green pepper
1 cup frozen peas
3 celery ribs with leaves, finely chopped
3 chicken bouillon cubes
2 tablespoons dried parsley flakes
1 teaspoon *each* Cajun seasoning, chili powder, Creole seasoning, pepper and crushed red pepper flakes
1 bay leaf

In a soup kettle or Dutch oven, cook beef and onion over medium heat until meat is no longer pink; drain. Add the remaining ingredients; bring to a boil. Reduce heat; simmer, uncovered, for 25 minutes or until vegetables are tender. Discard bay leaf before serving. **Yield:** 18 servings (4-1/2 quarts).

SIMPLE SUBSTITUTION:

If your grocery store doesn't carry condensed Italian tomato soup, use regular condensed tomato soup and add 1/2 teaspoon Italian seasoning.

NACHO CHILI

2 pounds lean ground beef
2 cans (14-1/2 ounces *each*) stewed tomatoes, cut up
2 cups chopped celery
1 jar (16 ounces) salsa
1 can (16 ounces) kidney beans, rinsed and drained
1 can (16 ounces) refried beans
1 medium onion, chopped
1 cup water
1 envelope taco seasoning
1/2 teaspoon pepper
1 can (11 ounces) condensed nacho cheese soup, undiluted

Crumble beef into a large bowl. Add the next nine ingredients and mix well. Transfer to a greased ovenproof Dutch oven or roasting pan. Cover and bake at 350° for 1 hour or until the meat is no longer pink, stirring once. Let stand for 5 minutes. Garnish individual servings with a dollop of cheese soup. **Yield:** 14 servings (3-1/2 quarts).

SERVING SUGGESTIONS:

Serve warmed tortillas or corn chips with Nacho Chili. Or use some of the chili as a topping for baked potatoes or cooked pasta.

My husband and I work together and arrive home at the same time. So I appreciate quick and easy dishes like this. The nacho cheese topping is a great addition to a tasty chili.
—Sally Roos
Osakis, Minnesota

BAKED BEEF CHOWDER

3 cups water
3 medium potatoes, cubed
1 can (14-1/2 ounces) stewed tomatoes
1 medium onion, chopped
2 large carrots, chopped
1/2 pound ground beef, cooked and drained
1/4 cup chopped celery
1/4 cup uncooked long grain rice
2 teaspoons salt
1/2 teaspoon pepper

In a large bowl, combine all ingredients. Transfer to an ungreased ovenproof Dutch oven or 13-in. x 9-in. x 2-in. baking dish. Cover and bake at 350° for 1-1/2 hours or until vegetables are tender. **Yield:** 6 servings.

HELPFUL HINT:

One medium celery rib yields about 1/2 cup chopped or sliced celery.

This hearty dish really warms up the kitchen on cold days and pleases empty tummies! I like the fact that I can combine all the ingredients, pop it into the oven and forget about it. I learned to cook in 4-H as a child. Now I'm a 4-H leader and enjoy teaching kitchen skills to others.
—Sarah Carpenter
Trumansburg, New York

MICROWAVE CLASSIC CHILI

1 pound ground beef
1 medium onion, finely chopped
2 cans (14-1/2 ounces *each*) stewed tomatoes
2 teaspoons chili powder
1-1/2 teaspoons prepared mustard
1 can (16 ounces) kidney beans, rinsed and drained
Salt and pepper to taste

Crumble the beef into a 2-qt. microwave-safe bowl. Add onion; mix well. Cover and microwave on high for 5 minutes or until meat is no longer pink; drain. Stir in the tomatoes, chili powder and mustard; mix well. Cover and microwave on high for 10 minutes. Add beans and mix well. Cover and microwave on high 3 minutes longer. Add salt and pepper. **Yield:** 4-6 servings. **Editor's Note:** This recipe was tested in a 700-watt microwave.

SIMPLE SUBSTITUTION:

Is your family not fond of kidney beans? Eliminate them in Microwave Classic Chili and stir in a 15-1/4-ounce can of whole kernel corn (drained).

GRANDMA'S CORN STEW

1 pound ground beef
1 medium onion, chopped
1/3 cup chopped green pepper
1 can (15-1/4 ounces) whole kernel corn, drained
1 can (10-3/4 ounces) condensed tomato soup, undiluted
1 tablespoon Worcestershire sauce
2 teaspoons sugar
1-1/2 teaspoons salt

In a large saucepan, cook beef, onion and green pepper over medium heat until the meat is no longer pink; drain. Add the remaining ingredients; bring to a boil. Reduce heat; cover and simmer for 1 hour. **Yield:** 4 servings.

HELPFUL HINT:

If a recipe only calls for a small amount of chopped bell pepper, chop the remaining pepper and freeze for 3 to 6 months in a freezer bag or airtight container. Use directly from the freezer in a variety of dishes.

HAMBURGER GARDEN SOUP

(Pictured above)

1 pound ground beef
1 cup chopped onion
1 garlic clove, minced
4 medium tomatoes, chopped *or* 1 can (28 ounces) diced tomatoes, undrained
2 cups fresh *or* frozen corn
2 cups water
3 tablespoons minced fresh parsley *or* 1 tablespoon dried parsley flakes
2 tablespoons minced fresh basil *or* 2 teaspoons dried basil
2 tablespoons minced fresh thyme *or* 2 teaspoons dried thyme
1-1/2 teaspoons minced fresh rosemary *or* 1/2 teaspoon dried rosemary, crushed
1 teaspoon salt
1/2 teaspoon pepper

In a large saucepan, cook the beef, onion and garlic over medium heat until meat is no longer pink; drain. Add the remaining ingredients; bring to a boil. Reduce heat; simmer, uncovered, for 30 minutes or until heated through. **Yield:** 5 servings.

MINCING FRESH HERBS

Wash and dry the herbs; place in a glass measuring cup or small bowl. Snip with kitchen shears until minced.

On our 4 acres in the country, we have a large vegetable and herb garden and raise our own steer. The only thing I need to buy for this soup is the garlic! Make this soup in summer with fresh produce, then freeze some for a hearty autumn meal.
—Alma Grady
Falls Creek,
Pennsylvania

GREEN CHILI STEW

(Pictured above)

Mexican cooking is rare here. So we've enjoyed treating our friends to some of our favorite recipes, like this zesty stew, that we acquired when living in New Mexico.
—Kerrie McFarland
Colstrip, Montana

1 pound ground beef
2 cans (14-1/2 ounces *each*) chicken broth
2 cups cubed peeled potatoes
1/2 cup chopped onion
3 garlic cloves, minced
1 can (15 ounces) pinto beans, rinsed and drained
1 cup frozen corn, thawed
1 can (4 ounces) chopped green chilies
Optional toppings: shredded lettuce, sour cream, diced tomatoes, shredded cheddar cheese

In a skillet, cook beef over medium heat until no longer pink. Meanwhile, in a large saucepan, combine broth, potatoes, onion and garlic; bring to a boil. Reduce heat; simmer, uncovered, for 15 minutes. Add the beans, corn and chilies. Drain beef; add to soup. Simmer for 15 minutes or until heated through. Garnish with your choice of toppings. **Yield:** 6 servings.

SIMPLE SUBSTITUTION:

To give Green Chili Stew a tasty flavor twist, substitute beef broth for the chicken broth.

PEPPER SOUP

1 pound ground beef
1 *each* large green, sweet red and yellow pepper, chopped
1 large onion, chopped
1 can (46 ounces) V-8 juice
1/2 to 1 teaspoon cayenne pepper
Salt and pepper to taste

In a large saucepan, cook beef, peppers and onion over medium heat until meat is no longer pink; drain. Add the remaining ingredients; bring to a boil. Reduce heat; simmer, uncovered, for 15 minutes or until vegetables are tender. **Yield:** 8 servings (2 quarts).

SERVING SUGGESTION:

Pepper Soup already has some zip from the cayenne pepper. But if you like foods even hotter, stir in some chopped jalapeno peppers.

This is my version of a soup we enjoyed at a restaurant. With green, red and yellow peppers, it's so colorful. I like to serve this slightly spicy soup with grilled cheese sandwiches.
—Debbie Fails
Neenah, Wisconsin

MEATY VEGETABLE CHILI

1 pound ground beef
2 medium onions, chopped
4 cups chopped zucchini
2 cans (16 ounces *each*) kidney beans, rinsed and drained
1 jar (28 ounces) spaghetti sauce with mushrooms
1 can (14-1/2 ounces) diced tomatoes, undrained
1 cup water
2 tablespoons chili powder
1 teaspoon ground cumin

In a large saucepan, cook beef and onions over medium heat until meat is no longer pink; drain. Add the remaining ingredients; bring to a boil. Reduce heat; cover and simmer for 20 minutes or until the vegetables are tender. **Yield:** 12 servings (3 quarts).

Spaghetti sauce gives an Italian twist to this chunky chili, which my husband can't get enough of. I always reach for this recipe when my zucchini crop is booming.
—Amy Dekker
Demotte, Indiana

HELPFUL HINTS:

Look for brightly colored zucchini that has few blemishes. In general, the smaller the squash, the more tender it will be. Store zucchini in a plastic bag in the refrigerator for up to 5 days. Two pounds yields about 4-1/2 cups chopped zucchini.

A touch of baking cocoa gives this chili a rich flavor without adding sweetness. When I was growing up in the North, we served chili over rice. But after I married a Texan, I began serving it with chopped onions, shredded cheese and, of course, corn bread!
—Audrey Byrne
Lillian, Texas

I'm fortunate to have a husband who loves to cook. He's always digging through cookbooks in search of new recipes. We enjoy grocery shopping and coming home to spend time together in the kitchen.
—Miriam Wages
Arnoldsville, Georgia

HEARTWARMING CHILI

1 pound ground beef
1 large onion, chopped
2 cans (16 ounces *each*) kidney beans, rinsed and drained
2 cans (14-1/2 ounces *each*) diced tomatoes, undrained
1 can (8 ounces) tomato sauce
1 medium green pepper, diced
3 tablespoons chili powder
1 tablespoon ground cumin
2 garlic cloves, minced
1 teaspoon baking cocoa
1 teaspoon dried oregano
1 teaspoon Worcestershire sauce, optional
Salt and pepper to taste

In a large saucepan, cook beef and onion over medium heat until the meat is no longer pink; drain. Add the remaining ingredients; bring to a boil. Reduce heat; cover and simmer for 3 hours, stirring occasionally. **Yield:** 4 servings.

CHUNKY BEEF STEW

2 quarts water
3 medium potatoes, peeled and cubed
3 medium carrots, sliced
1 medium onion, chopped
2 celery ribs, chopped
1 teaspoon salt
1 pound ground beef, cooked and drained
1 can (15-1/4 ounces) whole kernel corn, drained
1 can (14-1/2 ounces) diced tomatoes, undrained
1 can (8-1/4 ounces) peas, drained
1 can (8 ounces) tomato sauce
3/4 cup ketchup
2 tablespoons prepared mustard
1 tablespoon chili powder
1 garlic clove, minced
1 teaspoon garlic salt
1 teaspoon dried thyme
Dash hot pepper sauce
Dash pepper
1 cup elbow macaroni, cooked and drained

In a Dutch oven or soup kettle, combine the first six ingredients; bring to a boil. Reduce heat; cover and simmer for 20 minutes or until vegetables are tender. Add the beef, corn, tomatoes, peas, tomato sauce, ketchup, mustard and seasonings. Simmer for 30 minutes. Add macaroni; simmer 10 minutes longer. **Yield:** 20 servings.

SIMPLE SUBSTITUTION:

Out of prepared mustard? Make your own!
For every tablespoon of prepared mustard, combine
1/2 teaspoon ground mustard and 2 teaspoons vinegar.

CHEESY MEATBALL SOUP

(Pictured below)

1 egg
1/4 cup dry bread crumbs
1/2 teaspoon salt
1 pound ground beef
2 cups water
1 cup diced celery
1 cup whole kernel corn
1 cup cubed peeled potatoes
1/2 cup sliced carrot
1/2 cup chopped onion
2 beef bouillon cubes
1/2 teaspoon hot pepper sauce
1 jar (16 ounces) process cheese sauce

In a bowl, combine egg, bread crumbs and salt. Crumble beef over mixture and mix well. Shape into 1-in. balls. In a large saucepan, brown meatballs; drain. Add the water, celery, corn, potatoes, carrot, onion, bouillon and hot pepper sauce; bring to a boil. Reduce heat; cover and simmer for 25 minutes or until meat is no longer pink and potatoes are tender. Stir in the cheese sauce; heat through. **Yield:** 4-6 servings.

With meat, potatoes and other vegetables, this rich-tasting soup is really a meal in one. Process cheese sauce makes it taste like a cheeseburger. I serve this soup with a nice crusty loaf of French bread.
—Ione Sander Carlton, Minnesota

TORTELLINI SOUP
(Pictured below)

This soup is delicious, pretty and unbelievably fast to make. For a creamy variation, I sometimes substitute cream of mushroom soup for the French onion soup. If there are any leftovers, they taste even better the next day.
—Marsha Farley
Bangor, Maine

1 pound ground beef
3-1/2 cups water
1 can (28 ounces) diced tomatoes, undrained
1 can (10-1/2 ounces) condensed French onion soup, undiluted
1 package (9 ounces) frozen cut green beans
1 package (9 ounces) refrigerated cheese tortellini
1 medium zucchini, chopped
1 teaspoon dried basil

In a large saucepan, cook beef over medium heat until no longer pink; drain. Add the remaining ingredients; bring to a boil. Cook, uncovered, for 5 minutes or until heated through. **Yield:** 6-8 servings.

PERFECT PARTNERS:
Alongside Tortellini Soup, serve refrigerated crescent rolls. Before baking, sprinkle the dough with Parmesan cheese.

CLASSIC KETTLE CREATIONS

BLACK BEAN POTATO CHILI

1 pound dry black beans
6 cups water
1 can (28 ounces) diced tomatoes, undrained
1 pound ground beef, cooked and drained
4 medium potatoes, peeled and cubed
2 medium onions, chopped
1 can (16 ounces) enchilada sauce
1 envelope chili seasoning
1 tablespoon sugar
2 teaspoons salt
1 teaspoon garlic powder

Place the beans in a soup kettle or Dutch oven; add water to cover by 2 in. Bring to a boil; boil for 2 minutes. Remove from the heat; cover and let stand for 1 hour. Drain and discard liquid. Add 6 cups water to the beans; bring to a boil. Reduce heat; cover and simmer for 2 hours or until beans are almost tender. Add remaining ingredients. Cover and simmer for 1 hour or until soup reaches desired consistency. **Yield:** 12 servings (3 quarts).

Although I was always interested in cooking, I never got a chance to do much of it until I got married. I used to only rely on cookbooks, but over time, I became more confident and started creating my own recipes. This is one I'm especially proud of.
—Giovanna Garver
Paonia, Colorado

POTLUCK PASTA SOUP

1-1/2 pounds ground beef
2 quarts water
2 cans (14-1/2 ounces *each*) Italian stewed tomatoes
2 cups diced carrots
1-1/2 cups diced celery
1 cup chopped onion
1 can (8 ounces) tomato sauce
1 envelope onion soup mix
1 tablespoon sugar
1 teaspoon Italian seasoning
2 garlic cloves, minced
2 bay leaves
1/2 teaspoon pepper
3 cups cooked elbow macaroni
1 can (15 ounces) garbanzo beans, rinsed and drained
1/2 cup chopped green pepper

In a soup kettle or Dutch oven, cook beef over medium heat until no longer pink; drain. Add water, tomatoes, carrots, celery, onion, tomato sauce, soup mix and seasonings; bring to a boil. Reduce heat; simmer, uncovered, for 1 hour. Stir in macaroni, beans and green pepper; heat through. Discard bay leaves before serving. **Yield:** 20 servings (5 quarts).

In an attempt to duplicate a soup served at an Italian restaurant, I came up with this recipe. Friends and family are willing dinner guests when it's on the menu.
—Marilyn Foss
Beavertown, Ohio

TIMELY TIP:

To reduce preparation time when making Potluck Pasta Soup, chop the carrots, celery and onion early in the day or even the night before. Store in separate plastic bags in the refrigerator.

MASHED POTATO SOUP

This is my mom's recipe and a family favorite. Along with grilled cheese sandwiches, this chunky soup makes a quick lunch or dinner.
—Jo Boring
Silver Lake, Indiana

1-1/2 **pounds ground beef**
  1 **large onion, diced**
  6 **medium potatoes, peeled and cubed**
  3 **cups water**
  1 **cup diced celery**
  4 **cups milk**
  2 **cups cold mashed potatoes (prepared with milk and butter)**
  1 **can (12 ounces) evaporated milk**
Salt and pepper to taste

In a soup kettle or Dutch oven, cook beef and onion over medium heat until meat is no longer pink; drain. Add the cubed potatoes, water and celery; bring to a boil. Reduce heat; cover and simmer for 15-20 minutes or until vegetables are tender. Add milk, mashed potatoes, evaporated milk, salt and pepper. Heat through but do not boil. **Yield:** 16 servings (4 quarts).

SIMPLE SUBSTITUTION:

If you don't have time to make mashed potatoes from scratch, make instant mashed potatoes instead.

PORK AND BEANS STEW

My mom and dad, who are both great cooks, instilled in me a love of cooking. I enjoy experimenting with different recipes and couldn't wait to try this unique stew. I prepare it for my family at least once a month.
—Keli Lamb
Coupeville, Washington

  3 **pounds ground beef**
  1 **cup chopped onion**
  2 **cans (10-3/4 ounces** *each***) condensed tomato soup, undiluted**
2-2/3 **cups water**
  2 **envelopes taco seasoning**
  2 **cups** *each* **diced carrots and celery**
  2 **cups cubed potatoes**
  1 **can (28 ounces) pork and beans, undrained**
Salt and pepper to taste

In a skillet, cook beef and onion over medium heat until no longer pink. Meanwhile, in a soup kettle or Dutch oven, combine the soup, water and taco seasoning; bring to a boil. Add the carrots, celery and potatoes; bring to a boil. Reduce heat; cover and simmer for 20 minutes or until vegetables are tender. Drain beef; add to stew. Simmer, uncovered, for 5 minutes. Stir in pork and beans; simmer 5 minutes longer. Add salt and pepper. **Yield:** 12 servings.

MEAT 'N' POTATO STEW

1 pound ground beef
1 pound boneless pork loin, cut into 1-inch cubes
1 can (14-1/2 ounces) beef broth
2 large potatoes, peeled and cut into 1-inch cubes
1 can (14-1/2 ounces) diced tomatoes, undrained
1 large onion, chopped
1/2 cup ketchup
1/4 cup Worcestershire sauce
1 tablespoon lemon juice
1 tablespoon vinegar
1 cup whole kernel corn
Hot pepper sauce to taste
Salt and pepper to taste

In a skillet, cook beef and pork over medium heat until no longer pink; drain. Add the broth, potatoes, tomatoes, onion, ketchup, Worcestershire sauce, lemon juice and vinegar. Bring to a boil. Reduce heat; cover and simmer for 30 minutes. Add the corn, hot pepper sauce, salt and pepper. Simmer for 10 minutes, stirring occasionally. **Yield:** 6-8 servings.

HELPFUL HINT:

To remove kernels from cooked corncobs, stand one end of the cob on a cutting board. Run a sharp knife down the cob, cutting deeply to remove kernels. Lightly pack into freezer containers or plastic bags, leaving 1/2-inch headspace. Freeze for up to 10 months. Two medium ears yield about 1 cup kernels.

FAST MINESTRONE

1 pound ground beef
1 small onion, chopped
2 cans (10 ounces *each*) condensed minestrone soup, undiluted
2-1/2 cups water
1 can (10 ounces) diced tomatoes and green chilies

In a large saucepan, cook beef and onion over medium heat until the meat is no longer pink; drain. Add soup, water and tomatoes. Cook, uncovered, over medium heat until heated through. **Yield:** 8 servings (2 quarts).

SERVING SUGGESTION:

Stir some cooked pasta or rice into Fast Minestrone. Sprinkle individual servings with grated Parmesan or Romano cheese.

My sons are real meat-and-potatoes men, so they request this recipe quite often. The addition of pork adds a tempting taste twist.
—Mildred Sherrer
Bay City, Texas

My sister-in-law had this soup simmering on her stove to welcome our family to her home in Oklahoma. We quickly gobbled it up and took the recipe when we left.
—Beverly Moss
Phoenix, Arizona

CABBAGE PATCH STEW

3 pounds ground beef
2 medium heads cabbage, chopped
2 large onions, chopped
2 cans (15 ounces *each*) pinto beans, rinsed and drained
2 cans (14-1/2 ounces *each*) diced tomatoes, undrained
2 tablespoons vinegar
2 teaspoons sugar
Salt to taste

In a large skillet, cook beef over medium heat until no longer pink. Meanwhile, in a soup kettle or Dutch oven, combine cabbage and onions. Cook and stir over medium heat for 10 minutes or until crisp-tender. Add the beans, tomatoes, vinegar, sugar and salt. Drain beef; add to stew. Bring to a boil. Reduce heat; cover and simmer for 2 hours. **Yield:** 16-18 servings.

HELPFUL HINT:

Choose green cabbage with crisp-looking leaves that are firmly packed. Avoid heads with withered leaves or brown spots. Refrigerate cabbage, tightly wrapped in a plastic bag, for up to 1 week. One medium head weighs about 2 pounds.

BEEF BARLEY SOUP

1-1/2 pounds ground beef
1 medium onion, chopped
3 celery ribs, sliced
3 cans (10-1/2 ounces *each*) condensed beef consomme, undiluted
1 can (28 ounces) diced tomatoes, undrained
4 medium carrots, sliced
2 cups water
1 can (10-3/4 ounces) condensed tomato soup, undiluted
1/2 cup medium pearl barley
1 bay leaf

In a soup kettle or Dutch oven, cook beef, onion and celery over medium heat until the meat is no longer pink and the vegetables are tender; drain. Add the remaining ingredients; bring to a boil. Reduce heat; simmer, uncovered, for 2 hours or until barley is tender. Discard bay leaf before serving. **Yield:** 12 servings (3 quarts).

QUICK PIZZA SOUP

(Pictured above)

1 pound ground beef
2 cans (26 ounces *each*)
condensed tomato soup,
undiluted
6-1/2 cups water
1 jar (28 ounces) spaghetti
sauce
1 tablespoon Italian
seasoning
2 cups (8 ounces) shredded
cheddar cheese
Additional shredded cheddar
cheese, optional

In a soup kettle or Dutch oven, cook beef over medium heat until no longer pink; drain. Add soup, water, spaghetti sauce and Italian seasoning; bring to a boil. Reduce heat; simmer, uncovered, for 15 minutes. Add cheese; cook and stir until melted. Garnish with additional cheese if desired. **Yield:** 16 servings (4 quarts).

PERFECT PARTNERS:

Make Quick Pizza Soup a complete satisfying meal
by serving it with grilled cheese or sub sandwiches.

My kids first sampled this soup in the school cafeteria. They couldn't stop talking about it, so I knew I had to get the recipe. This quick and easy soup warms us up on cold winter evenings.
—Penny Lanxon
Newell, Iowa

Cooking and creating new recipes is a favorite pastime of mine. As a matter of fact, this is an original recipe, which earned me first place in the Wisconsin Beef Cookoff some years ago.
—Lynn Ireland
Lebanon, Wisconsin

SOUTH-OF-THE-BORDER SOUP

(Pictured below and on page 120)

1 egg
1/4 cup dry bread crumbs
1/2 teaspoon salt
1/4 teaspoon pepper
1 pound ground beef
1 jar (16 ounces) picante sauce
1 can (15-1/4 ounces) whole kernel corn, drained
1 can (15 ounces) black beans, rinsed and drained
1 can (14-1/2 ounces) diced tomatoes, undrained
1-1/4 cups water

In a bowl, combine the first four ingredients. Crumble beef over mixture and mix well. Shape into 1-in. balls. In a large saucepan, brown meatballs; drain. Add the picante sauce, corn, beans, tomatoes and water; bring to a boil. Reduce heat; cover and simmer for 20 minutes or until the meat is no longer pink. **Yield:** 8 servings (2 quarts).

HELPFUL HINT:

To make dry bread crumbs, arrange bread slices on a baking sheet. Bake at 300° until completely dry and golden; cool. Place in a resealable plastic bag; crush with a rolling pin. Season with salt, pepper and dried herbs if desired. One slice of bread yields about 1/3 cup dry crumbs.

CAMPFIRE STEW

2 pounds ground beef
6 medium potatoes, peeled and cubed
1-1/2 pounds carrots, sliced
4 cups water
1 can (15-1/4 ounces) whole kernel corn, drained
1 can (15 ounces) peas, drained
1 can (14-1/2 ounces) cut green beans, drained
2 medium onions, chopped
1 cup ketchup
3/4 cup medium pearl barley
1 tablespoon Worcestershire sauce
Dash vinegar
Salt and pepper to taste

In a soup kettle or Dutch oven, cook beef over medium heat until no longer pink; drain. Add the potatoes, carrots and water. Bring to a boil. Reduce heat; cover and simmer for 20 minutes or until vegetables are tender. Add remaining ingredients. Cover and simmer for 2 hours. **Yield:** 20 servings.

ABC SOUP

1 pound ground beef
1 medium onion, chopped
2 quarts tomato juice
1 can (15 ounces) mixed vegetables, undrained
1 cup water
2 beef bouillon cubes
1 cup alphabet pasta *or* small pasta
Salt and pepper to taste

In a large saucepan, cook beef and onion over medium heat until the meat is no longer pink; drain. Add tomato juice, vegetables, water and bouillon; bring to a boil. Add pasta. Cook, uncovered, for 6-8 minutes or until pasta is tender, stirring frequently. Add salt and pepper. **Yield:** 10-12 servings (2-3/4 quarts).

SIMPLE SUBSTITUTIONS:

If you don't have small pasta on hand for ABC Soup, use quick-cooking barley or instant rice. Cook until tender. If you're out of bouillon cubes, 2 teaspoons of bouillon granules can be used instead.

Instead of opening a can of alphabet soup, why not make some from scratch? Kids of all ages love this traditional soup with a tomato base, ground beef and alphabet pasta.
—Sharon Brockman
Appleton, Wisconsin

MUSHROOM BURGER STEW

*This stew is so easy
to make, yet it always
gets rave reviews from
my family and friends.
It's very hearty, and
the bold mushroom
flavor is unbeatable.
—Sue Ellen Dillard
El Dorado, Arkansas*

1 pound ground beef
1 small onion, chopped
4 cups water
4 medium potatoes, cubed
5 medium carrots, chopped
1 can (14-1/2 ounces) stewed tomatoes
1 envelope onion soup mix
Salt and pepper to taste
1/2 pound fresh mushrooms, quartered

In a large saucepan, cook beef and onion over medium heat until the meat is no longer pink; drain. Add the water, potatoes, carrots, tomatoes, soup mix, salt and pepper; bring to a boil. Reduce heat; simmer, uncovered, for 20-25 minutes or until vegetables are tender. Add mushrooms; simmer 5 minutes longer. **Yield:** 6-8 servings.

HELPFUL HINT:

*Look for fresh mushrooms that are firm with tightly closed caps.
Avoid those that are broken, discolored or have soft spots. Store unwashed
mushrooms in a brown paper bag in the refrigerator for up to 3 days.
Before using in a recipe, rinse mushrooms lightly in a colander (do not soak).
Then pat gently with paper towels to dry. Trim 1/4 inch off the stem.*

MEATBALL NOODLE SOUP

*Chicken noodle soup
is a sure-to-please
standby in every
kitchen. This version,
which includes
meatballs, is a
newfound favorite
at our house.
—Debbie Guntz
Collegeville,
Pennsylvania*

1 egg
1 tablespoon dry bread crumbs
1 teaspoon dried parsley flakes
1/2 teaspoon salt
1/8 teaspoon pepper
Pinch dried oregano
1 pound lean ground beef
2 cans (14-1/2 ounces *each*) chicken broth
1 cup uncooked fine egg noodles

In a bowl, combine the first six ingredients. Crumble beef over mixture and mix well. Shape into 1/2-in. balls; set aside. In a large saucepan, bring broth to a boil; add meatballs. Reduce heat; simmer, uncovered, for 20 minutes. Add noodles; cook 15 minutes longer or until the meat is no longer pink and the noodles are tender. **Yield:** 4 servings.

SPICY CHILI

(Pictured above)

1-1/2 **pounds ground beef**
1-1/2 **pounds bulk Italian**
sausage
3 **cans (14-1/2 ounces** *each*)
stewed tomatoes
2 **cans (16 ounces** *each*)
kidney beans, rinsed and
drained
1 **cup chopped onion**
1 **large green pepper,**
chopped
1 **can (6 ounces) tomato**
paste
2 **jalapeno peppers, finely**
chopped*
2 **tablespoons brown sugar**
2 **tablespoons chili powder**
2 **tablespoons vinegar**
1 **tablespoon spicy brown**
mustard

1 **tablespoon dried oregano**
2 **garlic cloves, minced**
1-1/2 **teaspoons ground cumin**
1-1/2 **teaspoons hot pepper**
sauce
1 **teaspoon salt**
1 **teaspoon paprika**

In a soup kettle or Dutch oven, cook beef and sausage over medium heat until no longer pink; drain. Add the remaining ingredients; bring to a boil. Reduce heat; simmer, uncovered, for 30 minutes, stirring frequently. **Yield:** 12 servings (3 quarts).
*Editor's Note: When cutting or seeding hot peppers, use rubber or plastic gloves to protect your hands. Avoid touching your face.

SERVING SUGGESTION:

Sprinkle individual servings of Spicy Chili with shredded cheddar cheese and chopped onion if you like. Plus, a dollop of sour cream can cut some of the spiciness.

This recipe is the culmination of several years' worth of experimenting to get just the right flavor. For those who like their chili very hot, the secret is to add more jalapenos. The most I ever used in a recipe was five ...was it ever spicy!
—Liesha Hoek
Somerset, New Jersey

Meaty Vegetable Entrees

By combining hearty ground
beef and garden-fresh
vegetables, you have a
head start on preparing
wholesome meals.
The possibilities for fine
dining are endless with these
oven entrees, skillet suppers
and microwave dishes.

SOUTH SEAS
SKILLET (P. 185)

BROCCOLI BEEF SUPPER (P. 162)
ZUCCHINI BOATS (P. 162)

BROCCOLI BEEF SUPPER

(Pictured on page 161)

4 cups frozen cottage fries
1 pound ground beef
1 package (10 ounces) frozen chopped broccoli, thawed
1 can (2.8 ounces) french-fried onions, *divided*
1 medium tomato, chopped
1 can (10-3/4 ounces) condensed cream of celery soup, undiluted
1 cup (4 ounces) shredded cheddar cheese, *divided*
1/2 cup milk
1/4 teaspoon garlic powder
1/4 teaspoon pepper

Line bottom and sides of a greased 13-in. x 9-in. x 2-in. baking dish with cottage fries. Bake, uncovered, at 400° for 10 minutes. Meanwhile, in a skillet, cook beef over medium heat until no longer pink; drain. Layer beef, broccoli, half of the onions and the tomato over fries. In a bowl, combine soup, 1/2 cup cheese, milk, garlic powder and pepper; pour over top. Cover and bake at 400° for 20 minutes. Uncover; sprinkle with remaining cheese and onions. Bake 2 minutes longer or until cheese is melted. **Yield:** 8 servings.

ZUCCHINI BOATS

(Pictured on page 161)

2 medium zucchini (about 8 inches)
3/4 pound ground beef
1 small onion, chopped
1/2 cup sliced fresh mushrooms
1/2 cup chopped sweet red pepper
1/2 cup chopped green pepper
1 cup (4 ounces) shredded cheddar cheese, *divided*
2 tablespoons ketchup
Salt and pepper to taste

Trim the ends of zucchini. Cut in half lengthwise; scoop out pulp, leaving a 1/2-in. shell. Finely chop pulp. In a skillet, cook beef, zucchini pulp, onion, mushrooms and peppers over medium heat until meat is no longer pink; drain. Remove from the heat. Add 1/2 cup cheese, ketchup, salt and pepper; mix well. Spoon into the zucchini shells. Place in a greased 13-in. x 9-in. x 2-in. baking dish. Sprinkle with remaining cheese. Bake, uncovered, at 350° for 25-30 minutes or until zucchini is tender. **Yield:** 4 servings.

TIMELY TIP:

When scooping out the pulp for Zucchini Boats, a teaspoon is just the right size. Use your food processor or blender to finely chop the pulp quickly.

SPINACH SKILLET BAKE

(Pictured above)

1 pound ground beef
1 medium onion, chopped
1 package (10 ounces) frozen
   chopped spinach
1 can (4 ounces) mushroom
   stems and pieces, drained
1 teaspoon garlic salt
1 teaspoon dried basil
1/4 cup butter *or* margarine
1/4 cup all-purpose flour
1/2 teaspoon salt
2 cups milk
1 cup (4 ounces) shredded
   Monterey Jack *or*
   mozzarella cheese

In an ovenproof skillet, cook beef and onion over medium heat until no longer pink; drain. Add the spinach, mushrooms, garlic salt and basil. Cover and cook for 5 minutes. In a saucepan, melt butter. Stir in the flour and salt until smooth. Gradually add milk. Bring to a boil; cook and stir for 2 minutes or until thickened. Pour over meat mixture; mix well. Sprinkle with cheese. Bake, uncovered, at 350° for 20-30 minutes or until heated through. **Yield:** 4-6 servings.

HELPFUL HINT:

To avoid ending up with lumps in the white sauce for Spinach Skillet Bake, stir it with a whisk while it cooks.

Over the years, I've tried to instill a love of cooking in our seven children. And we've enjoyed a variety of delicious recipes, including this one.
—Nancy Robaidek
Krakow, Wisconsin

TWO-MEAT MACARONI

1/2 pound ground beef
1/2 pound ground pork
2 cans (14-1/2 ounces *each*) diced tomatoes, undrained
2 cups (8 ounces) shredded cheddar cheese
2 cups uncooked elbow macaroni
1 medium onion, finely chopped
1 cup frozen peas, thawed
2 cans (2-1/2 ounces *each*) sliced ripe olives, drained
1 jar (2 ounces) diced pimientos, drained

1 teaspoon salt
1/2 teaspoon paprika
1/4 teaspoon celery salt

In a large skillet, cook beef and pork over medium heat until no longer pink; drain. Add the remaining ingredients. Transfer to a greased 3-qt. baking dish. Bake, uncovered, at 350° for 1-1/2 hours or until the macaroni is tender, stirring every 30 minutes. **Yield:** 8 servings.

SIMPLE SUBSTITUTION:

If you're unable to find fresh ground pork for Two-Meat Macaroni, use 1/2 pound bulk pork sausage instead.

SCALLOPED POTATOES AND HAMBURGER

1 pound ground beef
6 medium potatoes, peeled and sliced
1 large onion, sliced
Salt and pepper to taste
1 can (10-3/4 ounces) condensed cream of mushroom soup, undiluted
1 cup milk
1/4 cup chopped green pepper

In a skillet, cook beef over medium heat until no longer pink; drain. In a greased 13-in. x 9-in. x 2-in. baking dish, layer half of the potatoes, onion and beef; sprinkle with salt and pepper. Repeat layers. In a bowl, combine the soup, milk and green pepper; mix well. Pour over top. Cover and bake at 350° for 45 minutes. Uncover; bake 15 minutes longer or until potatoes are tender. **Yield:** 6 servings.

HELPFUL HINT:

When a recipe instructs you to season with salt and pepper to taste, start with 1/4 teaspoon salt and 1/8 pepper. Taste the finished food and gradually add more if needed. If the recipe has many canned or packaged foods (which usually contain a lot of sodium), 1/8 teaspoon each salt and pepper will likely suffice.

:now
the ... ecipe,
I do know my mother has pleased family and friends with it for many years. It's a great dish to pass.
—Terri Linn Griffin
Eugene, Oregon

This reliable recipe has been in the family for years. I like the fact that it uses everyday ingredients, so there's no running to the store at the last minute.
—Doris Borneman
Forreston, Illinois

STUFFED ARTICHOKES

2 medium artichokes
Lemon juice
2 eggs
1/4 cup milk
3 tablespoons ketchup
1 cup dry bread crumbs
2 tablespoons minced fresh basil *or* 2 teaspoons dried basil
2 tablespoons minced fresh parsley *or* 2 teaspoons dried parsley flakes
1 garlic clove, minced
1 pound lean ground beef
1 can (8 ounces) tomato sauce
1/4 cup water

Rinse artichokes well; trim stem. Cut 1 in. off the top. Snip the tip of each leaf with a kitchen shears.

Brush cut edges with lemon juice. Spread artichoke open. Using a small knife, carefully cut around center choke. Scoop out and discard the fuzzy center. In a saucepan, place artichokes in a steam basket over 1 in. of boiling water. Cover; steam for 20-25 minutes or until crisp-tender. Invert on a paper towel to drain. In a bowl, combine the eggs, milk, ketchup, bread crumbs, basil, parsley and garlic. Crumble beef over mixture and mix well. Stuff meat mixture into center of artichokes and between leaves. Place in an ungreased 11-in. x 7-in. x 2-in. baking dish. Combine tomato sauce and water; pour over top. Cover and bake at 350° for 1 to 1-1/2 hours or until meat is no longer pink. **Yield:** 4 servings.

When I was a child, my mother often made these meat loaf-stuffed artichokes. They're a nice change from traditional stuffed peppers.
—Jean Castriota York, Pennsylvania

PREPARING ARTICHOKES FOR STUFFING

STEP 1
Trim stem. Cut 1 inch off the top of artichoke. Snip each leaf tip with a kitchen shears. Rub edges with lemon juice.

STEP 2
Using a small knife, cut around center choke. Remove fuzzy center with a spoon.

STEP 3
Stuff meat mixture into center of artichoke and between leaves.

TACO POTATO SHELLS

(Pictured below)

3 large baking potatoes
1 tablespoon butter *or* margarine, melted
1 pound ground beef
1 can (14-1/2 ounces) diced tomatoes, undrained
1 envelope taco seasoning
1/2 cup shredded cheddar cheese
1/3 cup sour cream
2 green onions, sliced

Scrub and pierce potatoes. Bake at 375° for 1 hour or until tender. When cool enough to handle, cut potatoes in half lengthwise. Carefully scoop out pulp, leaving a thin shell (refrigerate pulp for another use). Brush inside and outside of potato shells with butter. Place cut side up on an ungreased baking sheet. Bake, uncovered, at 375° for 20 minutes. Meanwhile, in a skillet, cook beef over medium heat until no longer pink; drain. Add tomatoes and taco seasoning. Bring to a boil. Reduce heat; simmer, uncovered, for 20 minutes. Spoon into potato shells; sprinkle with cheese. Bake, uncovered, 5-10 minutes longer or until cheese is melted. Top with sour cream and onions. **Yield:** 6 servings.

SERVING SUGGESTION:

Taco Potato Shells also make a hearty appetizer. Cut the potato shells into wedges, top with the meat mixture and cheese. Bake as directed; serve with sour cream and onions.

LAYERED BEEF CASSEROLE

6 medium potatoes, peeled
  and thinly sliced
1 can (15-1/4 ounces) whole
  kernel corn, drained
1/2 cup chopped green pepper
1 cup chopped onion
2 cups sliced carrots
1-1/2 pounds lean ground beef
1 can (8 ounces) tomato
  sauce
Salt and pepper to taste
1 cup (4 ounces) shredded
  process American cheese

In a greased 13-in. x 9-in. x 2-in. baking dish, layer potatoes, corn, green pepper, onion and carrots. Crumble beef over the vegetables. Pour tomato sauce over top. Sprinkle with salt and pepper. Cover and bake at 350° for 2 hours. Sprinkle with cheese. Let stand 10 minutes before serving. **Yield:** 8 servings.

TIMELY TIP:

Layered Beef Casserole can be divided between two 1-1/2-quart baking dishes. Bake one casserole to enjoy now and freeze the other for another meal. When ready to use, thaw in the refrigerator overnight. Bake as directed and sprinkle with cheese before serving.

treasure [...] recipes like this. Toss together a salad, and dinner is ready in no time.
—Dorothy Wiedeman Eaton, Colorado

WINTER DAY DINNER

1-1/2 pounds ground beef
1 medium onion, chopped
2 tablespoons Worcestershire
  sauce
1 teaspoon salt
1/2 teaspoon pepper
8 medium potatoes, sliced
1 package (16 ounces) frozen
  peas, thawed
CHEESE SAUCE:
1/4 cup butter *or* margarine
1/3 cup all-purpose flour
1/2 teaspoon salt
1/4 teaspoon pepper
2 cups milk
4 ounces process American
  cheese, cubed

In a skillet, cook the beef, onion, Worcestershire sauce, salt and pepper over medium heat until meat is no longer pink; drain. In a greased 13-in. x 9-in. x 2-in. baking dish, layer half of the potatoes. Top with the meat mixture, peas and remaining potatoes; set aside. In a saucepan, melt butter over medium heat. Stir in flour, salt and pepper until smooth. Gradually stir in milk. Bring to a boil; cook and stir for 2 minutes or until thickened. Stir in cheese until melted. Pour over potatoes. Cover and bake at 350° for 1-1/2 hours or until the potatoes are tender. **Yield:** 8 servings.

In the middle of winter, I often rely on this recipe to warm us up! My husband doesn't care for noodles, so I look for different ways to serve potatoes.
—Linda Hagedorn Rockville, Maryland

CABBAGE CASSEROLE

5 cups shredded cabbage
6 medium potatoes, sliced
4 medium carrots, sliced
1 small onion, chopped
1 teaspoon salt
1/2 teaspoon pepper
1 pound lean ground beef
1 can (10-3/4 ounces) condensed cream of mushroom soup, undiluted
1 can (10-1/2 ounces) condensed vegetable beef soup, undiluted

In a bowl, combine the first six ingredients; mix well. Crumble beef over mixture; toss gently. Transfer to a greased 3-qt. baking dish. Spread soups over top. Cover and bake at 350° for 1-1/2 hours or until the meat is no longer pink and the vegetables are tender. **Yield:** 10 servings.

SIMPLE SUBSTITUTION:

You can easily use any kind of cream soup for the cream of mushroom in Cabbage Casserole.

BREAKFAST SCRAMBLE

1 pound ground beef
1 medium onion, chopped
3 cups diced peeled potatoes
1/2 cup water
Salt and pepper to taste
1 can (14-1/2 ounces) diced tomatoes, undrained
4 eggs, beaten
4 slices process American cheese

In a skillet, cook beef and onion over medium heat until meat is no longer pink; drain. Add potatoes, water, salt and pepper. Cover and simmer for 20 minutes or until the potatoes are tender. Add tomatoes; cook for 5 minutes. Pour eggs over mixture. Cook and stir until eggs are completely set. Top with cheese. Cover and cook for 1 minute or until the cheese is melted. **Yield:** 4-6 servings.

HELPFUL HINT:

Freshly squeezed orange juice is a nice accompaniment to Breakfast Scramble. One medium orange yields 1/4 to 1/3 cup juice. To extract the most juice, roll the orange on the countertop with your palm a few times before squeezing.

HERBED VEGETABLE MEDLEY

(Pictured above)

2 pounds ground beef
1 medium eggplant, cubed
2 medium zucchini, cubed
1 medium onion, chopped
1 medium sweet yellow
   pepper, chopped
3 garlic cloves, minced
1 can (28 ounces) stewed
   tomatoes
1 cup cooked rice
1 cup (4 ounces) shredded
   cheddar cheese, *divided*
1/2 cup beef broth
1/2 teaspoon *each* dried
   oregano, savory and thyme
1/2 teaspoon salt
1/4 teaspoon pepper

In a Dutch oven, cook beef over medium heat until no longer pink; drain. Add the eggplant, zucchini, onion, yellow pepper and garlic; cook until tender. Add tomatoes, rice, 1/2 cup of cheese, broth and seasonings; mix well. Transfer to a greased 13-in. x 9-in. x 2-in. baking dish. Sprinkle with the remaining cheese. Bake, uncovered, at 350° for 30 minutes or until heated through. **Yield:** 10 servings.

If your family is resistant to eating vegetables, offer them this dish! Eggplant, zucchini, onion and yellow pepper are disguised in a beefy tomato sauce.
—Betty Blandford
Johns Island,
South Carolina

DINNER IN A DISH

1	**pound ground beef**
1	**medium onion, chopped**
1/2	**cup julienned green pepper**
1/2	**teaspoon salt**
1/4	**teaspoon pepper**
2	**eggs, beaten**
2	**cups fresh *or* frozen corn**
4	**medium tomatoes, sliced**
1/2	**cup dry bread crumbs**
1	**tablespoon butter *or* margarine**

In a skillet, cook beef, onion, green pepper, salt and pepper over medium heat until meat is no longer pink. Remove from the heat. Add eggs; mix well. In a greased 11-in. x 7-in. x 2-in. baking dish, layer 1 cup corn and half of the meat mixture and tomato. Repeat layers. Sprinkle with bread crumbs. Dot with butter. Bake, uncovered, at 375° for 35 minutes or until golden brown. **Yield:** 4 servings.

HELPFUL HINT:

To dot a casserole with butter, cut small pieces from a stick of butter and drop onto the meat and vegetable mixture.

CASSEROLE ITALIANO

1-1/2	**pounds ground beef**
1	**medium onion, chopped**
1	**jar (14 ounces) spaghetti sauce**
1/3	**cup water**
1-1/2	**teaspoons salt**
1	**teaspoon sugar**
1	**teaspoon dried basil**
1	**teaspoon pepper**
4	**medium potatoes, peeled and thinly sliced**
1/2	**cup shredded mozzarella cheese**

In a skillet, cook beef and onion over medium heat until meat is no longer pink; drain. Add the spaghetti sauce, water and seasonings. In a greased 13-in. x 9-in. x 2-in. baking dish, layer half of the potatoes and meat mixture; repeat layers. Bake, uncovered, at 375° for 50 minutes. Sprinkle with cheese. Bake 10 minutes longer or until the potatoes are tender. **Yield:** 6 servings.

PERFECT PARTNERS:

Serve Casserole Italiano with warmed breadsticks and tomato wedges drizzled with Italian salad dressing.

SUMMER SQUASH BAKE

1 pound ground beef
4 to 6 medium yellow
  summer squash, chopped
  (about 1-1/2 pounds)
1 medium onion, chopped
3/4 cup dry bread crumbs
3/4 teaspoon salt
1/4 teaspoon pepper
1/4 teaspoon dried thyme
SAUCE:
1/4 cup plus 1 tablespoon
  butter *or* margarine,
  divided
1/4 cup all-purpose flour
1/2 teaspoon salt
2 cups milk
1-1/4 cups (6 ounces) shredded
  cheddar cheese
3/4 cup dry bread crumbs

In a skillet, cook beef, squash and onion over medium heat until the meat is no longer pink; drain. Add bread crumbs, salt, pepper and thyme; mix well and set aside. In a saucepan, melt 1/4 cup butter. Stir in the flour and salt until smooth. Gradually add milk. Bring to a boil; cook and stir for 2 minutes or until thickened. Reduce heat. Stir in cheese until melted. In a greased 11-in. x 7-in. x 2-in. baking dish, layer half of the meat mixture and cheese sauce; repeat layers. Melt the remaining butter and toss with bread crumbs. Sprinkle over cheese sauce. Bake, uncovered, at 350° for 35 minutes or until golden brown. **Yield:** 4-6 servings.

TIMELY TIP:

Prepare Summer Squash Bake up to 24 hours in advance; cover and chill. Remove from the refrigerator 30 minutes before baking.

My daughter, a home economist, serves this garden-fresh casserole at church functions in summer when squash is at its best. It's a good main dish for lunch or dinner.
—Rose Duggins Massie
Louisa, Virginia

SAUSAGE HOT DISH

1 pound lean ground beef
3 medium potatoes, peeled
  and cut into 1/4-inch slices
2 medium carrots, thinly
  sliced
1 small onion, thinly sliced
1 teaspoon dried thyme
1 teaspoon salt
1/8 teaspoon pepper
1/4 cup water
1 pound bulk pork sausage
2 cups (8 ounces) shredded
  cheddar cheese

Crumble half of the beef into a 2-1/2-qt. microwave-safe dish. Layer with half of the potatoes, carrots and onion. Sprinkle with half of the thyme, salt and pepper. Repeat layers. Pour water over top. Cover and microwave at 70% power for 25 minutes. Meanwhile, in a skillet, cook sausage over medium heat until no longer pink; drain. Spoon over beef mixture. Microwave, uncovered, on high for 8-10 minutes. Sprinkle with cheese. Heat 1 minute longer. Let stand for 5 minutes before serving. **Yield:** 8 servings. **Editor's Note:** This recipe was tested in a 700-watt microwave.

I normally don't cook foods in the microwave, but this meal is the exception! The flavorful combination of ground beef and sausage makes it unique. We like it a lot.
—Carol Rydman
Midland, Michigan

I came across this in my grandmother's recipe collection a few years back. It's easy to vary the vegetables to suit different people's tastes.
—Jody Summersett
New Haven, Indiana

MEAL IN A PACKET
(Pictured below)

1 pound lean ground beef
8 medium carrots, julienned
1 medium green pepper, julienned
1 envelope onion gravy mix
2 firm fresh tomatoes, halved

Shape beef into four patties. Place each on an ungreased 14-in. square of heavy-duty foil. Arrange carrots and green pepper around patties. Sprinkle with gravy mix. Place a tomato half, cut side down, on each patty. Fold foil around meat and vegetables; seal tightly. Place on an ungreased baking sheet. Bake at 350° for 45 minutes or until meat is no longer pink. **Yield:** 4 servings.

TIMELY TIP:

It's simple to take Meal in a Packet with you on a picnic. Assemble the packets and put them in a cooler. Grill over medium-high heat for about 1 hour or until meat is no longer pink.

MEATY VEGETABLE ENTREES

COMPANY CASSEROLE

4 medium carrots, cut into
  1-inch pieces
2 celery ribs, chopped
1 medium onion, sliced and
  separated into rings
1 can (14-1/2 ounces) whole
  tomatoes, drained
1 cup beef broth
1 can (8 ounces) sliced water
  chestnuts, drained
1 can (4 ounces) mushroom
  stems and pieces, drained
3 tablespoons quick-cooking
  tapioca

1 tablespoon sugar
1 teaspoon salt
2 pounds lean ground beef
Hot cooked rice *or* noodles

In a bowl, combine the first 10 ingredients; mix well. Crumble beef over mixture; toss gently. Transfer to a greased 13-in. x 9-in. x 2-in. baking dish. Cover and bake at 350° for 2 hours or until hot and bubbly. Serve over rice or noodles. **Yield:** 8 servings.

HELPFUL HINT:

In addition to being served as a dessert, quick-cooking tapioca is also often used as a thickener. Store uncooked tapioca in a cool dry place for up to 2 years.

I first tried this casserole at a family dinner years ago. It's a great dish because it goes into the oven before guests arrive. Just before serving, make rice or noodles and toss a salad.
—Barbara Treiuthick
Aurora, Colorado

FARMHOUSE DINNER

1 pound ground beef
2 eggs
1/4 cup milk
1 can (14-3/4 ounces) cream-
  style corn
1 cup soft bread crumbs
1/4 cup finely chopped onion
2 teaspoons prepared
  mustard
1 teaspoon salt
1/2 cup dry bread crumbs
2 tablespoons butter *or*
  margarine, melted

In a skillet, cook beef over medium heat until no longer pink; drain and set aside. In a bowl, combine eggs and milk. Add the corn, soft bread crumbs, onion, mustard, salt and beef; mix well. Transfer to a greased 9-in. square baking dish. Toss dry bread crumbs with butter; sprinkle over meat mixture. Bake, uncovered, at 350° for 30 minutes or until golden brown. **Yield:** 4-6 servings.

After a hard day of working on our farm, we look forward to a down-home dinner like this. Buttered bread crumbs enhance the mellow flavor of cream-style corn.
—Deborah Binstock
South Heart,
North Dakota

STUFFED ACORN SQUASH

2 large acorn squash, halved and seeded
1 cup water
3/4 pound ground beef
1 celery rib, chopped
1 small onion, chopped
1 medium tart apple, chopped
1 cup cooked rice
1/4 cup sunflower kernels
1 teaspoon curry powder
1 egg, beaten
5 teaspoons brown sugar, *divided*
1-1/2 teaspoons salt, *divided*
4 teaspoons butter *or* margarine

Invert squash in an ungreased 13-in. x 9-in. x 2-in. baking dish. Add water and cover with foil. Bake at 375° for 50-60 minutes or until tender. Meanwhile, cook beef, celery and onion over medium heat until meat is no longer pink and vegetables are tender; drain. Add the apple, rice, sunflower kernels and curry powder. Cook and stir for 3 minutes or until apple is tender. Remove from the heat. Stir in egg, 1 teaspoon brown sugar and 1 teaspoon salt. Place squash cut side up on a baking sheet. Place 1 teaspoon of brown sugar and 1 teaspoon butter in each. Sprinkle with remaining salt. Fill with meat mixture. Bake, uncovered, at 375° for 15-20 minutes or until heated through. **Yield:** 4 servings.

TIMELY TIP:

Acorn squash are easier to cut in half if you first soften them in the microwave for a few minutes. Always pierce squash with a fork before microwaving to allow steam to escape.

POTATO CORN CASSEROLE

1 pound lean ground beef
Salt and pepper to taste
1/4 cup diced onion
4 medium potatoes, peeled and diced
1 can (14-3/4 ounces) cream-style corn
1 tablespoon butter *or* margarine

Crumble beef into a shallow 2-qt. microwave-safe dish. Sprinkle with salt and pepper. Layer with onion, potatoes and corn. Dot with butter. Cover and microwave on high for 15 minutes; stir. Cover and heat 10-12 minutes longer or until meat is no longer pink and potatoes are tender. Let stand 5 minutes before serving. **Yield:** 4 servings. **Editor's Note:** This recipe was tested in a 700-watt microwave.

POTATO BEEF CROQUETTES

2 eggs
1 pound ground beef, cooked and drained
2 cups cold mashed potatoes (prepared with milk and butter)
1 medium onion, chopped
1/2 teaspoon salt
1/4 teaspoon pepper
1 cup crushed saltines (about 30 crackers)
Vegetable oil for frying

In a large bowl, beat 1 egg. Add the beef, potatoes, onion, salt and pepper; mix well. Shape into 12 balls. Beat remaining egg; dip balls into egg, then roll in the cracker crumbs. Shape each ball into a cone. In a Dutch oven or deep-fat fryer, heat 2 in. of oil to 375°. Fry croquettes, four at a time, for 2 minutes or until golden brown, turning occasionally. Drain on paper towels. **Yield:** 1 dozen.

MAKING CROQUETTES

Roll egg-coated balls in cracker crumbs. Shape each ball into a cone shape.

My daughter brought this recipe home from her high school home economics class more than 30 years ago. It's one of the few dishes everyone in my family will eat.
—Violet Gertsch
Darlington, Wisconsin

CREAMY SAUSAGE 'N' BEEF BAKE

1-1/2 pounds ground beef
1-1/2 pounds fully cooked smoked sausage links, sliced
1 package (16 ounces) frozen mixed vegetables, thawed
1 can (8 ounces) mushroom stems and pieces, drained
4 cups milk
1 can *each* (10-3/4 ounces) condensed cream of celery soup, cream of chicken soup and cream of mushroom soup, undiluted
1 package (5-1/4 ounces) au gratin potatoes
Dash onion powder
Grated Parmesan cheese
1 cup crushed potato chips

In a skillet, cook beef and sausage over medium heat until the beef is no longer pink; drain. In a greased roasting pan, layer meat mixture, mixed vegetables and mushrooms. In a large bowl, combine the milk, soups, contents of potato package and onion powder; mix well. Pour over vegetables. Sprinkle with Parmesan cheese and potato chips. Bake, uncovered, at 350° for 1 hour or until hot and bubbly. **Yield:** 12 servings.

HELPFUL HINT:

If you don't have a roasting pan for making Creamy Sausage 'n' Beef Bake, you can use two 13- x 9- x 2-inch baking dishes or two round or oval 3-quart baking dishes.

This delicious big-batch dish is perfect for potlucks. It's packed with meat and vegetables, so all that's needed to complete the meal is some dinner rolls and dessert.
—Mrs. Herbert Kohler
Wapakoneta, Ohio

BROCCOLI BISCUIT SQUARES
(Pictured at right)

1 pound ground beef
1 can (4 ounces) mushroom stems and pieces, drained
1 small onion, chopped
2 cups biscuit/baking mix
2 cups (8 ounces) shredded cheddar cheese, *divided*
1/4 cup grated Parmesan cheese
1/2 cup water
1 package (10 ounces) frozen chopped broccoli, thawed and drained
4 eggs
1/2 cup milk
1 teaspoon salt
Dash pepper

In a skillet, cook beef, mushrooms and onion over medium heat until meat is no longer pink; drain. In a bowl, combine biscuit mix, 1/2 cup cheddar cheese, Parmesan cheese and water until a soft dough forms. Press dough onto the bottom and 1/2 in. up the sides of a greased 13-in. x 9-in. x 2-in. baking dish. Stir remaining cheddar cheese into the beef mixture; spread over dough. Sprinkle with broccoli. In a bowl, beat eggs, milk, salt and pepper. Pour over meat mixture. Bake, uncovered, at 400° for 25 minutes or until a knife inserted near center comes out clean. **Yield:** 6 servings.

PERFECT PARTNERS:

Broccoli Biscuit Squares are a nice brunch item served with fresh fruit and muffins.

GARDEN SKILLET
(Pictured at right)

2 pounds ground beef
3 medium zucchini, julienned
4 medium carrots, julienned
1 can (16 ounces) bean sprouts, drained
1 medium onion, cut into thin wedges
3/4 cup julienned green pepper
1 garlic clove, minced
1 medium tomato, cut into wedges
1 teaspoon salt
1 teaspoon ground cumin

In a skillet, cook beef over medium heat until no longer pink; drain. Add the zucchini, carrots, bean sprouts, onion, green pepper and garlic. Cook and stir for 3-4 minutes or until crisp-tender. Add the tomato, salt and cumin. Cook 2 minutes longer or until heated through. **Yield:** 6-8 servings.

SIMPLE SUBSTITUTION:

To give the Garden Skillet a little more heat, toss in strips of jalapeno peppers and serve with taco sauce on the side.

BROCCOLI BISCUIT SQUARES
GARDEN SKILLET

SNOWCAPPED CASSEROLE

1 **pound ground beef**
1 **medium onion, chopped**
2 **cans (14-1/2 ounces *each*) cut green beans, drained**
1 **can (8 ounces) tomato sauce**
1 **teaspoon salt**
1/4 **teaspoon pepper**
2-1/2 **cups hot mashed potatoes (prepared with milk and butter)**
1/4 **cup butter *or* margarine, melted**
Paprika

In a skillet, cook beef and onion over medium heat until meat is no longer pink; drain. Add beans, tomato sauce, salt and pepper; mix well. Transfer to a greased shallow 2-qt. baking dish. Top with eight mounds of mashed potatoes. Drizzle with butter; sprinkle with paprika. Bake, uncovered, at 350° for 30 minutes or until potatoes are browned. **Yield:** 4 servings.

MASHING POTATOES

After cooking and draining potatoes, mash with a potato masher. Add milk and butter; mash until potatoes are light and fluffy. Over-mashing can make them sticky.

HELPFUL HINT:

*To cook potatoes for mashing, peel and cut into chunks.
Place in a saucepan; cover with water. Bring to a boil;
cover and cook for 15-30 minutes or until tender. Drain well and mash.
One large potato will yield about 1 cup mashed potatoes.*

EASY SKILLET SUPPER

1 **pound lean ground beef**
4 **medium potatoes, peeled and diced**
2 **cups fresh *or* frozen corn**
1 **small onion, chopped**
Salt and pepper to taste
1 **can (10-3/4 ounces) condensed cream of mushroom soup, undiluted**

In a skillet, crumble beef. Top with potatoes, corn and onion. Sprinkle with salt and pepper. Spread soup over the top. Cover and cook over medium heat for 10 minutes. Reduce heat; cover and simmer for 30-45 minutes or until meat is no longer pink and potatoes are tender. **Yield:** 4-6 servings.

HAMBURGER 'N' FRIES DINNER

1 pound ground beef
1 small onion, chopped
2 cups frozen french fries, thawed
1 can (15-1/4 ounces) whole kernel corn, drained
1 can (10-3/4 ounces) condensed cream of mushroom soup, undiluted
1/2 cup shredded process American cheese

In a skillet, cook beef and onion over medium heat until the meat is no longer pink; drain. Line a greased 9-in. square baking dish with french fries. Top with beef mixture, corn, soup and cheese. Bake, uncovered, at 375° for 30 minutes or until hot and bubbly. **Yield:** 4-6 servings.

SIMPLE SUBSTITUTION:

Don't have french fries in the freezer for Hamburger 'n' Fries Dinner? Use shredded or cubed hash browns instead.

TATER-TOPPED CASSEROLE

1-1/2 pounds ground beef, cooked and drained
1 package (16 ounces) frozen vegetables, thawed
1 can (2.8 ounces) french-fried onions
1/4 cup butter *or* margarine
1 can (10-3/4 ounces) condensed cream of celery soup, undiluted
1 can (10-3/4 ounces) condensed cream of chicken soup, undiluted
1/2 cup milk
1 package (16 ounces) frozen Tater Tots, thawed

In a greased 13-in. x 9-in. x 2-in. baking pan, layer beef, vegetables and onions. Dot with butter. In a bowl, combine soups and milk; spread over vegetables. Top with Tater Tots. Bake, uncovered, at 350° for 1 hour or until golden brown. **Yield:** 6-8 servings.

SERVING SUGGESTION:

When you remove the Tater-Topped Casserole from the oven, sprinkle with a little shredded cheddar, mozzarella or Swiss cheese.

One day I was having trouble deciding what to make for dinner. So I combined whatever was in the refrigerator and freezer. To my surprise, everyone loved it!
—Elizabeth Martz
Pleasant Gap, Pennsylvania

MEATBALL SAUSAGE DINNER

(Pictured below)

1 package (10 ounces) frozen chopped broccoli, thawed
2 medium potatoes, peeled and cubed
3 medium carrots, sliced
1 medium onion, chopped
1 pound fully cooked kielbasa *or* Polish sausage, halved and cut into 1-inch pieces
1/2 pound lean ground beef
1 can (14-1/2 ounces) beef broth
Lemon-pepper seasoning to taste

In a large bowl, combine the first four ingredients. Transfer to a greased 13-in. x 9-in. x 2-in. baking pan. Sprinkle with sausage. Shape beef into 1-in. balls; arrange over top. Pour broth over the casserole. Sprinkle with lemon-pepper. Bake, uncovered, at 350° for 1 hour or until heated through. **Yield:** 6-8 servings.

PERFECT PARTNERS:

Prepare a brownie mix and pop it into the oven when the Meatball Sausage Dinner is done...dessert will be baking while you're eating. Serve the brownies warm with vanilla ice cream.

GOLDEN BROCCOLI BAKE

1 pound ground beef, cooked
   and drained
1 can (10-3/4 ounces)
   condensed cream of
   mushroom soup, undiluted
1 package (10 ounces) frozen
   chopped broccoli, thawed
1 egg
2 cups (8 ounces) shredded
   cheddar cheese, *divided*
2 cups hot mashed potatoes
   (prepared with milk and
   butter)

In a bowl, combine the first four ingredients; mix well. Stir in 1 cup cheese. Transfer to a greased 11-in. x 7-in. x 2-in. baking dish. In a bowl, combine potatoes with remaining cheese; mix well. Spread over the meat mixture. Bake, uncovered, at 350° for 30 minutes or until lightly browned. **Yield:** 6 servings.

TIMELY TIP:

For even quicker preparation, assemble Golden Broccoli Bake the night before; cover and chill. Remove from the refrigerator 30 minutes before baking.

CHEESE-TOPPED PEPPERS

4 medium green peppers
1 pound ground beef
1 medium onion, chopped
1 cup cooked rice
1 can (10-3/4 ounces)
   condensed tomato soup,
   undiluted, *divided*
2 teaspoons Worcestershire
   sauce
1/2 teaspoon salt
Dash pepper
2 slices process American
   cheese, cut into strips

Cut tops off peppers and remove seeds. In a large kettle, cook peppers in boiling water for 3 minutes. Drain and rinse with cold water; invert on paper towels. In a skillet, cook beef and onion over medium heat until meat is no longer pink; drain. Add rice, 1 cup soup, Worcestershire sauce, salt and pepper; mix well. Spoon into peppers. Place in a greased 9-in. square baking dish. Bake, uncovered, at 375° for 25 minutes. Top with remaining soup and cheese. Bake 5 minutes longer or until cheese is melted. **Yield:** 4 servings.

HELPFUL HINT:

After parboiling peppers for Cheese-Topped Peppers, use tongs to easily remove them from the water. Rinsing the peppers in cold water stops them from cooking. Overcooked peppers can turn mushy and fall apart.

DOWN-HOME DINNER

1 pound ground beef
1 small onion, chopped
2 medium potatoes, peeled and thinly sliced
1 can (15 ounces) peas, drained
1 can (10-3/4 ounces) condensed cream of mushroom soup, undiluted
1 can (10-1/2 ounces) condensed vegetable beef soup, undiluted
Salt and pepper to taste

In a skillet, cook beef and onion over medium heat until meat is no longer pink; drain. Add the potatoes, peas, soups, salt and pepper; mix well. Transfer to a greased 11-in. x 7-in. x 2-in. baking dish. Cover and bake at 350° for 1 hour until potatoes are tender. **Yield:** 4-6 servings.

TIMELY TIP:

Down-Home Dinner can also be made in a slow cooker. Brown the beef and onion; drain. Combine with the remaining ingredients in a slow cooker. Cover and cook on high for 4 to 6 hours (on low for 8 to 12 hours) or until potatoes are tender.

MIXED VEGGIE CASSEROLE

1 pound ground beef
1 small onion, chopped
Salt and pepper to taste
1 can (11-1/8 ounces) condensed Italian tomato soup, undiluted
1 can (16 ounces) mixed vegetables, drained
2 cups hot mashed potatoes (prepared with milk and butter)
1 cup cubed process American cheese

In a skillet, cook beef, onion, salt and pepper over medium heat until meat is no longer pink; drain. Add soup; mix well. Transfer to a greased 9-in. square baking dish. Sprinkle with the vegetables. In a bowl, combine mashed potatoes and cheese; spread over vegetables. Bake, uncovered, at 350° for 30 minutes or until hot and bubbly. **Yield:** 4 servings.

Beef Potato Supper

1-1/2 pounds ground beef
1 large onion, chopped
4 cups sliced peeled potatoes
1 can (14-1/2 ounces) cut green beans, drained
1 can (10-3/4 ounces) condensed cream of mushroom soup, undiluted
2/3 cup milk
2/3 cup water
1 can (2.8 ounces) french-fried onions
1 cup (4 ounces) shredded cheddar cheese

In a skillet, cook beef and onion over medium heat until meat is no longer pink; drain. Meanwhile, place the potatoes in a saucepan and cover with water; bring to a boil. Cook for 7 minutes; drain. In a greased 13-in. x 9-in. x 2-in. baking dish, layer beef mixture, beans and potatoes. In a bowl, combine soup, milk and water; pour over potatoes. Sprinkle with onions and cheese. Bake, uncovered, at 350° for 35 minutes or until browned. **Yield:** 6-8 servings.

Simple Substitution:

Rushed for time? Instead of slicing and cooking potatoes for Beef Potato Supper, use 4 cups frozen hash browns. (Quickly thaw the hash browns by placing them in a colander and running hot water over them. Be sure to drain well.)

Five-Vegetable Delight

2 cups *each* diced carrots, celery and onion
2 cups diced peeled potatoes and rutabagas
1 pound lean ground beef
1 can (10-3/4 ounces) condensed tomato soup, undiluted
1-1/3 cups water
1 teaspoon salt
1/4 teaspoon pepper

In a bowl, combine the vegetables; mix well. Crumble beef over mixture and toss gently. Transfer to a greased 13-in. x 9-in. x 2-in. baking dish. In a bowl, combine soup, water, salt and pepper. Pour over vegetable mixture. Bake, uncovered, at 350° for 1-1/2 hours or until vegetables are tender. **Yield:** 8 servings.

Helpful Hint:

Rutabagas are available year-round, but fall and winter are the peak seasons. Buy small (3 to 4 inches in diameter) rutabagas that feel firm and have smooth skin. Refrigerate in a plastic bag for up to 1 month.

This recipe has been in our family for ages. We take it to just about every get-together...folks always rave about it. I like that it's so simple to prepare.
—Eileen Jahn
Detroit, Michigan

A friend of mine often made this lasagna without meat. But I thought ground beef would make it more flavorful. This recipe is a nice way to use up a bumper crop of zucchini.
—Charlotte McDaniel
Williamsville, Illinois

GREEN BEAN BEEF BAKE

1 pound ground beef
1 medium onion, chopped
3/4 teaspoon salt
Dash pepper
1 can (14-1/2 ounces) cut *or* French-style green beans, drained
1 can (10-3/4 ounces) condensed tomato soup, undiluted
1 can (4 ounces) mushroom stems and pieces, drained
2 cups mashed potatoes (without added milk and butter)
1 egg
1/4 cup milk
1/4 cup shredded cheddar cheese

In a skillet, cook beef, onion, salt and pepper over medium heat until meat is no longer pink; drain. Add the beans, soup and mushrooms; mix well. Transfer to a greased 8-in. square baking dish. In a bowl, combine the mashed potatoes, egg and milk; mix until light and fluffy. Spread over beef mixture. Sprinkle with cheese. Bake, uncovered, at 350° for 30-35 minutes or until heated through. **Yield:** 4-6 servings.

ZUCCHINI LASAGNA

1 pound ground beef
1 medium onion, chopped
1 can (15 ounces) tomato sauce
1/2 teaspoon salt
1/2 teaspoon dried oregano
1/4 teaspoon dried basil
Dash pepper
4 medium zucchini, cut lengthwise into 1/4-inch strips
2 tablespoons all-purpose flour
1 cup small-curd cottage cheese
1 egg
1 cup (4 ounces) shredded mozzarella cheese
1/2 cup grated Parmesan cheese

In a skillet, cook beef and onion over medium heat until meat is no longer pink; drain. Stir in tomato sauce, salt, oregano, basil and pepper. Bring to a boil. Reduce heat; simmer, uncovered, for 10 minutes, stirring occasionally. In a greased 11-in. x 7-in. x 2-in. baking dish, layer half of the zucchini; sprinkle with 1 tablespoon flour. In a bowl, combine cottage cheese and egg; mix well. Spread over zucchini. Layer with half of the meat mixture, remaining zucchini and remaining flour. Top with mozzarella cheese and the remaining meat mixture. Sprinkle with Parmesan cheese. Bake, uncovered, at 375° for 40 minutes or until heated through. Let stand 5-10 minutes before serving. **Yield:** 4-6 servings.

SIMPLE SUBSTITUTIONS:

For a splash of color, replace some of the zucchini in Zucchini Lasagna with slices of yellow summer squash. Or toss a cup of sliced mushrooms into the sauce.

SOUTH SEAS SKILLET

(Pictured above and on page 160)

1 pound ground beef
1 package (10 ounces) frozen peas
1 can (8 ounces) sliced water chestnuts, drained
2 jars (4-1/2 ounces *each*) sliced mushrooms, drained
1/2 cup beef broth
1/2 cup golden raisins
1/2 cup soy sauce
2 teaspoons ground ginger
1/2 cup slivered almonds, toasted
Fresh orange slices
Hot cooked rice

In a skillet, cook beef over medium heat until no longer pink; drain. Add peas, water chestnuts, mushrooms, broth, raisins, soy sauce and ginger; mix well. Bring to a boil. Reduce heat; cover and simmer for 15 minutes or until vegetables are tender. Garnish with almonds and orange slices. Serve over rice. **Yield:** 6-8 servings.

HELPFUL HINT:

*To toast nuts, bake them in a shallow baking pan at 350°
for 5 to 10 minutes, stirring twice. Or brown in a skillet over
medium heat for 5 to 7 minutes, stirring occasionally.*

Soy sauce, raisins, water chestnuts and toasted almonds lend to this dish's tropical flavor. Served over rice, it's a filling entree that satisfies my family.
—Bernice Muilenburg
Molalla, Oregon

EGGPLANT CASSEROLE

    4 **cups water**
    1 **medium eggplant, peeled and cubed**
1-1/2 **pounds ground beef**
    1 **medium onion, chopped**
    1 **medium green pepper, chopped**
    3 **medium tomatoes, chopped**
Salt and pepper to taste
  1/2 **cup milk**
    1 **egg, beaten**
  1/2 **cup dry bread crumbs**
    2 **tablespoons butter *or* margarine, melted**

In a saucepan, bring the water to a boil; add eggplant. Boil for 5-8 minutes or until tender; drain and set aside. In a skillet, cook beef, onion and green pepper over medium heat until the meat is no longer pink; drain. Add the tomatoes, salt and pepper. Cook and stir for 5 minutes or until tomato is tender. Remove from the heat. Stir in milk, egg and eggplant; mix well. Transfer to a greased 13-in. x 9-in. x 2-in. baking dish. Toss bread crumbs and butter; sprinkle over top. Bake, uncovered, at 375° for 30 minutes or until heated through. **Yield:** 8 servings.

PEELING AN EGGPLANT

Cut stem end off of the eggplant. Use a vegetable peeler or small kitchen knife to remove peel.

HELPFUL HINT:

Keep unwashed eggplant in an open plastic bag in the refrigerator for up to 3 days. Cut eggplant discolors quickly, so peel and dice just before cooking.

HARVEST STIR-FRY

    1 **pound ground beef**
    1 **medium onion, chopped**
    6 **small yellow summer squash, chopped**
    6 **medium tomatoes, quartered**
1-1/2 **cups whole kernel corn**
    1 **tablespoon minced fresh oregano *or* 1 teaspoon dried oregano**
    1 **teaspoon salt**
  1/2 **teaspoon coarsely ground pepper**

In a skillet, cook beef and onion over medium heat until the meat is no longer pink; drain. Add squash, tomatoes, corn, oregano, salt and pepper. Cook and stir for 5-10 minutes or until vegetables are tender. **Yield:** 8-10 servings.

PEPPER BEEF WITH CASHEWS

1-1/2 pounds ground beef
   2 teaspoons coarsely ground pepper
   1 small onion, chopped
   2 garlic cloves, minced
   4 tablespoons beef broth, *divided*
   1 *each* large sweet red, yellow and green pepper, chopped
   2 tablespoons oyster sauce, optional
   1 tablespoon soy sauce
   2 teaspoons cornstarch
3/4 cup cashew halves

In a skillet, cook beef and pepper over medium heat until no longer pink. Remove with a slotted spoon and keep warm. Add onion and garlic to skillet; saute for 2 minutes. Add 2 tablespoons broth; mix well. Stir in the peppers. Cover and steam for 1 minute. Return beef to pan. Stir in oyster sauce if desired and soy sauce. Combine cornstarch with remaining broth until smooth; gradually add to skillet. Bring to a boil. Cook and stir for 2 minutes or until thickened. Stir in cashews. **Yield:** 6 servings.

SERVING SUGGESTION:

Served over hot cooked rice or pasta, Pepper Beef with Cashews is special enough for company yet quick enough for every day.

I created this recipe after seeing an Oriental version of pepper steak. The pretty peppers make this dish look so attractive and are a nice sweet contrast to the peppery beef.
—Sharon Wolf Camrose, Alberta

POTATO LEEK SKILLET

1/2 pound ground beef
   2 medium potatoes, cubed and cooked
   3 large leeks (white part only), cut into 1/2-inch slices
1/2 cup water
   2 tablespoons olive *or* vegetable oil
   1 teaspoon salt
1/2 teaspoon pepper
1/2 teaspoon dill weed

In a skillet, cook beef over medium heat until no longer pink; drain. Add the potatoes, leeks, water, oil, salt, pepper and dill. Bring to a boil. Reduce heat; simmer, uncovered, until leeks are tender, about 5 minutes. **Yield:** 4 servings.

HELPFUL HINT:

Leeks are part of the onion family and resemble a large green onion. Sand is often found between their many layers. So if a leek is to be sliced, cut it open lengthwise down one side and rinse under cold running water, separating the leaves.

Before sampling this recipe from a neighbor, I never had eaten leeks. I've since fallen in love with their mellow, slightly sweet flavor. This is a nice brunch dish.
—Sharon Boyajian Linden, California

BALTIMORE HASH
(Pictured above)

*My mother-in-law
created this recipe
while living in Baltimore.
I make many batches
of it with our garden
vegetables and freeze
in serving-size
portions for later.
—Betty Cannell
Reading, Pennsylvania*

1 pound ground beef
1 small onion, diced
1 can (28 ounces) diced
tomatoes, undrained
1 cup diced carrots
1 cup diced celery
1 cup cubed peeled potatoes
Salt and pepper to taste

In a skillet, cook beef and onion over medium heat until meat is no longer pink; drain. Add tomatoes, carrots, celery and potatoes. Bring to a boil. Reduce heat; cover and simmer for 30 minutes or until vegetables are tender. Sprinkle with salt and pepper. **Yield:** 4-6 servings.

SIMPLE SUBSTITUTION:

The canned diced tomatoes in Baltimore Hash can be replaced with a quart of fresh tomatoes that have been peeled and diced.

MEATY VEGETABLE ENTREES

BEEF-STUFFED ONIONS

4 large sweet onions
1/2 pound ground beef, cooked and drained
1/4 cup soft bread crumbs
1/4 cup condensed fiesta nacho cheese soup, undiluted
1/4 cup finely chopped green pepper
1/2 teaspoon dried oregano
1/2 teaspoon salt
1/2 teaspoon pepper
1/2 teaspoon beef bouillon granules
1/4 cup hot water

Cut tops off onions and peel them. Scoop out centers to within 1/4 in. of edge; set shells aside. Chop the removed onion; set aside 1/4 cup (refrigerate remaining onion for another use). In a bowl, combine the beef, bread crumbs, soup, green pepper, oregano, salt, pepper and chopped onion; mix well. Stuff the onions. Arrange in a 9-in. microwave-safe pie plate. In a small bowl, dissolve bouillon in water. Pour over onions. Cover and microwave on high for 10-15 minutes, turning and basting after 5 minutes. **Yield:** 4 servings. **Editor's Note:** This recipe was tested in a 700-watt microwave.

TIMELY TIP:

When preparing Beef-Stuffed Onions, use a grapefruit spoon or melon baller to scoop out the centers of onions with ease.

SUNRISE SKILLET

1/2 pound ground beef
2 medium potatoes, peeled, cubed and cooked
1 medium onion, chopped
1 celery rib, chopped
4 eggs
Salt and pepper to taste

In a skillet, cook beef over medium heat until no longer pink; drain. Add potatoes, onion and celery. Cook and stir for 10-15 minutes or until potatoes are browned and celery is tender. Make four wells in beef mixture; break an egg into each well. Cover and cook over medium heat until eggs are completely set, about 10 minutes. Sprinkle with salt and pepper. **Yield:** 4 servings.

HELPFUL HINTS:

To make wells in the Sunrise Skillet beef mixture, use the back of a large serving spoon or the bottom of a measuring cup or small glass. To prevent eggshells from getting into the beef mixture, first break the eggs, one at a time, into a custard cup or saucer. Then gently slide into the well.

My son-in-law gave me the idea for this recipe as an alternative to stuffed tomatoes. He and the rest of the family love the incredible flavor.
—Clara Honeyager
Mukwonago,
Wisconsin

I learned to cook at an early age. Instead of relying on recipes, most of my dishes come about from trial and error, including this skillet. We always make this when we go camping.
—Mary Stickney
Cortland, Nebraska

HAMBURGER HASH BROWNS

4 cups frozen shredded hash brown potatoes, thawed
3 tablespoons vegetable oil
1/8 teaspoon pepper
1 pound ground beef
1 envelope brown gravy mix
1 cup water
1 package (10 ounces) frozen mixed vegetables, thawed
1/2 teaspoon garlic powder
1 cup (4 ounces) shredded cheddar cheese, *divided*
1 can (2.8 ounces) french-fried onions, *divided*

In a bowl, combine hash browns, oil and pepper. Press onto the bottom and 1 in. up the sides of an ungreased 9-in. square baking dish. Bake, uncovered, at 350° for 15 minutes. Meanwhile, in a skillet, cook beef over medium heat until no longer pink; drain. Stir in gravy mix and water. Add vegetables and garlic powder. Bring to a boil. Reduce heat; cover and simmer for 5 minutes. Stir in 1/2 cup cheese and half of the onions. Spoon into the potato shell. Bake, uncovered, at 350° for 15 minutes. Sprinkle with the remaining cheese and onions. Bake 5 minutes longer. **Yield:** 4-6 servings.

SIMPLE SUBSTITUTION:

When making Hamburger Hash Browns, you can use 1 cup of prepared gravy (homemade or purchased) instead of the gravy mix and 1 cup water.

HURRY-UP CASSEROLE

1 pound ground beef
1 medium onion, chopped
2 celery ribs, chopped
1 package (10 ounces) frozen pea pods
2 cups chow mein noodles
1 can (10-3/4 ounces) condensed cream of mushroom soup *or* cream of celery soup, undiluted

In a skillet, cook beef, onion and celery over medium heat until the meat is no longer pink and vegetables are tender; drain. Add pea pods, noodles and soup; mix well. Transfer to a greased 9-in. square baking dish. Bake, uncovered, at 350° for 30 minutes or until heated through. **Yield:** 4 servings.

SIMPLE SUBSTITUTION:

To give Hurry-Up Casserole a heartier crunch, try replacing the chow mein noodles with toasted cashews or almonds.

SAVORY STUFFED PEPPERS

6 medium green peppers
1 pound ground beef, cooked and drained
1/2 pound ground pork, cooked and drained
1 cup quick-cooking oats
1 medium onion, chopped
1/2 cup sliced fresh mushrooms
1 egg, beaten
1 tablespoon salsa
1 tablespoon hot pepper sauce
2 garlic cloves, minced
1 teaspoon *each* dried basil, oregano, thyme, Italian seasoning and parsley flakes
1/2 teaspoon pepper
2/3 cup tomato sauce

Cut tops off peppers and remove seeds. In a large kettle, cook peppers in boiling water for 3 minutes. Drain and rinse in cold water; invert on paper towels. In a bowl, combine meat, oats, onion, mushrooms, egg, salsa and seasonings. Spoon into peppers. Place in a greased 13-in. x 9-in. x 2-in. baking dish. Spoon tomato sauce over peppers. Bake, uncovered, at 350° for 1 hour or until heated through. **Yield:** 6 servings.

The filling for these stuffed peppers is loaded with meat, mushrooms and herbs. I like to serve them with cooked pasta or rice.
—Catherine Faubert
Embrun, Ontario

CHILI-TOPPED TATERS

6 large potatoes
2 pounds ground beef
1 medium onion, chopped
1 can (16 ounces) kidney beans, rinsed and drained
1 can (16 ounces) pork and beans, undrained
1 can (15 ounces) tomato sauce
2 tablespoons chili powder
1 tablespoon dried parsley flakes
1 teaspoon dried oregano
1/2 teaspoon garlic powder
Salt and pepper to taste
3/4 cup shredded cheddar cheese

Scrub and pierce potatoes. Bake at 375° for 1 hour or until tender. Meanwhile, in a large saucepan, cook beef and onion over medium heat until meat is no longer pink; drain. Add beans, tomato sauce and seasonings; mix well. Bring to a boil. Reduce heat; simmer, uncovered, for 30 minutes. When potatoes are cool enough to handle, cut an X in the top of each with a sharp knife. Fluff pulp with a fork; top with chili and cheese. **Yield:** 6 servings.

HELPFUL HINT:

If you prefer a soft-skinned baked potato, wrap in foil or brush with oil before baking.

I usually bake extra potatoes in anticipation of making this recipe. When our kids come in from sledding, I just reheat the potatoes in the microwave, top them with the chili... and they have a warm, hearty lunch.
—Marlys Withrow-Hill
Walsenburg, Colorado

BEAN & RICE BONANZA

Don't just serve
beans and rice solo
as simple side dishes.
Pair these tasty
legumes and grains with
ground beef—and
a host of other ingredients
—for a roundup of
showstopping meals!

HEARTY SKILLET SUPPER (P. 216)

CAJUN RICE DISH (P. 196)
COWBOY BAKED BEANS (P. 196)
BEEFY SPANISH RICE (P. 197)

GREAT
NORTHERN BEANS

LIMA
BEANS

BLACK-EYED
PEAS

PINTO BEANS

KIDNEY BEANS

BLACK BEANS

BEAN BASICS

• You can use canned or dry beans interchangeably in most recipes. One 15-1/2-ounce can of beans equals about 1-1/2 cups cooked beans or 1/2 cup uncooked dry beans. One pound uncooked dry beans equals about 2 cups dry or 6 cups cooked.

• Allow about 1/2 cup cooked beans for each serving.

• Most dry beans (except split peas and lentils) need to be soaked before cooking. Follow one of the soaking methods suggested below.

• Canned beans can be stored in their original sealed cans for up to 1 year.

• Dry beans can be stored in an airtight container at room temperature for up to 1 year and frozen indefinitely. Cooked dry beans can be refrigerated for 3 days or frozen for up to 3 months.

SOAKING METHODS FOR DRY BEANS

1-HOUR SOAK

Sort and rinse beans. Place in a soup kettle or Dutch oven; add enough water to cover beans by 2 inches. Bring to a boil; boil for 2 minutes. Remove from the heat; cover and let stand for 1 hour. Drain and rinse beans; discard liquid unless recipe directs otherwise.

OVERNIGHT SOAK

Sort and rinse beans. Place in a soup kettle or Dutch oven; add enough water to cover beans by 2 inches. Cover and let stand 6 to 8 hours or overnight. Drain and rinse beans; discard liquid unless recipe directs otherwise.

COMMON TYPES OF RICE

INSTANT WHITE RICE

LONG GRAIN WHITE RICE

BROWN RICE

WILD RICE

RICE FACTS

- Store white and wild rice in airtight containers indefinitely in a cool dry place. Store brown rice in the refrigerator in an airtight container for up to 6 months.

- Leftover rice can be refrigerated for up to 1 week.

- Allow 1/2 to 3/4 cup cooked rice for each side-dish serving.

RICE YIELDS

- 1 cup uncooked long grain and wild rice equals about 3 cups cooked, while 1 cup uncooked brown rice will yield about 4 cups cooked.

- For 2 cups cooked instant rice, start with 1 cup uncooked.

- To make 3-1/2 cups cooked converted rice, use 1 cup uncooked.

TIPS FOR COOKING RICE

- For whiter rice, add 1 to 2 teaspoons lemon juice to the cooking water.

- 1 to 2 teaspoons vegetable oil in the water will keep grains from sticking and help avoid boil-overs.

- Near the end of the cooking time, remove a grain from the cooking water. It's finished cooking if you can no longer feel a hard core when you bite into it.

- Toss just-cooked rice with a fork. This lets the steam escape, which separates the grains and makes for fluffier rice.

- Unless the recipe directs otherwise, don't lift the cover when cooking rice. Otherwise, valuable steam is lost and the cooking process is slowed.

- Wild rice may become tender without absorbing all the cooking liquid. If necessary, drain before serving or combining with other ingredients.

- To reheat leftover rice, place it in a saucepan with water (allow 2 tablespoons for each cup of rice). Cover and simmer for about 5 minutes or until heated through.

CAJUN RICE DISH

(Pictured on page 193)

5 cups beef broth
2 cups uncooked long grain rice
1 pound ground beef
1 medium onion, chopped
1 cup sliced carrots
1/2 cup sliced celery
1/2 cup frozen corn
1/2 cup frozen peas
1/2 cup chopped sweet red pepper
1 teaspoon salt
1 teaspoon Cajun seasoning

In a roasting pan, combine broth and rice; mix well. Cover and bake at 350° for 30 minutes. Meanwhile, in a skillet, cook beef and onion over medium heat until meat is no longer pink; drain. Add to rice with vegetables, salt and Cajun seasoning; mix well. Cover and bake 30 minutes longer or until rice is tender. **Yield:** 6-8 servings.

COWBOY BAKED BEANS

(Pictured on page 193)

1-1/2 pounds ground beef
1 large onion, chopped
1 can (16 ounces) kidney beans, undrained
1 can (15-1/2 ounces) great northern beans, rinsed and drained
1 can (15 ounces) lima beans, rinsed and drained
1 can (15 ounces) chili beans, undrained
1 can (14-1/2 ounces) wax beans, drained
1 can (10-3/4 ounces) condensed tomato soup, undiluted

1 cup packed brown sugar
2 celery ribs, sliced
2 teaspoons ground mustard

In an ovenproof Dutch oven, cook beef and onion over medium heat until meat is no longer pink; drain. Add the remaining ingredients; bring to a boil. Bake, uncovered, at 350° for 1-1/2 hours or until heated through, stirring occasionally. **Yield:** 6-8 servings.

TIMELY TIP:

Cowboy Baked Beans can also be heated in a slow cooker on low for 5 to 6 hours. Cook and drain the beef and onion as directed before adding to the slow cooker with the remaining ingredients.

BEEFY SPANISH RICE

(Pictured on page 193)

1 cup uncooked brown rice
1 pound ground beef
1 medium onion, chopped
1 can (28 ounces) stewed
  tomatoes
1 teaspoon celery salt
1 teaspoon salt
1 teaspoon honey
1/2 teaspoon garlic salt
1/2 teaspoon pepper
1 cup (4 ounces) shredded
  cheddar cheese

Cook rice according to package directions. Meanwhile, in a skillet, cook beef and onion over medium heat until meat is no longer pink; drain. Stir in tomatoes, seasonings and rice. Transfer to a greased 2-qt. baking dish. Cover and bake at 350° for 50-55 minutes. Sprinkle with cheese. Bake, uncovered, 5-10 minutes longer or until cheese is melted. **Yield:** 8 servings.

SIMPLE SUBSTITUTIONS:

Using instant brown rice in Beefy Spanish Rice recipe cuts down on the cooking time. Try substituting cheddar cheese with a more mild Monterey Jack cheese.

This recipe came from my husband's grandmother. It's quick to make and very tasty. Hearty helpings of this specially seasoned rice disappear in a hurry at our dinner table.
—Ruth Ann Klassen
Aberdeen, Idaho

HAMBURGER HASH

1/2 pound ground beef
1 can (11-1/2 ounces)
  condensed chicken with
  rice soup, undiluted
1-1/3 cups water
1/2 cup uncooked long grain
  rice

In a skillet, cook beef over medium heat until no longer pink; drain. Add soup, water and rice; mix well. Bring to a boil. Reduce heat; cover and simmer for 20 minutes or until rice is tender. **Yield:** 3 servings.

PERFECT PARTNERS:

To steam broccoli to serve with Hamburger Hash, place broccoli florets in a steamer basket over 1 inch of boiling water in a saucepan. Cover; steam for 5 to 8 minutes or until crisp-tender. Remove from the heat and toss with a little butter or margarine.

Traditional hash recipes call for potatoes, but this version uses rice with terrific results. Busy folks like this recipe's short ingredient list and quick preparation time.
—Rose Marie Shebetka
Cedar Rapids, Iowa

CRUNCHY RICE CASSEROLE

(Pictured above)

I tried this at a church potluck years ago and begged for the recipe. The crunchy cornflake topping pairs well with the creamy rice casserole.
—Beth Logan
Lakefield, Ontario

1 pound ground beef
1 large onion, chopped
1/2 cup chopped green pepper
2 tablespoons ketchup
1/2 teaspoon ground mustard
1/4 teaspoon salt
1-1/2 cups cooked long grain rice
1-1/2 cups (6 ounces) shredded cheddar cheese
1 can (10-3/4 ounces) condensed cream of mushroom soup, undiluted
1 cup milk
1 teaspoon Worcestershire sauce
2 cups cornflakes, coarsely crushed
3 tablespoons butter *or* margarine, melted

In a skillet, cook beef, onion and green pepper over medium heat until meat is no longer pink; drain. Add the ketchup, mustard and salt; mix well. Transfer to a greased 2-qt. baking dish. Top with rice. In a bowl, combine the cheese, soup, milk and Worcestershire sauce. Pour over rice. Combine cornflakes and butter; sprinkle over the top. Bake, uncovered, at 375° for 35 minutes or until heated through. **Yield:** 6-8 servings.

TIMELY TIP:

Divide Crunchy Rice Casserole between two 1-quart baking dishes. Sprinkle 1 cup buttered cornflake crumbs on top of one casserole and bake as directed. Freeze the other dish for later; sprinkle with 1 cup buttered cornflake crumbs just before baking.

BEEF FRIED RICE

3 **eggs**
Dash pepper
3 **tablespoons vegetable oil**
1 **pound ground beef, cooked**
 and drained
2 **cups cooked long grain rice**
2 **small onions, chopped**
3 **tablespoons soy sauce**
1 **teaspoon sugar**

In a bowl, beat eggs and pepper. In a skillet, heat oil. Add eggs. Cook until partially set. Lift the edges, letting the uncooked egg flow underneath. When eggs are completely set but still moist, remove from skillet. Cut into strips; return to pan. Add remaining ingredients; mix well. Gently cook and stir for 5 minutes or until heated through. **Yield:** 6 servings.

HELPFUL HINT:

If you're using cold leftover rice in Beef Fried Rice, let it come to room temperature before adding it to the skillet so it doesn't cool down the other ingredients.

Years ago, I frequently depended on economical ground beef to feed my three hungry kids. I fixed it every way imaginable. This was one of our favorites.
—Edith Haney
Erie, Pennsylvania

GERMAN SKILLET

3 **tablespoons butter** *or*
 margarine
1 **can (27 ounces) sauerkraut,**
 rinsed and drained
2/3 **cup uncooked long grain**
 rice
1 **large onion, diced**
2 **pounds lean ground beef**
1-1/2 **teaspoons salt**
Pepper to taste
2 **cups water**
1 **can (8 ounces) tomato**
 sauce

In a skillet, melt butter. Layer with sauerkraut, rice, onion and beef. Sprinkle with salt and pepper. In a bowl, combine water and tomato sauce; mix well. Pour over beef mixture. Bring to a boil. Reduce heat; cover and simmer for 50 minutes or until meat is no longer pink and rice is tender (do not stir). **Yield:** 8 servings.

Sauerkraut lovers enjoy hearty helpings of this dish. I've been preparing this recipe for more than 20 years...we have yet to tire of it!
—Peggy Heitzman
Geneseo, Illinois

PERFECT PARTNERS:

Caraway and apples are natural companions to sauerkraut. So serve German Skillet with caraway rye bread and fresh apple slices.

SPAGHETTI-STYLE RICE

1 pound ground beef, cooked and drained
1 jar (15-1/2 ounces) garden-style spaghetti sauce
1-1/2 cups (6 ounces) shredded Monterey Jack cheese
1 cup uncooked instant rice
1 can (4 ounces) mushroom stems and pieces, drained

In a large bowl, combine all ingredients. Transfer to a greased 11-in. x 7-in. x 2-in. baking dish. Bake, uncovered, at 375° for 15 minutes; stir. Bake 10 minutes longer or until rice is tender. **Yield:** 4 servings.

SIMPLE SUBSTITUTION:

Any variety of spaghetti sauce would work in Spaghetti-Style Rice.

COVERED DISH DINNER

1 pound lean ground beef
1 can (10-3/4 ounces) condensed cream of mushroom soup, undiluted
1 large onion, chopped
1 cup uncooked long grain rice
1 cup water
1 envelope onion soup mix
1 cup (4 ounces) shredded cheddar cheese

Crumble beef into a large bowl. Stir in soup, onion, rice, water and soup mix; mix well. Transfer to a greased 13-in. x 9-in. x 2-in. baking dish. Cover and bake at 350° for 1 hour. Uncover; sprinkle with cheese. Bake 5 minutes longer or until the cheese is melted. **Yield:** 4-6 servings.

TIMELY TIP:

If you plan on taking Covered Dish Dinner to a potluck, prepare as directed (omit the cheese until ready to bake) and freeze. Thaw in the refrigerator overnight. Sprinkle with cheese and bake 1 hour before leaving for the potluck.

BISCUIT-TOPPED BEEF 'N' BEANS

(Pictured above)

1 pound ground beef
1/4 cup chopped green pepper
1 can (16 ounces) kidney beans, rinsed and drained
1 cup spaghetti sauce
1 can (4 ounces) mushroom stems and pieces, drained
1 tablespoon onion soup mix
1/4 teaspoon garlic powder
1 block (4 ounces) cheddar cheese, cut into 1/2-inch cubes
1 tube (12 ounces) refrigerated buttermilk biscuits
1 tablespoon butter *or* margarine, melted

In a skillet, cook beef and green pepper over medium heat until meat is no longer pink; drain. Stir in beans, spaghetti sauce, mushrooms, soup mix and garlic powder; mix well. Bring to a boil. Meanwhile, place a cheese cube in the center of each biscuit. Fold dough over cheese to cover; pinch to seal. Transfer hot meat mixture to a greased 2-qt. baking dish. Place biscuits seam side down over beef mixture. Brush with butter. Bake, uncovered, at 400° for 18-20 minutes or until the biscuits are golden brown. **Yield:** 5 servings.

MAKING CHEESE-STUFFED BISCUITS

Place a cheese cube in the center of each biscuit. Shape dough around the cheese cube to cover completely, pinching seams to seal.

I entered this recipe for the annual cookbook put out by our local newspaper and was thrilled to win a prize! I shared my winnings with the dear friend who gave the recipe to me.
—Eleanor McQuiston Harrisville, Pennsylvania

SWEET-AND-SOUR SUPPER

(Pictured below)

1 pound ground beef
1-1/2 teaspoons chili powder
1-1/2 teaspoons dried oregano
1-1/2 teaspoons salt
Pepper to taste
3 cups cooked long grain rice
1 can (7 ounces) mushroom stems and pieces, drained
1 medium green pepper, sliced
SAUCE:
1 cup plus 2 tablespoons sugar
1/3 cup cornstarch
2-1/2 cups cold water
1/3 cup vinegar
1/3 cup ketchup
1-1/2 teaspoons salt
Pepper to taste

In a skillet, cook beef over medium heat until meat is no longer pink; drain. Stir in chili powder, oregano, salt and pepper. In a greased 3-qt. baking dish, layer rice, beef mixture, mushrooms and green pepper; set aside. In a saucepan, combine sugar and cornstarch; stir in the remaining sauce ingredients until smooth. Bring to a boil; cook and stir for 2 minutes or until thickened. Pour over layered ingredients. Bake, uncovered, at 350° for 30 minutes or until heated through. **Yield:** 4-6 servings.

RANCH BEANS

2 pounds ground beef
1 medium onion, chopped
2 cans (15 ounces *each*) ranch-style beans *or* chili beans
2 cans (10-3/4 ounces *each*) condensed cream of chicken soup, undiluted
2 cans (10 ounces *each*) diced tomatoes and green chilies
1 jar (8 ounces) taco sauce

In a soup kettle or Dutch oven, cook beef and onion over medium heat until the meat is no longer pink; drain. Add the remaining ingredients. Cook, uncovered, over medium heat until heated through, about 10 minutes. **Yield:** 8-10 servings.

SERVING SUGGESTIONS:

You can present Ranch Beans in a variety of ways. Use them in place of seasoned ground beef next time you make tacos (don't forget the shredded lettuce and cheese, and chopped tomatoes, onions and olives!). Generous helpings can also be served over hot dogs, corn chips or corn bread.

With two men in the house, I need to put together stick-to-your-ribs meals. My husband and son are never disappointed when these saucy beans are the featured fare.
—Sue Neeld
Duncan, Oklahoma

CORN BREAD BEEF BAKE

1 pound ground beef
2 cans (16 ounces *each*) pork and beans
1/4 cup ketchup
2 tablespoons brown sugar
1/8 teaspoon pepper
1 package (8-1/2 ounces) corn bread/muffin mix
1/3 cup milk
1 egg

In a skillet, cook beef over medium heat until no longer pink; drain. Add the beans, ketchup, brown sugar and pepper; mix well. Transfer to a greased 11-in. x 7-in. x 2-in. baking dish. In a bowl, combine dry corn bread mix, milk and egg just until combined. Spoon over bean mixture. Bake, uncovered, at 350° for 35 minutes or until a toothpick inserted in the corn bread comes out clean. **Yield:** 4-6 servings.

PERFECT PARTNERS:

Serve Corn Bread Beef Bake with deli coleslaw, green beans and ice cream sandwiches.

My friend gave me this recipe one day when I was desperate for a quick yet wholesome meal. When my family knows this is in the oven, they come running!
—Mary Jane Ogmundson
Danbury,
New Hampshire

MANDARIN BEEF SKILLET

1 pound ground beef
1 small onion, sliced
1 can (11 ounces) mandarin
   oranges
1-1/2 cups water, *divided*
1/4 cup soy sauce
3/4 teaspoon ground ginger
2 tablespoons cornstarch
3 celery ribs, sliced
1 small green pepper,
   chopped
1 can (8 ounces) sliced water
   chestnuts, drained
1 can (4 ounces) mushroom
   stems and pieces, drained
Hot cooked rice

In a skillet, cook beef and onion over medium heat until meat is no longer pink; drain. Drain the oranges, reserving syrup. Add syrup to the meat mixture; set oranges aside. Stir in 1 cup of water, soy sauce and ginger. Cover and simmer for 5 minutes. Combine cornstarch and remaining water until smooth; stir into meat mixture. Bring to a boil; cook and stir for 2 minutes or until thickened. Add the celery, pepper, water chestnuts and mushrooms. Cover and cook over low heat for 5-7 minutes or until heated through. Serve over rice. Garnish with the oranges. **Yield:** 4-6 servings.

TIMELY TIP:

*If you want to save time, you can make
Mandarin Beef Skillet ahead and reheat it. But don't
garnish with the mandarin oranges until just before serving.*

TROPICAL BEANS

2 pounds ground beef
1 bottle (28 ounces) ketchup
2 cans (16 ounces *each*)
   kidney beans, undrained
1-3/4 cups water
1 large green pepper,
   chopped
5 celery ribs, chopped
1 can (8 ounces) pineapple
   tidbits, drained
2 envelopes onion soup mix

In a soup kettle or Dutch oven, cook beef over medium heat until no longer pink; drain. Add the remaining ingredients; mix well. Bring to a boil. Reduce heat; cover and simmer for 1 hour or until heated through. **Yield:** 12 servings.

SPICY BAKED RICE

(Pictured below)

1 pound ground beef
1 medium green pepper, chopped
1 medium onion, chopped
3 cups cooked long grain rice
1 can (14-1/2 ounces) stewed tomatoes
1-1/2 cups tomato juice
1 teaspoon salt
1 teaspoon chili powder
1 teaspoon ground mustard
1 teaspoon dried oregano
1/2 teaspoon hot pepper sauce
1 cup (4 ounces) shredded cheddar cheese

In a skillet, cook beef, green pepper and onion over medium heat until meat is no longer pink and the vegetables are tender; drain. Add the next eight ingredients; mix well. Transfer to a greased 2-qt. baking dish. Cover and bake at 350° for 35 minutes. Uncover and sprinkle with cheese. Bake 10 minutes longer or until the cheese is melted. **Yield:** 4-6 servings.

SIMPLE SUBSTITUTIONS:

Make Spicy Baked Rice as hot or as mild as you'd like. For extra zest, use Mexican-style stewed tomatoes. If you prefer a little less heat, omit the hot pepper sauce.

A close family friend shared this recipe with me years ago. It makes a filling main course, or serve it as a side dish with a meaty entree.
—Kim Kolb Dague
Huntsville, Alabama

BISCUITS AND BEANS
(Pictured above)

Biscuits and beans are common ingredients in traditional country cooking. This recipe earned an honorable mention when I entered it in a local cooking contest.
—Dolores Grossenbacher Beloit, Wisconsin

1 pound ground beef
1 can (16 ounces) pork and beans
3/4 cup barbecue sauce
2 tablespoons brown sugar
1 tablespoon dried minced onion
1/2 teaspoon salt
1 tube (12 ounces) refrigerated buttermilk biscuits
1/2 to 1 cup shredded cheddar cheese

In a skillet, cook beef over medium heat until no longer pink; drain. Add the beans, barbecue sauce, brown sugar, onion and salt; mix well. Bring to a boil. Transfer to a greased 2-qt. baking dish. Separate biscuits and arrange over the hot beef mixture. Sprinkle with cheese. Bake, uncovered, at 400° for 18-20 minutes or until the biscuits are golden brown. **Yield:** 5 servings.

PERFECT PARTNERS:

Corn on the cob would go great with Biscuits and Beans. Remove husk and silk from ears of corn. Bring water to a rapid boil in a large kettle; add corn. Cover and return to a boil; cook for 3 to 5 minutes or until tender. Remove from the water with tongs.

TACO RICE

1 pound ground beef
1 medium onion, chopped
1 jar (16 ounces) salsa
1 can (15 ounces) tomato
  sauce
1 chicken bouillon cube
1-1/2 cups instant rice, cooked
Tortilla chips
Optional toppings: shredded
  cheddar cheese, kidney beans,
  sour cream, sliced ripe olives

In a skillet, cook beef and onion over medium heat until meat is no longer pink; drain. Add the salsa, tomato sauce and bouillon. Bring to a boil. Reduce heat; cover and simmer for 5 minutes. Stir in rice. Cover and simmer for 30 minutes or until rice is tender. Serve with tortilla chips and toppings of your choice. **Yield:** 4 servings.

TIMELY TIP:

Serve Taco Rice at your next buffet dinner by making a double batch in advance and reheating it in a slow cooker. Ask each guest to bring a taco topping, such as diced tomatoes, chopped onions, shredded lettuce or any of the optional toppings listed in the recipe.

BAKED BLACK-EYED PEAS

1-1/2 pounds ground beef
1 medium onion, chopped
2 garlic cloves, minced
1 can (15-1/2 ounces)
  black-eyed peas, rinsed and
  drained
1 can (10-3/4 ounces)
  condensed cream of
  mushroom soup, undiluted
1 can (10 ounces) enchilada
  sauce
1 cup tortilla chips, crushed
3 cups (12 ounces) shredded
  cheddar cheese

In a skillet, cook beef, onion and garlic over medium heat until the meat is no longer pink; drain. Add peas, soup and enchilada sauce; mix well. Sprinkle tortilla chips in a greased 11-in. x 7-in. x 2-in. baking dish. Layer with half of the beef mixture and cheese. Repeat layers. Bake, uncovered, at 350° for 35 minutes or until heated through. **Yield:** 6 servings.

SERVING SUGGESTION:

Baked Black-Eyed Peas can be served as an appetizer with tortilla chips for dipping.

Most of my favorite recipes—including this one—come from my mother-in-law, who's a truly terrific cook. By including rice in this taco-type dish, you can forgo the tortillas.
—Mary McCann
Falmouth, Virginia

Black-eyed peas are a nice change of pace in this cheesy casserole. Use whatever type of enchilada sauce you prefer...or try a blend of cheddar and Monterey Jack cheeses.
—Janelle Buschman
Waka, Texas

ONE-POT CASSEROLE

1 pound ground beef, cooked and drained
2 medium potatoes, cooked and cubed
2 cans (8 ounces *each*) tomato sauce
1 can (15-1/2 ounces) black-eyed peas, rinsed and drained
1 can (15 ounces) lima beans, rinsed and drained
1 can (8 ounces) mixed vegetables, drained
1 medium onion, chopped
1/2 teaspoon liquid smoke, optional
1/8 teaspoon garlic powder
Salt and pepper to taste

In a large bowl, combine all ingredients and mix well. Transfer to a greased 13-in. x 9-in. x 2-in. baking dish. Cover and bake at 350° for 1 hour or until heated through. **Yield:** 4-6 servings.

HELPFUL HINT:

Liquid smoke adds a distinctive hickory-smoke barbecue flavor to foods. If you don't care for the taste, you can omit it in One-Pot Casserole without affecting the flavor.

HUNGRY MAN'S DINNER

1-1/2 pounds ground beef
2 celery ribs, sliced
1 medium onion, chopped
1/2 cup chopped green pepper
1 garlic clove, minced
1 can (16 ounces) pork and beans
1 can (15 ounces) garbanzo beans *or* chickpeas, undrained
1 can (6 ounces) tomato paste
3/4 cup water
1 teaspoon salt
1 teaspoon paprika

In a skillet, cook beef, celery, onion, green pepper and garlic over medium heat until the meat is no longer pink and vegetables are tender. Stir in the remaining ingredients. Simmer, uncovered, for 30 minutes or until heated through. **Yield:** 6-8 servings.

COLORFUL HAMBURGER RICE

(Pictured above)

3 cups water
1 pound ground beef, cooked and drained
1 medium onion, chopped
2 celery ribs, thinly sliced
2 medium carrots, sliced
1 cup *each* frozen corn, peas and cut green beans
1 tablespoon butter *or* margarine
1 teaspoon salt
1/2 teaspoon celery salt
1/2 teaspoon garlic powder
1/4 teaspoon pepper
1-1/2 cups uncooked long grain rice
Shredded Parmesan cheese

In a large saucepan, combine the water, beef, vegetables, butter and seasonings. Bring to a boil. Add the rice. Reduce heat; cover and simmer for 20 minutes or until rice is tender. Fluff with a fork. Sprinkle with Parmesan cheese. **Yield:** 8-10 servings.

PERFECT PARTNERS:

While Colorful Hamburger Rice is simmering, prepare any flavor instant pudding, pour into parfait glasses and garnish with whipped cream, coconut and toasted nuts. Chill until ready to serve.

With a pretty blend of vegetables, this skillet dish is an eye-catching addition to a potluck buffet. You can use garden-fresh vegetables instead of frozen.
—Drusilla Luckey Marathon, New York

ZESTY OVEN-FRIED RICE

2 cans (14-1/2 ounces *each*) chicken broth
1-1/2 cups uncooked long grain rice
1-1/2 pounds ground beef
2 large onions, thinly sliced
1 large green pepper, chopped
4 garlic cloves, minced
3 eggs, beaten
1 can (4 ounces) mushroom stems and pieces, drained
1/3 cup soy sauce
1 tablespoon hot pepper sauce

In a saucepan, bring broth to a boil. Add rice. Reduce heat; cover and simmer for 20 minutes. Meanwhile, in a skillet, cook beef, onions, green pepper and garlic over medium heat until meat is no longer pink and vegetables are tender. Drain and place in a large bowl. In the same skillet, cook and stir eggs until set but still moist. Add to meat mixture. Fluff rice with fork. Add rice, mushrooms, soy sauce and hot pepper sauce to meat mixture; mix well. Transfer to a greased 13-in. x 9-in. x 2-in. baking dish. Cover and bake at 350° for 30 minutes or until heated through. **Yield:** 10 servings.

BAKED BEEF AND BROWN RICE

1 cup uncooked brown rice
1 large onion, sliced
4 medium carrots, grated
1-1/2 pounds lean ground beef
1 medium green pepper, diced
2 teaspoons salt
2 cups tomato juice
2 tablespoons Worcestershire sauce
1/2 teaspoon dried basil
1-1/2 cups (6 ounces) shredded cheddar cheese
1/2 cup wheat germ

In a greased 13-in. x 9-in. x 2-in. baking dish, layer rice, onion, carrots, beef and green pepper. Sprinkle with salt. Combine the tomato juice, Worcestershire sauce and basil; pour over the top. Sprinkle with cheese and wheat germ. Cover and bake at 350° for 1-1/2 hours or until the rice is tender. **Yield:** 6 servings.

HELPFUL HINT:

Wheat germ is very perishable. So be sure to only store it tightly covered in the refrigerator for up to 3 months.

MUSHROOM WILD RICE

3 cups boiling water
1 cup uncooked wild rice
1-1/2 pounds ground beef
1 small onion, chopped
1 pound fresh mushrooms,
    halved
2 cans (10-3/4 ounces *each*)
    condensed cream of
    chicken soup, undiluted
1 can (10-1/2 ounces) beef
    consomme
1-1/3 cups water
1/2 cup slivered almonds
1 tablespoon minced fresh
    parsley
1 bay leaf
1/2 teaspoon salt
1/4 teaspoon *each* celery salt,
    garlic salt and onion salt
1/4 teaspoon poultry
    seasoning
1/4 teaspoon paprika
1/4 teaspoon pepper
Pinch dried thyme

In a bowl, combine water and rice; let stand 15 minutes. Meanwhile, in a large skillet, cook beef and onion over medium heat until the meat is no longer pink; drain. Add mushrooms; saute for 2 minutes. Stir in the remaining ingredients. Drain rice and stir into beef mixture. Remove from the heat; cool. Transfer to a greased 13-in. x 9-in. x 2-in. baking dish. Cover and refrigerate overnight. Cover and bake at 350° for 2 hours. Uncover and bake 30 minutes longer or until rice is tender. Discard the bay leaf before serving. **Yield:** 6-8 servings.

I love to cook and entertain. This is a favorite company's coming casserole, especially in fall. Mushrooms and wild rice make a terrific team.
—Edna Eggert
Bella Vista, Arkansas

VEGGIE CASSEROLE

1 pound ground beef
1 medium onion, chopped
1 can (10-1/2 ounces)
    condensed vegetable beef
    soup, undiluted
1-1/3 cups water
1/2 cup uncooked long grain
    rice
1/4 cup ketchup

In a skillet, cook beef and onion over medium heat until meat is no longer pink; drain. Add soup, water, rice and ketchup; mix well. Transfer to a greased 1-1/2-qt. baking dish. Bake, uncovered, at 350° for 30 minutes or until rice is tender. **Yield:** 4 servings.

PERFECT PARTNERS:

Top some sourdough bread with Swiss cheese slices and broil until melted. Serve with Veggie Casserole.

My mom was a great cook, and I have fond memories of her teaching me to cook for my dad and two brothers. Her recipes weren't fancy, but they were always delicious!
—Dorothy Ambroson
Leland, Iowa

KIDNEY BEANS AND RICE
(Pictured below)

1-1/2 pounds ground beef
1/4 cup chopped onion
  1 can (16 ounces) kidney beans, rinsed and drained
  1 can (14-1/2 ounces) stewed tomatoes
  1 teaspoon salt
  1 teaspoon chili powder
  1 bay leaf
1/2 teaspoon garlic powder
1/2 teaspoon seasoned salt
1/4 teaspoon dried oregano
1/4 teaspoon pepper
  2 cups cooked long grain rice

In a skillet, cook beef and onion over medium heat until meat is no longer pink; drain. Stir in the beans, tomatoes and seasonings. Cover and simmer for 5 minutes. Add rice; cover and simmer for 30 minutes or until heated through. Discard bay leaf before serving. **Yield:** 6-8 servings.

I developed this recipe while working for a rehabilitation home. It was a success with everyone who tried it. I soon started making it for my family, who gave it rave reviews.
—Cherie Gresham
Killen, Alabama

SIMPLE SUBSTITUTION:

Cajun-style diced tomatoes can be used in place of the regular stewed tomatoes in Kidney Beans and Rice.

CHEESY BROCCOLI RICE

1 pound ground beef
1 medium onion, diced
1 garlic clove, minced
3 cups cooked long grain rice
2 cups fresh *or* frozen
  chopped broccoli, thawed
2 cups (8 ounces) shredded
  cheddar cheese
2 tablespoons grated
  Parmesan cheese

In a skillet, cook beef, onion and garlic over medium heat until the meat is no longer pink; drain. Stir in the rice, broccoli and cheddar cheese. Transfer to a greased 13-in. x 9-in. x 2-in. baking dish. Sprinkle with Parmesan cheese. Bake, uncovered, at 350° for 30-40 minutes or until heated through. **Yield:** 4 servings.

SERVING SUGGESTION:

Making Cheesy Broccoli Rice for a holiday dinner? Give it a festive look by stirring in some drained diced pimientos.

Looking for a new side dish for your holiday dinners? Try this recipe that combines tender rice, nutritious broccoli and savory cheese!
—Karen Weavill
Johnston, Rhode Island

THREE-BEAN BAKE

3 pounds ground beef
1 large onion, chopped
1/2 cup chopped sweet red
  pepper
2 cans (16 ounces *each*) pork
  and beans, drained
1 can (15 ounces) chili beans,
  undrained
1 can (15 ounces) pinto
  beans, rinsed and drained
1 cup ketchup
1/2 cup packed brown sugar
3 to 4 tablespoons chili
  powder
1 tablespoon vinegar

1 teaspoon salt
1 teaspoon ground cumin
1 teaspoon cayenne pepper
1/2 teaspoon hot pepper sauce
1/8 teaspoon garlic powder
1/8 teaspoon pepper

In an ovenproof Dutch oven, cook beef, onion and red pepper over medium heat until meat is no longer pink; drain. Add the remaining ingredients; mix well. Cover and bake at 350° for 1-1/2 to 2 hours or until heated through, stirring once. **Yield:** 12-14 servings.

Being big eaters, my three sons love this recipe that I created. Leftovers can be used as a taco filling or a topping for baked potatoes.
—Meredith Mabe
Columbus, Indiana

TIMELY TIP:

For added convenience, make Three-Bean Bake in a slow cooker.
Cook the beef, onion and red pepper as directed; drain.
Transfer to a slow cooker. Add remaining ingredients; mix well.
Cover and cook on low for 4 to 5 hours or until heated through.

BEEF AND BAKED BEANS

1 pound ground beef
1 medium onion, chopped
1 medium green pepper, chopped
1 can (16 ounces) baked beans
1 can (4 ounces) mushrooms stems and pieces, drained

In a skillet, cook beef, onion and green pepper over medium heat until meat is no longer pink and vegetables are tender; drain. Add beans and mushrooms; mix well. Cover and simmer for 5 minutes or until heated through. **Yield:** 4 servings.

SERVING SUGGESTION:

Perk up boring brown-bag lunches by sending along some Beef and Baked Beans. It heats up fast in the microwave for a hearty hot lunch.

OLIVE RAISIN RICE

4 cups water
2 cups uncooked long grain rice
4 beef bouillon cubes
1 pound ground beef
3 medium green peppers, chopped
3 medium onions, chopped
2 garlic cloves, minced
1 cup water
3/4 cup raisins
3/4 cup sliced ripe olives
3 bay leaves
Salt and pepper to taste

In a large saucepan, combine the water, rice and bouillon. Bring to a boil. Reduce heat; cover and simmer for 15 minutes. Meanwhile, in a large skillet, cook beef, green peppers, onions and garlic over medium heat until the meat is no longer pink; drain. Add water, raisins, olives and bay leaves. Cover and simmer for 30 minutes or until heated through. Discard bay leaves. Stir in rice, salt and pepper. **Yield:** 8-10 servings.

HELPFUL HINT:

Store raisins at room temperature in a tightly sealed plastic bag for several months. To store for up to 1 year, refrigerate or freeze. One pound of raisins yields about 3 cups.

RICE-STUFFED TOMATOES

(Pictured above and on front cover)

6 large tomatoes
1 pound ground beef, cooked and drained
1 cup cooked long grain rice
2 tablespoons minced fresh parsley
1 teaspoon dried basil
1 teaspoon salt
1 teaspoon pepper
1/2 cup grated Parmesan cheese
1 block (4 ounces) Swiss cheese, cut into 1/2-inch cubes

Cut a thin slice off the top of each tomato and discard; remove core. Carefully scoop out and reserve pulp, leaving a 1/2-in. shell. Invert tomatoes onto paper towels to drain. Chop reserved pulp. In a skillet, combine the beef, rice, parsley, basil, salt, pepper and tomato pulp; heat through. Remove from the heat; stir in cheeses. Spoon into tomato shells. Place stuffed side up in a greased shallow baking dish. Bake, uncovered, at 350° for 35 minutes or until heated through. **Yield:** 6 servings.

I learned to put an Italian twist on my cooking after getting married since my husband is of Italian descent. I don't have many occasions to cook anymore. But when I'm expecting company, this is the dish I'll likely prepare.
—Marion Amonte
Hingham,
Massachusetts

MAKING TOMATO SHELLS

STEP 1
Cut a thin slice from the top of each tomato. Using a small kitchen knife, remove tomato core. With a spoon, gently scoop out tomato pulp, leaving a 1/2-inch shell.

STEP 2
Drain excess moisture from tomatoes by inverting onto paper towels.

HEARTY SKILLET SUPPER

(Pictured above and on page 192)

When the weather starts turning cooler, I start to hear requests for this dish. The light soy, onion and garlic flavors blend nicely with fresh carrots and potatoes in this budget-minded recipe.
—Pat Jensen
Cottonwood,
Minnesota

1 pound ground beef
1 large onion, chopped
1 garlic clove, minced
1 cup chopped carrots
1 cup cubed peeled potatoes
1 cup water
1/2 cup uncooked long grain rice
2 tablespoons soy sauce
1 teaspoon salt
1/8 teaspoon pepper

In a skillet, cook beef, onion and garlic over medium heat until the meat is no longer pink; drain. Add the carrots, potatoes, water and rice; mix well. Cover and simmer for 30 minutes or until the rice and vegetables are tender. Just before serving, stir in soy sauce, salt and pepper. **Yield:** 4 servings.

HELPFUL HINT:

Long grain rice has a length 4 to 5 times that of its width. When cooked, it produces light dry grains that separate easily.

CORNY SPANISH RICE

3/4 **pound ground beef**
1 **can (14-1/2 ounces) stewed tomatoes**
1 **package (10 ounces) frozen corn** *or* **mixed vegetables**
1 **cup water**
1/2 **teaspoon salt**
1/2 **teaspoon chili powder**
1/2 **teaspoon dried oregano**
1/4 **teaspoon garlic powder**
1/8 **teaspoon pepper**
1-1/2 **cups uncooked instant rice**

In a skillet, cook beef over medium heat until no longer pink; drain. Add the tomatoes, corn, water and seasonings; mix well. Bring to a boil; cook for 2 minutes. Stir in rice; cover and remove from the heat. Let stand for 5 minutes or until rice is tender. Fluff with a fork. **Yield:** 4 servings.

Corn—a staple here in Iowa—stars in this easy recipe that I received from a niece. It's a quick-to-fix meal after a busy day in the fields.
—Evelyn Massner
Oakville, Iowa

SERVING SUGGESTION:

Corny Spanish Rice can be served by itself as a hearty meal. But for something different, spoon some of it onto warmed flour tortillas, sprinkle with shredded Monterey Jack cheese and roll up. Serve with salsa and sour cream.

LIMA BEAN BAKE

1 **pound dry lima beans**
1/2 **pound ground beef**
1 **medium onion, chopped**
2 **cans (15 ounces** *each***) tomato sauce**
1 **tablespoon brown sugar**
1-1/2 **teaspoons salt**
Dash poultry seasoning

Cook the lima beans according to package directions. Drain, reserving 1/2 cup liquid; set beans and liquid aside. In a skillet, cook beef and onion over medium heat until meat is no longer pink; drain. Add tomato sauce, brown sugar, salt, poultry seasoning and reserved bean liquid. Place the beans in a greased 13-in. x 9-in. x 2-in. baking dish. Top with tomato mixture. Bake, uncovered, at 350° for 30-35 minutes or until bubbly. Stir before serving. **Yield:** 16 servings.

This was my mother's recipe, and I enjoyed it often growing up. Now I make it for my husband. The delicious taste has stood the test of time.
—Sharon Lemke
Quincy, Michigan

WILD RICE CASSEROLE

2 pounds ground beef, cooked and drained
2 cans (11-1/2 ounces *each*) condensed chicken with rice soup, undiluted
1 cup sliced onion
1 cup uncooked wild rice
1 can (4 ounces) mushroom stems and pieces, drained
1 teaspoon salt
1 teaspoon dried oregano
1/4 teaspoon *each* celery salt, garlic salt and onion salt
1/4 teaspoon curry powder
1/4 teaspoon paprika
1/4 teaspoon soy sauce
1 cup (4 ounces) shredded cheddar cheese

In a large bowl, combine the beef, soup, onion, rice, mushrooms and seasonings; mix well. Transfer to a greased 13-in. x 9-in. x 2-in. baking dish. Sprinkle with cheese. Cover and bake at 350° for 1 hour or until rice is tender. **Yield:** 8 servings.

CLASSIC RED BEANS 'N' RICE

1 pound dry kidney beans
2 quarts water
1 ham hock
2 bay leaves
1 teaspoon onion powder
1 pound ground beef
1 large onion, chopped
1 garlic clove, minced
1 teaspoon salt
1/2 teaspoon pepper
Hot cooked rice

Place beans in a large saucepan; add water to cover by 2 in. Bring to a boil; boil for 2 minutes. Remove from the heat; cover and let stand for 1 hour. Drain and discard liquid. Add 2 qts. water, ham hock, bay leaves and onion powder to the beans. Bring to a boil. Reduce heat; cover and simmer for 1 hour. In a skillet, cook beef, onion, garlic, salt and pepper over medium heat until meat is no longer pink; drain. Add to bean mixture. Simmer, uncovered, for 1 hour. Discard bay leaves. Remove ham hock. Remove ham from bones; cut into bite-size pieces and return to broth. Serve over rice. **Yield:** 8 servings.

HELPFUL HINT:

Smoked or cured ham hocks are usually available in your grocer's meat department. If you can't find them, ask your butcher for some leftover ham bones.

SOUTHWEST SKILLET

(Pictured below)

1 pound ground beef
3/4 cup chopped onion
1 can (16 ounces) kidney beans, rinsed and drained
1 can (14-1/2 ounces) diced tomatoes, undrained
1/2 cup uncooked instant rice
1/2 cup water
3 tablespoons chopped green pepper
1-1/2 teaspoons chili powder
1/2 teaspoon garlic salt
1/2 teaspoon salt
1 cup corn chips
3/4 cup shredded cheddar cheese

In a skillet, cook beef and onion over medium heat until meat is no longer pink; drain. Add beans, tomatoes, rice, water, green pepper and seasonings; mix well. Bring to a boil. Reduce heat; cover and simmer for 20 minutes, stirring occasionally. Remove from the heat. Sprinkle with the corn chips and cheese. Cover and let stand for 3 minutes or until cheese is melted. **Yield:** 4 servings.

TIMELY TIP:

Make a double batch of Southwest Skillet and freeze half. Thaw, reheat and sprinkle with corn chips and cheese just before serving.

I was born and raised on a farm and still live on one with my husband and kids. We build up hearty appetites, and this Mexican-style dish always pleases.
—Becky Paxton
Afton, Iowa

BEAN & RICE BONANZA

PORK 'N' BEANS BAKE

(Pictured below)

1-1/2 **pounds ground beef**
   1 **medium onion, chopped**
   1 **medium green pepper, chopped**
 3/4 **cup chopped celery**
   2 **cans (16 ounces *each*) pork and beans**
   1 **can (8 ounces) tomato sauce**
   1 **tablespoon sugar**
   1 **tablespoon ground mustard**
   1 **tablespoon vinegar**
 1/4 **teaspoon dried thyme**

In a large skillet, cook beef, onion, green pepper and celery over medium heat until the meat is no longer pink and the vegetables are tender; drain. Add the remaining ingredients; mix well. Transfer to a greased 3-qt. baking dish. Bake, uncovered, at 375° for 30-35 minutes or until heated through. **Yield:** 6-8 servings.

TIMELY TIP:

You can make Pork 'n' Beans Bake even when it's too hot to turn on the oven. Cook the beef, onion, green pepper and celery in a Dutch oven; drain. Add the remaining ingredients; simmer for 30 to 35 minutes or until heated through.

FAST BEEF AND RICE

1 pound ground beef
1 package (6.8 ounces) beef-flavored rice mix
2 tablespoons butter *or* margarine
2-1/2 cups water

In a skillet, cook beef over medium heat until no longer pink; drain and set aside. In the same skillet, brown the rice in butter. Add water and contents of rice seasoning packet; mix well. Stir in beef. Cover and simmer for 15 minutes or until rice is tender. **Yield:** 4 servings.

SERVING SUGGESTION:

To make Fast Beef and Rice a complete meal, stir in 2 cups of your family's favorite cooked vegetable.

I'm not much of a cook, but I did receive many recipe requests the first time I made this dish. Using a packaged rice mix makes it so simple to prepare.
—Deborah Vahlkamp
Belleville, Illinois

CREAMY VEGETABLE RICE

2 pounds ground beef
1 large onion, chopped
1 cup chopped cabbage
1 cup chopped celery
1 cup frozen corn
1 cup frozen peas
1 cup water
2-1/4 cups cooked rice
1 can (10-3/4 ounces) condensed cream of celery soup, undiluted
1 can (10-3/4 ounces) condensed cheddar cheese soup, undiluted
1-1/3 cups milk
4 bacon strips, cooked and crumbled
Salt and pepper to taste

In a skillet, cook beef and onion until the meat is no longer pink; drain. Add the cabbage, celery, corn, peas and water. Bring to a boil. Cover and simmer for 5-10 minutes or until vegetables are tender. In a bowl, combine beef mixture, rice, soups, milk, bacon, salt and pepper; mix well. Transfer to a greased 13-in. x 9-in. x 2-in. baking dish. Cover and bake at 350° for 30 minutes or until heated through. **Yield:** 10 servings.

My husband really doesn't care for plain rice. So I combined it with lots of flavorful ingredients like ground beef, vegetables and canned soups. Now I can't make this often enough for him!
—Beth Deters
Baileyville, Kansas

SIMPLE SUBSTITUTIONS:

Instead of using corn and peas in Creamy Vegetable Rice, use 2 cups of frozen mixed vegetables. Or experiment with various canned soups for different taste combinations.

STOVETOP PINTO BEANS

1 pound ground beef
1 small onion, chopped
1 small green pepper, chopped
1 can (15 ounces) pinto beans, rinsed and drained
1 can (14-1/2 ounces) diced tomatoes, undrained
1 teaspoon salt
1/2 teaspoon ground mustard

In a skillet, cook beef, onion and green pepper over medium heat until meat is no longer pink; drain. Add the beans, tomatoes, salt and mustard; mix well. Simmer, uncovered, for 20 minutes or until thickened. **Yield:** 4 servings.

SIMPLE SUBSTITUTION:

You can substitute 1-1/2 cups of chopped fresh tomatoes for the canned diced tomatoes in Stovetop Pinto Beans.

POTLUCK MUSHROOM RICE

3 cups water
1-1/2 teaspoons beef bouillon granules
1-1/2 cups uncooked long grain rice
2 pounds ground beef
1 large onion, chopped
1 large green pepper, chopped
1 jar (6 ounces) whole mushrooms, drained
1 can (4 ounces) mushroom stems and pieces, drained
1 celery rib, sliced
1 can (10-3/4 ounces) condensed cream of celery soup, undiluted
1 can (10-3/4 ounces) condensed cream of mushroom soup, undiluted
2 tablespoons Worcestershire sauce
1/2 teaspoon garlic powder

In a saucepan, bring water and bouillon to a boil. Add rice. Reduce heat; cover and simmer for 15-20 minutes or until tender. Meanwhile, in a large skillet, cook beef, onion, green pepper, mushrooms and celery until the meat is no longer pink and the vegetables are tender; drain. Stir in rice, soups, Worcestershire sauce and garlic powder; mix well. Transfer to an ovenproof Dutch oven. Cover and bake at 350° for 30 minutes or until heated through. **Yield:** 12-14 servings.

ORIENTAL RICE

1-1/2 pounds ground beef
1-1/2 cups water
1 can (10-3/4 ounces) condensed cream of mushroom soup, undiluted
2 celery ribs, chopped
3/4 cup uncooked long grain rice
1 can (8 ounces) sliced water chestnuts, drained
1 medium onion, chopped
1/2 cup chopped green pepper
3 tablespoons soy sauce
1/2 teaspoon salt

In a skillet, cook beef over medium heat until no longer pink; drain. Add the remaining ingredients and mix well. Transfer to a greased 13-in. x 9-in. x 2-in. baking dish. Cover and bake at 350° for 1-1/2 hours or until heated through. **Yield:** 8 servings.

TIMELY TIP:

Oriental Rice can be assembled the night before and chilled. Remove from the refrigerator 30 minutes before baking.

I love hearty suppers after a long day on the ranch, but I don't look forward to spending a lot of time in the kitchen. This recipe is great because it can be made ahead and reheated in short order.
—Tammi Littrel
Chadron, Nebraska

QUICK TAMALE CASSEROLE

1 pound ground beef
1 can (15 ounces) chili with beans
1 jar (13-1/2 ounces) tamales
1 can (15-1/4 ounces) whole kernel corn, drained
4 slices process American cheese

In a skillet, cook beef over medium heat until no longer pink; drain. Spoon into a greased 9-in. square baking dish; top with chili. Remove papers from tamales; cut each into six slices. Arrange over chili. Sprinkle with corn and top with cheese. Bake, uncovered, at 350° for 30 minutes or until heated through. **Yield:** 4 servings.

SERVING SUGGESTION:

To give Quick Tamale Casserole more of a taco taste, add an envelope of taco seasoning and 3/4 cup water to the ground beef after browning and draining.

The filling ingredients in this casserole will satisfy hearty appetites. You can garnish individual servings with sliced ripe olives and serve with tortilla chips.
—Cecily Gates
Santa Ana, California

PASTA PLEASERS

Next time you're scratching your noodle deciding what to make for dinner, turn to these promising pasta dishes. With wholesome hearty spaghetti, lasagna, stuffed shells, macaroni and more, there any many palate-pleasing "pastabilities"!

STUFFED MANICOTTI (P. 253)

MEXICAN LASAGNA (P. 228)
SPANISH SPIRALS (P. 228)

COMMON PASTA SHAPES

ANGEL HAIR

BOW TIE

EGG NOODLES, MEDIUM

EGG NOODLES, WIDE

ELBOW MACARONI

FETTUCCINE

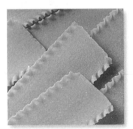

LASAGNA

LINGUINE

MANICOTTI

MOSTACCIOLI

ROTINI

SHELLS, JUMBO

SHELLS, MEDIUM

SPAGHETTI

VERMICELLI

PASTA PLEASERS

PASTA POINTERS

- Dried pasta can be stored indefinitely in an airtight container in a cool dry place.

- Fresh or refrigerated pasta should be put in an airtight container in the refrigerator for up to 5 days or in the freezer for up to 8 months.

- Keep frozen pasta in the freezer for up to 8 months.

- Pasta with similar sizes and shapes (like spaghetti and vermicelli or elbow macaroni and small shells) are interchangeable in most recipes.

- Leftover plain pasta can be refrigerated for 1 to 2 days in an airtight container. Reheat by placing in a colander and rinsing with hot water.

- To keep cooked pasta hot for a few minutes before using, return cooked and drained pasta to the warm cooking pan. Stir in any additional ingredients. Or, if you haven't added oil to the cooking water, toss plain pasta with a little oil, butter or margarine. Another option is to put the cooked and drained pasta in a warmed serving bowl.

- Letting lasagna stand for about 10 minutes after baking helps it "set up", making it easier to slice.

- You need about 2 cups of sauce for 1 pound of pasta.

- Allow 2 to 4 ounces of pasta per person for each main-dish serving.

COOKING PASTA

- Always cook pasta in a large kettle or Dutch oven to cook it more evenly, prevent it from sticking and avoid boil-overs. Unless you have a very large kettle, don't cook more than 2 pounds of pasta at a time.

- For 1 pound of dried pasta, bring 4 quarts of water to a full rolling boil. Add the pasta all at once and return to a rolling boil, stirring occasionally.

- To prevent pasta from sticking, add 1 tablespoon of olive or vegetable oil to the cooking water. If desired, you can also give a little flavor to the pasta by adding 1 tablespoon of salt.

- You don't need to break long pasta like spaghetti to fit it in the pan. Just hold the pasta in a bunch and put one end in the boiling water. As it softens, gradually push the rest into the pan.

- Cooking times vary for different sizes and shapes of pasta. So for best results, follow package directions.

- To test for doneness, remove a single piece of pasta from the boiling water with a fork; rinse under cold water and taste. Pasta should be cooked until "al dente", or firm yet tender.

- Test pasta often while cooking to avoid overcooking, which can result in a soft or mushy texture. If pasta will be used in a recipe that requires further cooking (such as a casserole), undercook it by one-third the recommended time.

- When pasta tests done, drain in a large colander. If you're using the pasta in a salad or at a later time, rinse with cold water. If you're using it immediately in a hot dish, there's no need to rinse.

- Use a large slotted spoon to carefully remove cooked filled pasta such as ravioli out of the boiling water.

PASTA EQUIVALENTS

- 1 cup of uncooked macaroni yields 2 cups cooked.

- 1 cup of uncooked egg noodles yields 1-1/4 cups cooked.

- If you want to make 2 cups of cooked spaghetti, start with 4 ounces of uncooked. (When held together in a bunch, 4 ounces of spaghetti has about a 1-inch diameter.)

MEXICAN LASAGNA

(Pictured on page 225)

2 pounds ground beef
1 can (16 ounces) refried beans
1 can (4 ounces) chopped green chilies
1 envelope taco seasoning
2 tablespoons hot salsa
4 cups (16 ounces) shredded Co-Jack *or* Monterey Jack cheese, *divided*
12 ounces uncooked lasagna noodles
1 jar (16 ounces) mild salsa
2 cups water
2 cups (16 ounces) sour cream
1 can (2-1/4 ounces) sliced ripe olives, drained
3 green onions, chopped

In a skillet, cook beef over medium heat until no longer pink; drain. Add the beans, chilies, taco seasoning and hot salsa; mix well. In a greased 13-in. x 9-in. x 2-in. baking dish, layer a third of the noodles and meat mixture. Sprinkle with 1 cup of cheese. Repeat layers twice. Combine mild salsa and water; pour over top. Cover and bake at 350° for 1 hour or until heated through. Uncover; top with sour cream, olives, onions and remaining cheese. Bake 5 minutes longer. Let stand 10-15 minutes before cutting. **Yield:** 12 servings.

TIMELY TIP:

You can prepare Mexican Lasagna up to 24 hours in advance. Cover and chill. Remove from the refrigerator 30 minutes before baking.

SPANISH SPIRALS

(Pictured on page 225)

1 pound ground beef
1 medium onion, chopped
1 can (28 ounces) diced tomatoes, undrained
2 cups uncooked rotini
2 teaspoons salt
1 teaspoon sugar
1 teaspoon chili powder
1/4 teaspoon garlic powder

In a skillet, cook beef and onion over medium heat until meat is no longer pink; drain. Stir in tomatoes, rotini, salt, sugar, chili powder and garlic powder. Bring to a boil. Reduce heat; cover and simmer for 25-30 minutes or until rotini is tender. **Yield:** 4-6 servings.

MEATY MACARONI

1 pound ground beef
1 medium onion, chopped
1/2 cup chopped green pepper
1 jar (15 ounces) spaghetti
   sauce
1-1/2 cups uncooked elbow
   macaroni
1 cup water
Salt and pepper to taste
1 cup (4 ounces) shredded
   mozzarella cheese

Crumble beef into a 2-qt. microwave-safe dish. Add onion and green pepper. Cover and microwave on high for 6-8 minutes or until meat is no longer pink, stirring once; drain. Stir in spaghetti sauce, macaroni, water, salt and pepper. Cover and microwave on high for 14 minutes, stirring once. Sprinkle with cheese. Let stand 5 minutes before serving. **Yield:** 6 servings. **Editor's Note:** This recipe was tested in a 700-watt microwave.

This recipe is always fast to make, and the kids certainly enjoy it. I sometimes use my homemade canned spaghetti sauce.
—Carolyn Rausch
St. Lucas, Iowa

PARMESAN PENNE

1 pound ground beef
1 medium onion, chopped
1 can (28 ounces) tomato
   sauce
1 cup grated Parmesan
   cheese, *divided*
1/2 teaspoon ground allspice
Salt and pepper to taste
1/2 cup butter *or* margarine,
   divided
1/4 cup all-purpose flour
2 cups milk
2 eggs, beaten
1 package (16 ounces) penne
   pasta *or* mostaccioli,
   cooked and drained

In a skillet, cook beef and onion over medium heat until meat is no longer pink; drain. Stir in tomato sauce, 1/3 cup Parmesan cheese, all-spice, salt and pepper. Bring to a boil. Reduce heat; simmer, uncovered, for 15 minutes. Meanwhile, in a saucepan, melt 1/4 cup butter. Stir in flour until smooth. Gradually add milk. Bring to a boil; cook and stir for 2 minutes or until thickened and bubbly. Stir in 1/3 cup Parmesan cheese. Remove from the heat. Add eggs; whisk until smooth. In a bowl, combine pasta and remaining Parmesan cheese. Melt remaining butter; add to pasta and toss to coat. Spread a third of the meat sauce in a greased 13-in. x 9-in. x 2-in. baking dish. Layer with half of the pasta, a third of the meat sauce and half of the white sauce. Repeat layers. Bake, uncovered, at 350° for 40-45 minutes or until bubbly. **Yield:** 12 servings.

My mother was not much of a cook. So I credit my husband for encouraging me to experiment in the kitchen. This is a fantastic all-in-one-meal that features both a cream sauce and a meat sauce.
—Vera Soghomonian
Maple Grove,
Minnesota

PERFECT PARTNERS:

Instead of a traditional tossed salad, serve Parmesan Penne with garden-fresh vegetables. Saute sliced zucchini, yellow squash and sweet red pepper in butter or margarine until crisp-tender. Season with garlic salt and pepper.

SPAGHETTI SUPREME

(Pictured above)

When friends and family rave about this skillet supper, I'm almost embarrassed to tell them how easy it is to prepare! I'm the oldest of 13 kids and have been cooking since I was 7.
—Shannon Donnan
Saskatoon, Saskatchewan

4 bacon strips, diced
1/2 pound ground beef
2 celery ribs, chopped
1 large onion, chopped
1 cup sliced fresh mushrooms
1/2 cup chopped green pepper
1 can (10-3/4 ounces) condensed tomato soup, undiluted
1 teaspoon Worcestershire sauce
1/4 teaspoon salt
Dash pepper
4 ounces spaghetti *or* angel hair pasta, cooked and drained

In a skillet, cook bacon until crisp. Remove with a slotted spoon and set aside. In the drippings, cook beef, celery, onion, mushrooms and green pepper over medium heat until meat is no longer pink and vegetables are tender; drain. Stir in the soup, Worcestershire sauce, salt, pepper and bacon; mix well. Stir in pasta. Cover and simmer for 20 minutes or until heated through. **Yield:** 4 servings.

PERFECT PARTNERS:

Toss salad greens with tomato wedges and cucumber slices. Sprinkle with Italian seasoning and drizzle with oil-and-vinegar dressing. Serve with Spaghetti Supreme.

BEEF AND CHEESE SHELLS

1 pound ground beef, cooked
  and drained
2 cups (16 ounces) small-curd
  cottage cheese
2 cups (8 ounces) shredded
  mozzarella cheese
1 egg, beaten
2 tablespoons dried parsley
  flakes
1 tablespoon dried minced
  onion
1/4 teaspoon garlic powder
1/4 teaspoon dried oregano
28 jumbo pasta shells, cooked
  and drained
2 cups spaghetti sauce
Grated Parmesan cheese

In a large bowl, combine the first eight ingredients. Stuff into pasta shells; arrange in a greased 13-in. x 9-in. x 2-in. baking dish. Top with spaghetti sauce. Cover and bake at 350° for 30 minutes or until heated through. Sprinkle with Parmesan cheese. **Yield:** 7-9 servings.

HELPFUL HINT:

To prevent cooked jumbo pasta shells from tearing, carefully remove them from the boiling water with a tongs. Pour out any water inside shells. Drain on lightly greased waxed paper.

LAZY LASAGNA

2 cups (8 ounces) shredded
  mozzarella cheese
1-1/2 cups (12 ounces) small-curd
  cottage cheese
2 eggs, beaten
1/3 cup minced fresh parsley
1 teaspoon onion powder
1/2 teaspoon dried basil
1/8 teaspoon pepper
1 jar (28 ounces) spaghetti
  sauce
3/4 pound ground beef, cooked
  and drained
9 uncooked lasagna noodles
1/4 cup water
Grated Parmesan cheese

In a large bowl, combine the first seven ingredients; set aside. In another bowl, combine the spaghetti sauce and beef; mix well. Spoon a fourth of the meat sauce into a greased 13-in. x 9-in. x 2-in. baking dish. Top with three noodles and half of the cheese mixture; repeat layers once. Top with a fourth of the meat sauce, remaining noodles and remaining meat sauce. Pour water around edges. Sprinkle with Parmesan cheese. Cover and bake at 375° for 45 minutes. Uncover and bake 15 minutes longer or until noodles are tender. Let stand 10 minutes before cutting. **Yield:** 8-10 servings.

This recipe was in a church cookbook my sister-in-law gave me after I got married. I make this casserole for new moms just home from the hospital, and it's always well received.
—Cindy Vanderweele
Sheboygan, Wisconsin

Using uncooked noodles makes the traditional time-consuming task of preparing lasagna a little easier. A few seasonings boost the flavor of store-bought spaghetti sauce.
—Kathy Demler
Emporia, Kansas

CASHEW NOODLE CASSEROLE

2 pounds ground beef
2 large onions, chopped
1 can (4 ounces) mushroom stems and pieces, drained
1 can (10-3/4 ounces) condensed cream of chicken soup, undiluted
1-1/4 cups milk
1/4 cup soy sauce
1 teaspoon Worcestershire sauce
1/2 teaspoon pepper
8 ounces fine egg noodles, cooked and drained
2 cups (8 ounces) shredded cheddar cheese
1 package (6 ounces) chow mein noodles
1 cup whole cashews

In a skillet, cook beef and onions over medium heat until meat is no longer pink; drain. Add the mushrooms; set aside. In a bowl, combine the soup, milk, soy sauce, Worcestershire sauce and pepper. In a greased 13-in. x 9-in. x 2-in. baking dish, layer egg noodles, beef mixture and soup mixture. Sprinkle with cheese and chow mein noodles. Bake, uncovered, at 350° for 20 minutes or until heated through. Sprinkle with cashews. **Yield:** 8-10 servings.

HELPFUL HINT:

Store roasted cashews in an airtight can or jar for about 1 month at room temperature. In the refrigerator or freezer, they'll stay fresh for about 1 year.

CREAMY BEEF STROGANOFF

1 pound ground beef
1/3 cup all-purpose flour
1/2 teaspoon salt
1 can (10-3/4 ounces) condensed cream of mushroom soup, undiluted
1 can (10-1/2 ounces) beef consomme
1 tablespoon prepared mustard
8 ounces wide egg noodles, cooked and drained
1 cup (8 ounces) sour cream

In a skillet, cook beef over medium heat until no longer pink; drain. Stir in flour and salt until blended. Stir in soup, consomme and mustard. Bring to a boil, stirring constantly. Reduce heat; simmer, uncovered, for 10 minutes. Stir in the noodles and sour cream; heat through (do not boil). **Yield:** 6-8 servings.

HERB GARDEN PASTA

1-1/2 pounds ground beef
1 medium onion, chopped
1 garlic clove, minced
1 can (28 ounces) diced tomatoes, undrained
1 small green pepper, chopped
1 small sweet red pepper, chopped
1 jar (6 ounces) sliced mushrooms, drained
1 can (6 ounces) tomato paste
1 teaspoon Italian seasoning
1 teaspoon dried parsley flakes
1/2 teaspoon celery salt
1/2 teaspoon dried basil
1/2 teaspoon dried thyme
1/4 teaspoon dried oregano
Salt and pepper to taste
3/4 cup elbow macaroni, cooked and drained
Grated Parmesan cheese

In a large saucepan, cook beef, onion and garlic over medium heat until no longer pink; drain. Add the tomatoes, peppers, mushrooms, tomato paste and seasonings. Bring to a boil. Reduce heat; cover and simmer for 15 minutes. Add macaroni; cover and simmer 10 minutes longer or until heated through. Sprinkle with Parmesan cheese. **Yield:** 6 servings.

DICING WHOLE TOMATOES

You can easily use home-canned whole tomatoes when a recipe calls for a can of diced tomatoes. Pour the tomatoes into a large glass measuring cup. Cut into small pieces with a kitchen shears. One 28-ounce can of diced tomatoes equals 3-1/2 cups.

I developed this dish after combining different features from a variety of recipes. Leftovers seem to taste even better the next day.
—Linda Hindle
Halifax, Nova Scotia

CHEDDAR BEEF BAKE

1 pound ground beef
1 small onion, chopped
Dash seasoned salt
1 cup small pasta shells, cooked and drained
1 can (15 ounces) tomato sauce
1 can (10-3/4 ounces) condensed cheddar cheese soup, undiluted
1 teaspoon ground mustard

In a skillet, cook beef, onion and seasoned salt over medium heat until meat is no longer pink; drain. Add the pasta, tomato sauce, soup and mustard; mix well. Transfer to a greased 1-1/2-qt. baking dish. Bake, uncovered, at 350° for 35 minutes or until heated through. **Yield:** 4 servings.

SIMPLE SUBSTITUTION:

To give Cheddar Beef Bake a more zippy taste, use nacho cheese soup in place of the cheddar cheese soup.

Kids love this saucy noodle casserole, and moms love the ease of preparation. You can use whatever type of small pasta you have in the pantry.
—Jean Aingworth
Painesville, Ohio

SPINACH-STUFFED SHELLS

1 pound ground beef
1 large onion, chopped
1 package (10 ounces) frozen chopped spinach, thawed and well drained
1 cup (8 ounces) small-curd cottage cheese
3/4 cup grated Parmesan cheese
1 large carrot, grated
1/2 teaspoon Creole *or* Cajun seasoning
1/2 teaspoon seasoned salt
1/4 teaspoon pepper
36 jumbo pasta shells, cooked and drained
1/4 cup butter *or* margarine
3 tablespoons all-purpose flour
2-1/4 cups milk
1/2 teaspoon salt
1/2 cup shredded mozzarella cheese

In a large skillet, cook beef and onion over medium heat until meat is no longer pink. Remove from the heat. Stir in the spinach, cottage cheese, Parmesan cheese, carrot and seasonings; mix well. Stuff into pasta shells. Arrange in a greased 13-in. x 9-in. x 2-in. baking dish; set aside. In a saucepan, melt butter; stir in flour until smooth. Gradually add milk and salt; bring to a boil. Cook and stir for 2 minutes or until thickened. Pour over shells; sprinkle with mozzarella cheese. Cover and bake at 350° for 30 minutes or until heated through. Uncover and bake 5 minutes longer or until browned. **Yield:** 8-10 servings.

PERFECT PARTNERS:

Round out rich servings of Spinach-Stuffed Shells with a light, refreshing dessert. Put fresh sliced strawberries in small bowls; top with whipped cream. Sprinkle with toasted almonds and drizzle with chocolate syrup.

WESTERN SPAGHETTI

2 pounds ground beef
1 large onion, chopped
1 garlic clove, minced
8 ounces process American cheese, cubed
1 can (15 ounces) chili with beans
1 can (14-1/2 ounces) stewed tomatoes
1/2 cup ketchup
Salt and pepper to taste
8 ounces thin spaghetti *or* vermicelli, cooked and drained

In a Dutch oven, cook beef, onion and garlic over medium heat until meat is no longer pink; drain. Add the cheese, chili, tomatoes, ketchup, salt and pepper. Cook, uncovered, over low heat until cheese is melted, stirring occasionally. Stir in spaghetti. Cover and simmer for 20 minutes or until heated through. **Yield:** 12-14 servings.

CAJUN FETTUCCINE

(Pictured above)

1-1/2 pounds ground beef
1 cup chopped green onions
1 medium onion, chopped
1 medium green pepper, chopped
1 celery rib, chopped
1 garlic clove, minced
1/4 cup butter *or* margarine
1 tablespoon all-purpose flour
8 ounces plain *or* Mexican-flavored process American cheese, cubed, *divided*
1 can (10 ounces) diced tomatoes and green chilies, undrained
1 can (5 ounces) evaporated milk
3/4 teaspoon Cajun *or* Creole seasoning
8 ounces fettuccine, cooked and drained
Grated Parmesan cheese

In a large skillet, cook beef over medium heat until no longer pink; drain and set aside. In the same skillet, saute the onions, green pepper, celery and garlic in butter until crisp-tender. Stir in flour until blended. Return beef to the pan. Cook, uncovered, over medium heat for 15 minutes, stirring occasionally. Add 1 cup American cheese, tomatoes, milk and Cajun seasoning. Simmer, uncovered, for 15 minutes, stirring occasionally. Add fettuccine; mix well. Transfer to a greased shallow 3-qt. baking dish. Top with remaining American cheese. Sprinkle with Parmesan cheese. Bake, uncovered, at 350° for 15 minutes or until heated through. **Yield:** 6-8 servings.

It's nice to serve this zesty creamy casserole when you want a change from pasta dishes with a tomato sauce. The Cajun flavor really reflects this region of the country.
—Jackie Turnage
New Iberia, Louisiana

BUSY DAY DINNER

(Pictured below)

1 pound ground beef
1/4 cup chopped onion
3/4 teaspoon salt
1/4 teaspoon pepper
Dash garlic powder
1 can (19 ounces) ready-to-serve chunky beef vegetable soup
4 ounces spaghetti, cooked and drained
1 cup (4 ounces) shredded cheddar cheese
Minced fresh parsley, optional

In a skillet, cook beef and onion over medium heat until meat is no longer pink; drain. Stir in salt, pepper and garlic powder. Transfer to a greased 2-qt. baking dish. Pour soup over meat mixture. Top with spaghetti and cheese. Bake, uncovered, at 350° for 15-20 minutes or until heated through. Sprinkle with parsley if desired. **Yield:** 4-6 servings.

PERFECT PARTNERS:

Add a pan of refrigerated biscuits to the oven while Busy Day Dinner bakes and you'll have a complete meal in minutes.

Mock Ravioli

1 pound ground beef
1 medium onion, chopped
1 garlic clove, minced
1 jar (28 ounces) spaghetti
  sauce
1 teaspoon salt
2 cups medium pasta shells,
  cooked and drained
1 package (10 ounces) frozen
  chopped spinach, thawed
  and drained
1/2 cup shredded cheddar
  cheese
1/2 cup grated Parmesan
  cheese

2 eggs, beaten
1/2 cup vegetable oil

In a skillet, cook beef, onion and garlic over medium heat until the meat is no longer pink; drain. Stir in spaghetti sauce and salt; set aside. In a bowl, combine the pasta, spinach, cheeses, eggs and oil. Transfer to a greased 13-in. x 9-in. x 2-in. baking dish. Top with the meat sauce. Bake, uncovered, at 350° for 30 minutes or until heated through. **Yield:** 6-8 servings.

Helpful Hint:

To quickly thaw frozen spinach, place it in a colander and rinse with warm water for 2 to 3 minutes. Drain thoroughly by squeezing out the water with your hands.

My Italian aunt makes homemade ravioli for special occasions. But when she has a taste for ravioli without all the fuss, this is the dish she prepares.
—Marsha Ransom
South Haven, Michigan

Hamburger Noodle Bake

1-1/2 pounds ground beef
1 medium onion, chopped
2 teaspoons salt
1 teaspoon chili powder
1/4 teaspoon pepper
1 package (16 ounces) elbow
  macaroni, cooked and
  drained
1 package (10 ounces) frozen
  mixed vegetables, thawed
2 cans (6 ounces *each*)
  tomato paste
2 cups water
1 cup (4 ounces) shredded
  process American cheese

In a skillet, cook beef and onion over medium heat until meat is no longer pink; drain. Stir in salt, chili powder and pepper. Place macaroni in a greased 4-qt. baking dish; top with mixed vegetables and beef mixture. Combine tomato paste and water; pour over meat. Sprinkle with cheese. Bake, uncovered, at 400° for 20 minutes or until heated through. **Yield:** 12 servings.

Timely Tip:

Cook the elbow macaroni for Hamburger Noodle Bake ahead of time. Rinse with cold water and drain. Toss with a little vegetable oil to prevent sticking and refrigerate in a resealable plastic bag.

I first started making this in the 1950s when I needed to feed many mouths on a budget. My husband and I are empty nesters now and I've had a hard time cutting back on serving sizes. It's a good thing my husband likes leftovers!
—Alice Marie Caldera
Tuolumne, California

BROCCOLI BEEF LO MEIN
(Pictured at right)

1 pound ground beef
1 large onion, thinly sliced
4 garlic cloves, minced
3/4 cup bean sprouts
1 jar (4-1/2 ounces) sliced mushrooms, drained
1 can (8 ounces) sliced water chestnuts, drained
6 ounces vermicelli *or* thin spaghetti, cooked and drained
2 to 3 cups broccoli florets, cooked
1/4 cup soy sauce
1/4 cup oyster sauce, optional
2 teaspoons ground ginger

In a large skillet, cook beef, onion and garlic over medium heat until meat is no longer pink; drain. Add bean sprouts, mushrooms and water chestnuts. Cook and stir for 3-5 minutes. Stir in the vermicelli, broccoli, soy sauce, oyster sauce if desired and ginger; toss to coat. Cover and cook for 5 minutes or until heated through. **Yield:** 4-6 servings.

HELPFUL HINT:
Select firm broccoli stalks with compact, deep green florets. Store unwashed in an airtight plastic bag in the refrigerator for up to 4 days. One pound of broccoli yields about 3-1/2 cups florets.

MOM'S MOSTACCIOLI
(Pictured at right)

1/2 pound ground beef
1 medium onion, chopped
1/2 cup chopped green pepper
1 can (14-1/2 ounces) diced tomatoes, undrained
1 can (6 ounces) tomato paste
1/2 cup water
1 bay leaf
1/2 teaspoon salt
1/4 teaspoon pepper
8 ounces mostaccioli, cooked and drained
8 ounces sliced process American cheese

In a skillet, cook beef, onion and green pepper over medium heat until meat is no longer pink; drain. Add the tomatoes, tomato paste, water, bay leaf, salt and pepper. Cover and simmer for 10 minutes; discard bay leaf. In a greased 11-in. x 7-in. x 2-in. baking dish, layer half of the mostaccioli, meat sauce and cheese; repeat layers. Bake, uncovered, at 350° for 30 minutes or until heated through. Let stand for 10 minutes before serving. **Yield:** 4-6 servings.

BROCCOLI BEEF LO MEIN
MOM'S MOSTACCIOLI

In this recipe, vermicelli noodles are first browned to develop a slightly nutty flavor. Then they simmer in a seasoned tomato sauce for a deliciously different dinner.
—Vicki Holmes
Kansas City, Missouri

GROUND BEEF VERMICELLI

8 ounces vermicelli *or* thin spaghetti, broken into 2-inch pieces
2 tablespoons butter *or* margarine
2 pounds lean ground beef
1 can (15 ounces) tomato sauce
4 celery ribs, chopped
2 large onions, finely chopped
1 can (15-1/4 ounces) whole kernel corn, drained
1/2 cup chopped green pepper
1 tablespoon garlic powder
1 tablespoon salt
1 teaspoon cayenne pepper
1 teaspoon chili powder
8 slices process American cheese

In a large skillet, saute vermicelli in butter until browned. Add beef; cook over medium heat until meat is no longer pink. Stir in the tomato sauce, celery, onions, corn, green pepper and seasonings; mix well. Cover and simmer for 25 minutes. Arrange cheese slices over the top. Cook, uncovered, until the cheese is melted, about 5 minutes. **Yield:** 12 servings.

Since I received this recipe from a friend several years ago, it's been a much-requested recipe by my family. Green olives are a great addition that give it a distinctive taste.
—Doris Baker
West Asheville,
North Carolina

OLIVE BEEF PASTA

1 pound ground beef
1 can (15 ounces) tomato sauce
1 medium onion, chopped
1 medium green pepper, chopped
1 can (11 ounces) whole kernel corn, drained
1 can (4 ounces) mushroom stems and pieces, drained
1/2 cup stuffed olives, sliced
1/2 teaspoon *each* garlic powder, chili powder and curry powder
Salt and pepper to taste
8 ounces medium egg noodles, cooked and drained
Grated Parmesan cheese

In a large saucepan, cook beef over medium heat until no longer pink; drain. Add tomato sauce, onion, green pepper, corn, mushrooms, olives and seasonings; mix well. Bring to a boil. Reduce heat; cover and simmer for 30 minutes. Stir in the noodles. Transfer to a greased 13-in. x 9-in. x 2-in. baking dish. Sprinkle with Parmesan cheese. Cover and bake at 350° for 30 minutes or until heated through. **Yield:** 8 servings.

HELPFUL HINT:

Unopened jars of olives can be stored in a cool dry place for 1 year. Once opened, they should be refrigerated and used within a month.

CREAMY BEEF CASSEROLE

2 pounds ground beef
1 large onion, chopped
6 ounces medium egg
　noodles, cooked and
　drained
1 can (15-1/4 ounces) whole
　kernel corn, drained
1 can (10-3/4 ounces)
　condensed cream of
　chicken soup, undiluted
1 can (10-3/4 ounces)
　condensed cream of
　mushroom soup, undiluted
1 cup (8 ounces) sour cream
1 can (2 ounces) diced
　pimientos, drained
3/4 teaspoon salt
1/4 teaspoon pepper
1 cup soft bread crumbs
1/4 cup butter *or* margarine,
　melted

In a skillet, cook beef and onion over medium heat until meat is no longer pink; drain. Add noodles, corn, soups, sour cream, pimientos, salt and pepper; mix well. Transfer to a greased 3-qt. baking dish. Toss bread crumbs and butter; sprinkle over casserole. Bake, uncovered, at 350° for 30 minutes or until heated through. **Yield:** 8 servings.

My mother and I own and operate a small baking business, so I have little free time to spend in the kitchen cooking for my family. I appreciate this easy recipe.
—Melanie Riley
McHenry, Illinois

BUTTERMILK NOODLE BAKE

1-1/2 pounds ground beef
1 large onion, finely chopped
1/4 cup butter *or* margarine
1/4 cup all-purpose flour
2-1/2 teaspoons salt
Dash pepper
2 cups buttermilk
1 can (4 ounces) mushroom
　stems and pieces,
　undrained
1/3 cup ketchup
1 tablespoon Worcestershire
　sauce
8 ounces medium egg
　noodles, cooked and
　drained

In a skillet, cook beef and onion over medium heat until meat is no longer pink; drain. In a large saucepan, melt butter. Stir in flour, salt and pepper until smooth. Gradually add buttermilk. Stir in mushrooms, ketchup and Worcestershire sauce. Bring to a boil; cook and stir for 2 minutes or until thickened. Add noodles and beef mixture; mix well. Transfer to a greased 2-1/2-qt. baking dish. Bake, uncovered, at 350° for 45 minutes or until heated through. **Yield:** 6 servings.

I enjoyed Mom's old-fashioned casserole as a child and made it often for my own family. Now that our children are grown, I make this for senior citizen lunches.
—Alice Fraser
Meridale, New York

SIMPLE SUBSTITUTION:

You don't need to run to the grocery store if you find you're out of buttermilk. Make your own! For every 1 cup of buttermilk, place 1 tablespoon of lemon juice or vinegar in a glass measuring cup. Add enough milk to measure 1 cup. Let stand 5 minutes before using.

PEPPERONI PASTA

(Pictured above)

I found this recipe in a cookbook from my mother's sorority. For a fun look, substitute half of the rotini with wagon wheel pasta.
—Carol Buckman
Colony, Kansas

1 pound ground beef
1 medium onion, chopped
1 medium green pepper, chopped
1 garlic clove, minced
1 jar (28 ounces) spaghetti sauce
1 can (4 ounces) mushroom stems and pieces, drained
1 package (3-1/2 ounces) sliced pepperoni
8 ounces rotini, cooked and drained
1 cup (4 ounces) shredded mozzarella cheese
4 ounces provolone cheese, shredded
Grated Parmesan cheese

In a large skillet, cook beef, onion, green pepper and garlic over medium heat until the meat is no longer pink; drain. Add spaghetti sauce, mushrooms and pepperoni. In a greased 13-in. x 9-in. x 2-in. baking dish, layer half of the rotini and beef mixture. Sprinkle with 1/2 cup each mozzarella and provolone. Repeat layers. Sprinkle with Parmesan cheese. Bake, uncovered, at 400° for 30-35 minutes or until heated through. Let stand for 15 minutes before serving. **Yield:** 6-8 servings.

PERFECT PARTNERS:

Need a new dessert idea? Top pound cake slices with miniature chocolate chips and miniature marshmallows. Broil for a few minutes or until the chips and marshmallows are melted.

CHEESEBURGER MACARONI

1 pound ground beef
1 medium onion, chopped
1 garlic clove, minced
1 can (10-3/4 ounces) condensed cheddar cheese soup, undiluted
1 can (10-3/4 ounces) condensed cream of mushroom soup, undiluted
1/2 cup milk
1/2 teaspoon dried basil
1/8 teaspoon pepper
2 cups elbow macaroni, cooked and drained
1 cup (4 ounces) shredded process American cheese
1/2 cup dry bread crumbs
1 tablespoon butter *or* margarine, melted

In a skillet, cook beef, onion and garlic over medium heat until meat is no longer pink; drain. In a bowl, combine soups, milk, basil and pepper; mix well. Stir in beef mixture. Fold in macaroni and cheese. Transfer to a greased 13-in. x 9-in. x 2-in. baking dish. Toss bread crumbs and butter; sprinkle over the top. Bake, uncovered, at 375° for 45 minutes or until heated through. **Yield:** 8 servings.

SIMPLE SUBSTITUTIONS:

Vary Cheeseburger Macaroni by using cream of onion soup for the cream of mushroom, small pasta shells for the elbow macaroni or Swiss cheese for the American cheese.

CHILI SPAGHETTI

1 can (25 ounces) chili with beans
1 pound ground beef, cooked and drained
8 ounces spaghetti, cooked and drained
1 can (14-1/2 ounces) stewed tomatoes
1 can (6 ounces) tomato paste
1/2 cup sour cream
3/4 teaspoon dried oregano
3/4 teaspoon salt
1/2 teaspoon sugar
1/4 teaspoon pepper
1-1/2 cups (6 ounces) shredded cheddar cheese, *divided*

In a large bowl, combine the first 10 ingredients. Stir in 1 cup cheese. Transfer to a greased 13-in. x 9-in. x 2-in. baking dish. Sprinkle with the remaining cheese. Bake, uncovered, at 350° for 30 minutes or until heated through. **Yield:** 8 servings.

Our family of four loves this creamy and cheesy casserole so much that we have few leftovers. It's a delicious quick meal for those busy days on the farm.
—Carol Funk
Richard,
Saskatchewan

I frequently depend on this dish when we have unexpected company because it calls for everyday ingredients. A hearty helping goes a long way.
—Cindie Peters
Moses Lake,
Washington

KID-PLEASING SPAGHETTI

1-1/2 **pounds ground beef**
1 **medium onion, chopped**
2-1/2 **cups spaghetti sauce**
8 **ounces spaghetti, cooked and drained**
3 **tablespoons butter *or* margarine**
2 **tablespoons all-purpose flour**
1/2 **teaspoon salt**
1-1/2 **cups milk**
1-1/2 **cups (6 ounces) shredded cheddar cheese, *divided***
1/4 **cup grated Parmesan cheese**

In a skillet, cook beef and onion over medium heat until meat is no longer pink; drain. Stir in spaghetti sauce. Cover and simmer for 10 minutes. Stir in spaghetti; set aside. In a saucepan, melt butter. Stir in flour and salt until smooth. Gradually add milk. Bring to a boil; cook and stir for 2 minutes or until thickened. Remove from the heat. Stir in 3/4 cup cheddar cheese and Parmesan cheese until melted. Place half of the spaghetti mixture in a greased 13-in. x 9-in. x 2-in. baking dish. Top with cheese sauce and the remaining spaghetti mixture. Sprinkle with remaining cheddar cheese. Bake, uncovered, at 350° for 30 minutes or until heated through. **Yield:** 10 servings.

PERFECT PARTNERS:

Try this quick dessert idea. Sprinkle warmed pear halves with cinnamon. Top with whipped cream, caramel ice cream topping and chopped walnuts.

ROUNDUP SUPPER

1 **pound ground beef**
1 **large onion, chopped**
1/2 **cup chopped green pepper**
8 **ounces wide egg noodles, cooked and drained**
1 **pound process American cheese, cubed**
1 **can (14-3/4 ounces) cream-style corn**
1 **can (14-1/2 ounces) diced tomatoes, undrained**
1 **can (4 ounces) chopped green chilies, undrained**
1 **can (4 ounces) mushroom stems and pieces, drained**
1/2 **teaspoon garlic powder**
1/2 **teaspoon cayenne pepper**
1/2 **teaspoon salt**
1/4 **teaspoon pepper**

In a skillet, cook beef, onion and green pepper over medium heat until the meat is no longer pink; drain. Add the remaining ingredients and mix well. Transfer to a greased 13-in. x 9-in. x 2-in. baking dish. Cover and bake at 350° for 30 minutes or until heated through. **Yield:** 8-10 servings.

SPICY MAC 'N' CHEESE

1 pound ground beef
1 large onion, chopped
1 medium green pepper, chopped
1 jalapeno pepper, finely chopped*
4 garlic cloves, minced
5 cups elbow macaroni, cooked and drained
1 cup milk
1 teaspoon salt
3/4 teaspoon cayenne pepper
3/4 teaspoon chili powder
3/4 teaspoon ground cumin
1 cup (4 ounces) shredded cheddar cheese

In a large saucepan, cook the beef, onion, peppers and garlic over medium heat until meat is no longer pink; drain. Stir in macaroni, milk and seasonings. Reduce heat. Stir in cheese until melted. **Yield:** 6-8 servings. ***Editor's Note:** When cutting or seeding hot peppers, use rubber or plastic gloves to protect your hands. Avoid touching your face.

SEEDING A JALAPENO PEPPER

To reduce the heat of jalapenos and other hot peppers, cut the peppers in half; remove and discard the seeds and membranes. If you like very spicy foods, add the seeds to the dish you're making instead of discarding them.

To give a little life to regular macaroni and cheese, my best friend and I decided to stir in ground beef and a chopped jalapeno.
—Debra Kind
Shawnigan Lake, British Columbia

TACO PASTA SHELLS

1-1/2 pounds ground beef
1 medium onion, chopped
1 package (8 ounces) cream cheese, cubed
2 envelopes taco seasoning
1 to 2 tablespoons minced chives
1 package (12 ounces) jumbo pasta shells, cooked and drained
2 cups taco sauce *or* salsa
2 cups (8 ounces) shredded plain *or* Mexican-flavored process American cheese
1 cup coarsely crushed tortilla chips

In a skillet, cook beef and onion over medium heat until meat is no longer pink; drain. Stir in cream cheese, taco seasoning and chives; cook until cream cheese is melted. Stuff into pasta shells. Place in a greased 4-qt. baking dish. Top with taco sauce. Bake, uncovered, at 350° for 20 minutes or until heated through. Sprinkle with cheese and tortilla chips. Bake 5 minutes longer or until the cheese is melted. **Yield:** 10-12 servings.

I tease my family that we have to save leftovers of this dish for my lunch the next day. This wonderful recipe uses pasta shells instead of taco shells or tortillas.
—Laura Pope
Bloomville, Ohio

HELPFUL HINT:

For best flavor, use fresh chives in recipes when possible. Wrap fresh chives in a paper towel, place in a plastic bag and refrigerate for up to 1 week. Or snip fresh chives and freeze in an airtight container for up to 6 months.

MACARONI ROYALE

8 ounces uncooked elbow macaroni
1 carton (6 ounces) whipped cream cheese with chives
2 pounds ground beef
2 large onions, thinly sliced
2 cans (8 ounces *each*) tomato sauce
4-1/2 teaspoons salt
1 tablespoon sugar
1 egg
1 cup (8 ounces) sour cream

Cook macaroni according to package directions; drain. Add cream cheese; toss until melted. Transfer to a greased 13-in. x 9-in. x 2-in. baking dish. In a skillet, cook beef and onions over medium heat until meat is no longer pink; drain. Add tomato sauce, salt and sugar; mix well. Spread over macaroni mixture. Combine egg and sour cream; spread over meat mixture. Bake, uncovered, at 350° for 45 minutes or until lightly browned. **Yield:** 8-10 servings.

SIMPLE SUBSTITUTION:

If your grocery store doesn't carry cream cheese with chives, stir 1 to 2 tablespoons of chopped fresh chives into 6 ounces of softened plain cream cheese.

CRUNCHY BEEF 'N' NOODLES

1 pound ground beef
1 medium onion, chopped
2-2/3 cups milk
1 can (10-3/4 ounces) condensed cream of mushroom soup, undiluted
1/2 cup shredded cheddar cheese
Salt and pepper to taste
1 package (16 ounces) medium egg noodles, cooked and drained
2 cups chow mein noodles

In a skillet, cook beef and onion over medium heat until the meat is no longer pink; drain. Add the milk, soup, cheese, salt and pepper; mix well. In a large bowl, toss meat mixture and egg noodles until coated. Transfer to a greased 13-in. x 9-in. x 2-in. baking dish. Cover and bake at 350° for 30 minutes. Uncover; sprinkle with chow mein noodles. Bake 15 minutes longer or until heated through. **Yield:** 12 servings.

HELPFUL HINT:

A 5-ounce can of chow mein noodles yields 2-1/2 cups. Store unused noodles in an airtight container to sprinkle on salads or casseroles.

CHURCH SUPPER SPAGHETTI

(Pictured above)

1 pound ground beef
1 large onion, chopped
1 medium green pepper, chopped
1 can (14-1/2 ounces) diced tomatoes, undrained
1 cup water
2 tablespoons chili powder
1 package (10 ounces) frozen corn, thawed
1 package (10 ounces) frozen peas, thawed
1 can (4 ounces) mushroom stems and pieces, drained
Salt and pepper to taste
1 package (12 ounces) spaghetti, cooked and drained
2 cups (8 ounces) shredded cheddar cheese, *divided*

In a skillet, cook beef, onion and green pepper over medium heat until meat is no longer pink. Add tomatoes, water and chili powder. Cover and simmer for 30 minutes. Add the corn, peas, mushrooms, salt and pepper. Stir in spaghetti. Layer half of the mixture in a greased 4-qt. baking dish. Sprinkle with 1 cup cheese; repeat layers. Bake, uncovered, at 350° for 20 minutes or until heated through. **Yield:** 12 servings.

Because this recipe feeds so many, I often take it to church dinners and potlucks. This colorful dish also comes in handy when we have lots of help to feed on our farm.
—Verlyn Wilson Wilkinson, Indiana

SIMPLE SUBSTITUTIONS:

To give Church Supper Spaghetti a new flavor twist, use Italian, Mexican or Cajun diced tomatoes in place of the plain diced tomatoes.

THREE-CHEESE JUMBO SHELLS

(Pictured below)

1	pound ground beef
2/3	cup chopped onion
2	cups water
2	cans (6 ounces *each*) tomato paste
1	tablespoon beef bouillon granules
1-1/2	teaspoons dried oregano
1	carton (15 ounces) ricotta cheese
2	cups (8 ounces) shredded mozzarella cheese, *divided*
1/2	cup grated Parmesan cheese
1	egg, beaten
24	jumbo pasta shells, cooked and drained

In a large skillet, cook beef and onion over medium heat until the meat is no longer pink; drain. Stir in water, tomato paste, bouillon and oregano. Cover and simmer for 30 minutes. Meanwhile, in a bowl, combine the ricotta cheese, 1 cup mozzarella, Parmesan cheese and egg; mix well. Stuff shells with the cheese mixture; arrange in a greased shallow 3-qt. baking dish. Spoon meat sauce over shells. Cover and bake at 350° for 30 minutes. Uncover; sprinkle with remaining mozzarella cheese. Bake 3-5 minutes longer or until cheese is melted. **Yield:** 6-8 servings.

HELPFUL HINT:

If there is no "Sell By" date on a ricotta cheese carton, it should be stored in the refrigerator no longer than 5 days after purchase. Ricotta and other soft cheeses should be discarded as soon as any mold appears.

OVEN SPAGHETTI

1/2 pound ground beef
1/4 cup chopped onion
1/3 cup instant nonfat dry milk powder
  3 tablespoons all-purpose flour, *divided*
  1 envelope onion soup mix, *divided*
1/2 teaspoon salt
Dash pepper
  1 cup water
1/2 cup sour cream
  4 ounces spaghetti, cooked and drained
1/2 cup dry bread crumbs
  1 tablespoon butter *or* margarine, melted

In a skillet, cook beef and onion over medium heat until meat is no longer pink; drain. Stir in milk powder, 2 tablespoons of flour, half of the soup mix, salt and pepper; mix well. Gradually add water. Bring to a boil. Cook and stir for 2 minutes or until thickened; set aside. In a bowl, combine remaining flour and soup mix with sour cream; stir until smooth. Add the spaghetti. Press onto the bottom and up the sides of a greased 1-qt. baking dish. Spoon beef mixture into shell. Toss bread crumbs and butter; sprinkle over beef mixture. Bake, uncovered, at 350° for 30 minutes or until heated through. **Yield:** 4 servings.

The rich, sour cream-coated noodles in this recipe resemble Stroganoff. Now that I'm cooking for two, I appreciate the fact that this dish yields only four servings.
—Martha Sherman
New Holstein, Wisconsin

BOW TIE BAKE

  1 pound ground beef
  1 large onion, chopped
  1 can (8 ounces) mushroom stems and pieces, drained
1/2 cup chopped green pepper
  1 package (16 ounces) bow tie pasta, cooked and drained
  1 can (10-3/4 ounces) condensed tomato soup, undiluted
  3 cups (12 ounces) shredded mozzarella cheese, *divided*
  1 can (10-3/4 ounces) condensed cream of mushroom soup, undiluted

In a skillet, cook beef, onion, mushrooms and green pepper over medium heat until the meat is no longer pink; drain. In a greased 3-qt. baking dish, layer half of the pasta, half of the meat mixture, all of the tomato soup and 1 cup of cheese. Top with the remaining pasta and meat mixture. Spread with mushroom soup. Sprinkle with the remaining cheese. Bake, uncovered, at 350° for 30-45 minutes or until heated through. **Yield:** 12 servings.

My cousin takes this dish to our annual family picnic. I make it for functions on my husband's side of the family and never bring home leftovers.
—Cindy Kemp
Forest, Ontario

PERFECT PARTNERS:

As a side dish for Bow Tie Bake, place fresh cut green beans in a saucepan; cover with water. Bring to a boil. Cook, uncovered, for 8 to 10 minutes or until crisp-tender; drain. Sprinkle with Italian seasoning.

POTLUCK HOT DISH

1 pound ground beef
1 pound ground pork
1 large onion, chopped
1 medium green pepper, chopped
1 package (7 ounces) elbow *or* ring macaroni, cooked and drained
2 cans (14-3/4 ounces *each*) cream-style corn
2 cans (11-1/2 ounces *each*) condensed chicken with rice soup, undiluted
1 can (10-3/4 ounces) condensed cream of mushroom soup, undiluted
1 teaspoon salt
1/2 teaspoon pepper
Seasoned salt to taste
1/2 cup dry bread crumbs
2 tablespoons butter *or* margarine, melted

In a skillet, cook meat, onion and green pepper over medium heat until meat is no longer pink; drain. Stir in macaroni, corn, soups and seasonings; mix well. Transfer to a greased 13-in. x 9-in. x 2-in. baking dish. Toss bread crumbs and butter; sprinkle over top. Cover and bake at 350° for 45 minutes. Uncover and bake 15 minutes longer or until heated through. **Yield:** 10-12 servings.

TIMELY TIP:

After preparing a double batch of Potluck Hot Dish on the stove, transfer half to a 13- x 9- x 2-inch baking dish and sprinkle with buttered bread crumbs. Bake as directed. Freeze the remaining portion in an airtight container. When ready to use, thaw, transfer to a 13- x 9- x 2-inch baking dish, sprinkle with buttered crumbs and bake as directed.

SIMPLE MANICOTTI

1-1/2 pounds ground beef
2 cups spaghetti sauce, *divided*
1 tablespoon onion powder
1 teaspoon salt
1/2 teaspoon pepper
1 cup (4 ounces) shredded mozzarella cheese
14 large manicotti shells, cooked and drained

In a skillet, cook beef over medium heat until no longer pink; drain. Remove from the heat. Stir in 1 cup spaghetti sauce, onion powder, salt and pepper. Cool for 5 minutes. Set 1/2 cup aside. Add cheese to the remaining meat mixture. Stuff into manicotti shells; arrange in a greased 13-in. x 9-in. x 2-in. baking dish. Combine remaining spaghetti sauce and reserved meat mixture; pour over shells. Bake, uncovered, at 350° for 10 minutes or until heated through. **Yield:** 7 servings.

SKILLET LASAGNA

2 pounds ground beef
1 envelope spaghetti sauce mix, *divided*
2 cups (16 ounces) small-curd cottage cheese
3 cups uncooked wide egg noodles
1 tablespoon dried parsley flakes
1 teaspoon salt
1 teaspoon dried basil
1 teaspoon Italian seasoning
1 can (14-1/2 ounces) stewed tomatoes
1 cup spaghetti sauce with meat
1 cup water
2 cups (8 ounces) shredded mozzarella cheese

In a skillet, cook beef over medium heat until no longer pink; drain. Sprinkle with half of the spaghetti sauce mix. Spoon cottage cheese over meat. Top with noodles. Sprinkle with parsley, salt, basil, Italian seasoning and remaining spaghetti sauce mix. Pour tomatoes, spaghetti sauce and water over the top. Bring to a boil. Reduce heat; cover and simmer for 35 minutes or until noodles are tender. Sprinkle with mozzarella cheese. Cover and simmer for 5 minutes or until the cheese is melted. **Yield:** 8 servings.

HELPFUL HINT:

Skillet Lasagna only uses 1 cup prepared spaghetti sauce. Leftover sauce can be frozen in an airtight container for up to 3 months. Use it as a dip for breadsticks or as sauce for homemade pizza.

ITALIAN PASTA SUPPER

1/2 pound ground beef
1 medium onion, chopped
1/4 cup minced fresh parsley
1 garlic clove, minced
1 can (14-1/2 ounces) diced tomatoes, drained
1 can (6 ounces) tomato paste
3/4 cup water
1 teaspoon sugar
1/2 teaspoon salt
1/2 teaspoon dried basil
1/4 teaspoon *each* dried marjoram, oregano and thyme

1-1/2 cups elbow macaroni, cooked and drained

In a skillet, cook beef, onion, parsley and garlic over medium heat until meat is no longer pink; drain. Add the tomatoes, tomato paste, water, sugar and seasonings; mix well. Cover and simmer for 30 minutes. Add macaroni; mix well. Simmer, uncovered, 5 minutes longer or until heated through. **Yield:** 4 servings.

SIMPLE SUBSTITUTION:

In summer, give Italian Pasta Supper a fresher flavor by using 1-1/2 teaspoons minced fresh basil and 3/4 teaspoon each minced fresh marjoram, oregano and thyme.

I like this recipe because you make it all in one skillet and don't have to hassle with cooking lasagna noodles separately. Its cheesy topping is delicious.
—Merry Roop
Washington, Kansas

When my husband and I lived on a farm, this wonderful stovetop dish satisfied hearty appetites after a long day of work in the fields. It's simple to prepare.
—Emily Smith
Orangeville, Ontario

STUFFED MANICOTTI

STUFFED MANICOTTI

(Pictured at left and on page 224)

1 pound ground beef
2 cups water
2 cans (6 ounces *each*) tomato paste
1 medium onion, chopped
6 tablespoons minced fresh parsley, *divided*
1 tablespoon dried basil
1 garlic clove, minced
2 teaspoons salt, *divided*
1/4 teaspoon pepper, *divided*
3 cups ricotta cheese
1-1/4 cups grated Romano *or* Parmesan cheese, *divided*
2 eggs, beaten
8 large manicotti shells, cooked and drained

In a skillet, cook beef over medium heat until no longer pink; drain. Add water, tomato paste, onion, 2 tablespoons parsley, basil, garlic, 1-1/2 teaspoons salt and 1/8 teaspoon pepper; mix well. Simmer, uncovered, for 30 minutes, stirring occasionally. Meanwhile, combine the ricotta cheese, 3/4 cup Romano cheese, eggs and remaining parsley, salt and pepper. Stuff into manicotti shells. Pour half of the meat sauce into a greased 11-in. x 7-in. x 2-in. baking dish. Arrange shells over sauce. Top with remaining sauce. Sprinkle with remaining Romano cheese. Bake, uncovered, at 350° for 30-35 minutes or until heated through. **Yield:** 4 servings.

STUFFING MANICOTTI SHELLS

An easy mess-free way to stuff manicotti shells is to combine the filling ingredients and place in a large resealable plastic bag. Cut a hole in one corner and squeeze filling into shells. Make sure the hole in the bag is slightly smaller than the opening of the shell.

TASTY GREEN BEAN BAKE

1 pound ground beef
1 large onion, chopped
1/2 cup chopped green pepper
2-1/4 cups uncooked wide egg noodles
1 can (14-1/2 ounces) cut green beans, drained
1 can (14-1/2 ounces) diced tomatoes, undrained
1 can (4 ounces) mushroom stems and pieces, drained
2 teaspoons salt
1 to 2 teaspoons chili powder

In a skillet, cook beef, onion and green pepper over medium heat until meat is no longer pink; drain. Add the remaining ingredients; mix well. Transfer to a greased 11-in. x 7-in. x 2-in. baking dish. Cover and bake at 350° for 1 hour or until noodles are tender, stirring occasionally. **Yield:** 6-8 servings.

ONION BEEF FETTUCCINE

3 cups thinly sliced onions
1/4 cup butter (no substitutes)
1 pound ground beef
3 tablespoons all-purpose flour
1 tablespoon brown sugar
1 teaspoon salt
1/2 teaspoon pepper
1/2 teaspoon ground cumin
2 cans (14-1/2 ounces *each*) beef broth
8 ounces fettuccine, cooked and drained
1 cup (4 ounces) shredded mozzarella cheese
1/2 cup grated Parmesan cheese

In a skillet, saute onions in butter for 10-15 minutes or until caramelized (do not overbrown). Remove onions with a slotted spoon. In the same skillet, cook beef over medium heat until no longer pink; drain. Return onions to skillet. In a bowl, combine the flour, brown sugar, salt, pepper and cumin. Gradually stir in the broth until smooth. Add to skillet; bring to a boil. Cook and stir for 2 minutes or until thickened. Place fettuccine in a greased 4-qt. baking dish. Top with beef mixture. Combine cheeses; sprinkle over the top. Bake, uncovered, at 450° for 15 minutes or until cheese is melted. **Yield:** 8 servings.

HELPFUL HINT:

Caramelizing onions brings out their natural sweetness and mellows their sharp flavor. To reduce the risk of burning, saute the onions in butter over low heat just until onions are coated with the browned butter.

CASSEROLE FOR A CROWD

2 pounds ground beef
1 large onion, chopped
8 ounces wide egg noodles, cooked and drained
1 can (15-1/4 ounces) whole kernel corn, drained
1 can (15-1/4 ounces) peas, drained
1 can (8 ounces) mushroom stems and pieces, drained
4 cups (16 ounces) shredded cheddar cheese, *divided*
1 can (10-3/4 ounces) condensed cream of celery soup, undiluted
1-1/4 cups milk
1 tablespoon chili powder
1 tablespoon Worcestershire sauce
2 teaspoons salt
1/4 teaspoon pepper
1/4 teaspoon garlic powder

In a skillet, cook beef and onion over medium heat until meat is no longer pink; drain. Transfer to a greased roasting pan. Add the noodles, corn, peas and mushrooms; mix well. In a saucepan, combine 2-1/2 cups cheese, soup, milk and seasonings. Cook and stir over low heat until cheese is melted. Pour over noodle mixture and mix well. Sprinkle with remaining cheese. Bake, uncovered, at 350° for 30 minutes or until heated through. **Yield:** 12-14 servings.

HOMEMADE PINWHEEL NOODLES

2-1/4 to 2-3/4 cups all-purpose
  flour
4 eggs
3/4 pound ground beef
1/4 cup *each* finely chopped
  celery, onion and green
  pepper
3/4 teaspoon garlic powder
3/4 teaspoon seasoned salt
1/2 teaspoon pepper
6 cups water
1 can (10-1/2 ounces)
  condensed beef broth,
  undiluted

Place 2-1/4 cups of flour in a bowl. Make a well in the center; add the eggs. Gradually mix with a wooden spoon until well blended. Knead on a floured surface until smooth, about 10 minutes. If necessary, add remaining flour to kneading surface or hands. On a lightly floured surface, roll dough into a 16-in. x 12-in. rectangle, dusting top of dough with flour to prevent sticking. Crumble beef over dough; lightly press into dough. Sprinkle with celery, onion, green pepper, garlic powder, seasoned salt and pepper. Roll up, jelly-roll style, starting with a short side. Using a sharp knife, cut into 2-in. slices. In a large kettle or Dutch oven, bring water and broth to a rapid boil. Drop pinwheels into the boiling liquid. Return to a gentle boil. Reduce heat; cover and simmer for 1 hour or until noodles are tender and meat is no longer pink. Serve with broth in soup bowls. **Yield:** 6 servings.

MAKING PINWHEEL NOODLES

STEP 1
Use masking tape, mark the work surface with a 16-in. x 12-in. rectangle. Lightly flour the surface and roll dough to marked dimensions. If needed, trim dough to form a rectangle.

STEP 2
Crumble beef over the rectangle and lightly press into the dough.

BEEF AND PEPPER LINGUINE

1 pound ground beef
1 large onion, chopped
2 medium green peppers,
  cubed
1 package (16 ounces)
  linguine, cooked and
  drained
4 to 6 tablespoons soy sauce
Dash garlic powder, optional

In a large skillet, cook beef, onion and green peppers over medium heat until meat is no longer pink; drain. Remove from the heat. Add linguine and soy sauce; mix well. Sprinkle with garlic powder if desired. **Yield:** 6 servings.

My family considers this recipe—from my husband's grandmother—a real treat. Homemade noodles simmer into delicious meat-filled puffs.
—Deb Shafer Dowling, Michigan

This recipe didn't sound so tasty when I first saw it, so I didn't make it for years. One day I decided to give it a try, and I'm glad I did!
—Marilyn Chigas Peabody, Massachusetts

PIZZAS, POCKETS & PIES

Everyone agrees that
piping-hot pizzas,
potpies, turnovers,
quiches and pasties packed
with flavorful fillings
are a slice of heaven!
Pocket these hearty recipes
so you can try them
on your family soon.

MEAT AND
POTATO PIE
(P. 278)

SUPER CALZONES

(Pictured on page 257)

1/2 pound ground beef
2 tablespoons finely chopped onion
2 tablespoons finely chopped green pepper
1 garlic clove, minced
1 can (15 ounces) tomato sauce
1 teaspoon Italian seasoning
1 tube (10 ounces) refrigerated pizza crust
1 package (3 ounces) cream cheese, softened
1 cup (4 ounces) shredded mozzarella cheese
1 can (4 ounces) mushroom stems and pieces, drained
1 can (2-1/4 ounces) sliced ripe olives, drained

In a skillet, cook the beef, onion, green pepper and garlic over medium heat until meat is no longer pink; drain and set aside. In a saucepan, bring tomato sauce and Italian seasoning to a boil. Reduce heat; cover and simmer for 5 minutes. Stir 1/2 cup into the meat mixture; keep remaining sauce warm. Unroll pizza crust on a floured surface. Roll into a 12-in. square; cut into four squares. Spread cream cheese over each to within 1/2 in. of edges. Top with meat mixture. Sprinkle with mozzarella cheese, mushrooms and olives. Fold dough over filling, forming a triangle; press edges with a fork to seal. Place on a greased baking sheet. Bake at 400° for 20-25 minutes or until golden brown. Serve with the remaining sauce. **Yield:** 4 servings.

PERSONAL PIZZAS

(Pictured on page 257)

2 packages (6-1/2 ounces *each*) pizza crust mix
1-1/2 cups pizza sauce
1 pound ground beef, cooked and drained
1 medium onion, chopped
1 cup chopped green pepper
2 cans (2-1/4 ounces *each*) sliced ripe olives, drained
2 cups (8 ounces) shredded mozzarella cheese

Prepare both packages of pizza dough according to directions. On a floured surface, knead dough several times; divide into six portions. Roll each into an 8-in. circle. Place on greased baking sheets. Bake at 425° for 10 minutes. Spread pizza sauce over crusts to within 1/2 in. of edge. Top with beef, onion, green pepper, olives and cheese. Return to the oven for 10-15 minutes or until crust is golden brown and cheese is melted. **Yield:** 6 servings.

TIMELY TIP:

After baking plain crusts for Personal Pizzas, cool, transfer to an airtight container and freeze. Spread sauce over frozen crusts and sprinkle with toppings. Bake at 425° for 10 to 15 minutes.

FINNISH MEAT PIE

(Pictured on page 257)

1 cup water
1 teaspoon salt
1 cup shortening
3 cups all-purpose flour
FILLING:
  4 cups shredded peeled
    potatoes
1-1/2 pounds lean ground beef
  2 cups shredded carrots
  1 medium onion, chopped
  1/2 cup shredded peeled
    rutabaga
1-1/2 teaspoons salt
  1/4 teaspoon pepper

In a saucepan, combine water and salt; bring to a boil. Remove from the heat. Stir in shortening until melted. Add flour; stir until a soft ball forms. Cover and refrigerate until cool, about 1 hour. Divide dough in half. On a floured surface, roll one portion of dough to fit the bottom of a 13-in. x 9-in. x 2-in. baking dish. Line ungreased dish with pastry. In a bowl, combine filling ingredients; mix well. Spoon into crust. Roll out remaining pastry to fit top of dish. Place over filling; press edges with a fork to seal. Cut slits in top. Bake at 350° for 1-1/4 hours or until golden brown. **Yield:** 6-8 servings.

HELPFUL HINT:

When a recipe instructs you to divide dough into portions, place the dough on a floured surface and flatten slightly. Cut the dough with a sharp knife, pizza cutter or dough cutter (sometimes called a pastry scraper). It's important not to tear the dough, so don't use a serrated knife.

CHEESEBURGER PIE

1 unbaked deep-dish pastry
  shell (9 inches)
1 pound ground beef
1 medium onion, finely
  chopped
1 garlic clove, minced
1/4 cup all-purpose flour
1/2 teaspoon salt
2 cups (8 ounces) shredded
  process American cheese
1/2 cup chopped dill pickles
1/3 cup dill pickle juice
1/3 cup milk

Bake the pastry shell at 425° for 15 minutes. Meanwhile, in a skillet, cook beef, onion and garlic over medium heat until the meat is no longer pink; drain. Sprinkle with flour and salt; stir until blended. Stir in the remaining ingredients. Spoon into pastry shell. Bake for 15 minutes or until crust is golden brown. Let stand 15 minutes before cutting. **Yield:** 6-8 servings.

We enjoy this hearty, traditional meat pie year-round, but it's especially appreciated during hunting season. This is one recipe I'll be sure to pass on to our seven children.
—Laurel Skoog
Frazee, Minnesota

This meat pie tastes so much like a cheeseburger—right down to the pickles in it! We home-school our children, so I like easy recipes like this that get them involved in cooking.
—Rhonda Cannady
Bartlesville, Oklahoma

GRANDMA'S POTPIE

(Pictured above)

My husband and father-in-law are both picky eaters, but they do enjoy this savory meat pie with flaky golden crust. The recipe is from my husband's grandmother.
—Annette Wheatley
Syracuse, New York

1-1/2 **pounds ground beef**
    1 **teaspoon onion powder**
Salt to taste
    1 **cup diced peeled potatoes**
    1 **cup frozen mixed**
      vegetables, thawed
1/4 **cup butter *or* margarine**
1/4 **cup all-purpose flour**
    1 **can (14-1/2 ounces) beef**
      broth
CRUST:
    2 **cups all-purpose flour**
    1 **tablespoon baking powder**
    1 **teaspoon salt**
1/4 **cup shortening**
3/4 **cup milk**
    1 **tablespoon butter *or***
      margarine, melted

In a skillet, cook beef over medium heat until no longer pink; drain. Stir in onion powder and salt. Transfer to a greased 9-in. square baking dish. Top with potatoes and vegetables. In a skillet, melt the butter. Stir in flour until smooth; gradually add broth. Bring to a boil; cook and stir for 2 minutes or until thickened. Pour over vegetables. For crust, combine the flour, baking powder and salt in a bowl. Cut in shortening until mixture resembles coarse crumbs. Stir in milk until a soft dough forms. On a floured surface, roll dough into a 9-in. square. Place over filling; flute edges and cut slits in top. Brush with butter. Bake at 350° for 45 minutes or until golden brown. **Yield:** 6 servings.

HELPFUL HINT:

Use a pastry blender or two knives to cut shortening into dry ingredients. The coarse crumbs should be the size of small peas when finished.

RICE CAKE PIZZAS

1 can (8 ounces) tomato
  sauce
1 package (4-1/2 ounces)
  plain *or* cheese-flavored
  rice cakes
Italian seasoning to taste
1 pound ground beef
1 medium onion, chopped
1 medium green pepper,
  chopped
2 cups (8 ounces) mozzarella
  cheese
1 can (2-1/4 ounces) sliced
  ripe olives, drained

Spread tomato sauce over the rice cakes. Sprinkle with Italian seasoning. In a skillet, cook beef, onion and green pepper over medium heat until meat is no longer pink; drain. Spoon over rice cakes. Sprinkle with cheese and olives. Place five pizzas on a microwave-safe plate. Microwave, uncovered, on high for 1 minute or until cheese is melted. Repeat with remaining pizzas. **Yield:** 14 servings. **Editor's Note:** This recipe was tested in a 700-watt microwave.

PERFECT PARTNERS:

For a quick accompaniment to Rice Cake Pizzas, toss together a bag of store-bought shredded cabbage and bottle of Italian or ranch salad dressing. Stir in some chopped green onions for added flavor.

Ordinary rice cakes get a taste lift with some simple pizza toppings. I keep small portions of the beef mixture in the freezer to quickly thaw for fast snacks.
—Gayle Richardson
Great Falls, Montana

HASH BROWN QUICHE

1 package (16 ounces) frozen
  shredded hash brown
  potatoes, thawed
1/3 cup butter *or* margarine,
  melted
3/4 pound ground beef
1 small onion, chopped
2 tablespoons cornstarch
2 eggs
1/2 cup milk
8 ounces process American
  cheese, cubed
1 teaspoon Worcestershire
  sauce
1/2 teaspoon salt
1/4 teaspoon pepper

Combine hash browns and butter in a greased 9-in. pie plate. Press onto the bottom and up the sides, forming a shell. Bake at 350° for 10 minutes. Meanwhile, in a skillet, cook beef and onion over medium heat until meat is no longer pink; drain. Cool for 5 minutes. In a bowl, combine cornstarch, eggs and milk until smooth. Stir into beef mixture. Add the remaining ingredients; mix well. Pour into shell. Bake at 350° for 30-35 minutes or until a knife inserted near the center comes out clean. Let stand 5-10 minutes before cutting. **Yield:** 4-6 servings.

TIMELY TIP:

If you want to serve overnight guests Hash Brown Quiche for breakfast, assemble it the night before. Remove it from the refrigerator 15 minutes before baking.

I got this recipe from an aunt some years ago, and it quickly became a favorite breakfast entree. You can't go wrong with ground beef, hash browns and cheese!
—Jamie Creamer
Bartlett, Tennessee

BASIC BEEF PIZZA

1 **pound ground beef**
1/2 **teaspoon salt**
1/4 **teaspoon celery salt**
1/4 **teaspoon pepper**
1 **loaf (1 pound) frozen bread dough, thawed**
1 **cup pizza sauce**
2 **cups (8 ounces) shredded mozzarella cheese**

In a skillet, cook beef over medium heat until no longer pink; drain. Add salt, celery salt and pepper; set aside. On a floured surface, roll dough into a 13-in. circle. Press onto the bottom and up the sides of a greased 12-in. pizza pan. Spread sauce over crust to within 1/2 in. of edge. Top with cheese and beef mixture. Bake at 350° for 20-25 minutes or until crust is golden and cheese is melted. **Yield:** 4-6 servings.

TIMELY TIP:

If you don't have time to thaw frozen bread dough for Basic Beef Pizza, you can use a refrigerated pizza crust instead.

CHILI RICE PIE

2 **cups cooked brown rice**
1/4 **cup shredded cheddar cheese**
1 **egg, beaten**
1 **teaspoon vegetable oil**
FILLING:
1/2 **pound ground beef**
1/4 **cup** *each* **finely chopped celery, onion and green and sweet red pepper**
1 **garlic clove, minced**
1 **cup canned diced tomatoes, drained**
1/2 **cup canned kidney beans, rinsed and drained**
1/4 **teaspoon chili powder**

In a bowl, combine the first four ingredients; mix well. Press onto the bottom and up the sides of a greased 9-in. pie plate; set aside. For filling, cook beef, celery, onion, peppers and garlic over medium heat until meat is no longer pink; drain. Add the tomatoes, beans and chili powder. Spoon into crust. Bake at 325° for 40 minutes or until heated through. Let stand 15 minutes before serving. **Yield:** 4 servings.

SIMPLE SUBSTITUTIONS:

You can also make the crust for Chili Rice Pie with 2 cups cooked white rice. Don't care for kidney beans? Use black or pinto beans instead. For a more spicy chili, stir in some finely chopped jalapeno pepper.

CHEESEBURGER POCKETS

(Pictured above)

1/2 **pound ground beef**
1 **tablespoon chopped onion**
1/2 **teaspoon salt**
1/8 **teaspoon pepper**
1 **tube (12 ounces) refrigerated buttermilk biscuits**
5 **slices process American cheese**

In a skillet, cook beef, onion, salt and pepper over medium heat until meat is no longer pink; drain and cool. Place two biscuits overlapping on a floured surface; roll out into a 5-in. oval. Place 3 tablespoons meat mixture on one side. Fold a cheese slice to fit over meat mixture. Fold dough over filling; press edges with a fork to seal. Repeat with remaining biscuits, meat mixture and cheese. Place on a greased baking sheet. Prick tops with a fork. Bake at 400° for 10 minutes or until golden brown. **Yield:** 5 servings.

HELPFUL HINT:

Pricking the tops of Cheeseburger Pockets helps steam escape during baking. If you don't do this, the pockets will puff up and may break open.

Ground beef is my favorite meat to cook with because it's so versatile, flavorful and economical. Refrigerated biscuits save you the trouble of making dough from scratch.
—Pat Chambless Crowder, Oklahoma

PUFFED PAN PIZZA

1/2 pound ground beef
1 medium onion, chopped
1 teaspoon Italian seasoning
Salt and pepper to taste
4 tubes (12 ounces *each*) refrigerated buttermilk biscuits
1/2 cup chopped green pepper
4 ounces fresh mushrooms, sliced
1 jar (28 ounces) spaghetti sauce
2 cups (8 ounces) shredded cheddar cheese

In a large skillet, cook beef and onion over medium heat until the meat is no longer pink; drain. Add Italian seasoning, salt and pepper. Simmer for 1 minute. Quarter the biscuits; place half in a large bowl. Add half of beef mixture, green pepper, mushrooms, and a third of the spaghetti sauce and cheese. Gently fold ingredients together. Transfer to a greased 13-in. x 9-in. x 2-in. baking dish. Repeat. Pour remaining sauce over biscuit mixture. Sprinkle with remaining cheese. Bake at 350° for 50 minutes or until center is puffed. Let stand 5-10 minutes before serving. **Yield:** 8 servings.

HELPFUL HINT:

Sharp cheddar cheese has a stronger flavor than mild and medium cheddar but doesn't melt as nicely. However, if you prefer the more pronounced flavor of sharp cheddar cheese, you'll find it melts better if finely shredded.

MUSHROOM BURGER POCKETS

1-1/2 pounds ground beef
1 can (10-3/4 ounces) condensed cream of mushroom soup, undiluted
1 can (4 ounces) mushroom stems and pieces, drained
1 medium onion, chopped
1 tablespoon Worcestershire sauce
Salt and pepper to taste
1 loaf (1 pound) frozen bread dough, thawed
1 cup (4 ounces) shredded cheddar cheese

In a skillet, cook beef over medium heat until no longer pink; drain. Stir in the soup, mushrooms, onion, Worcestershire sauce, salt and pepper. Remove from the heat. On a floured surface, roll dough into a 16-in. x 8-in. rectangle. Cut into eight squares. Place about 1/3 cup meat mixture in the center of each square; sprinkle with cheese. Bring the four corners to center over filling; pinch seams together to seal. Place seam side down on greased baking sheets. Cover and let rise in a warm place for 15-20 minutes. Bake at 350° for 20-25 minutes or until golden brown. **Yield:** 8 servings.

BEEF-SPINACH LATTICE PIE

Pastry for double-crust pie (9 inches)
- **1 package (10 ounces) frozen chopped spinach, thawed and squeezed dry**
- **2 cups cooked long grain rice**
- **1/2 pound ground beef, cooked and drained**
- **1 cup grated Parmesan cheese**
- **3 eggs, beaten**
- **1/2 cup dry bread crumbs**
- **1/3 cup olive *or* vegetable oil**
- **1/4 teaspoon ground nutmeg**

Salt and pepper to taste

On a floured surface, roll out half of pastry to fit the bottom and two-thirds up the sides of a 13-in. x 9-in. x 2-in. baking dish. Line ungreased dish with pastry. In a bowl, combine remaining ingredients. Spoon over crust. Roll out remaining pastry into a 15-in. x 10-in. rectangle; cut lengthwise into 3/4-in. strips. Place strips over the filling, forming a lattice crust. Press edges with a fork to seal. Bake at 350° for 50-60 minutes or until golden brown. **Yield:** 6-8 servings.

My grandmother initially used this filling for her homemade ravioli. One day she decided to bake the leftover filling in a crust...and another family favorite was born!
—Marjorie Goral Ridgefield, Connecticut

MAKING A LATTICE-TOPPED PIE

STEP 1
Roll out pastry into a 15-inch x 10-inch rectangle. Using a knife or pastry wheel, cut lengthwise into 3/4-inch strips. Lay five strips lengthwise and 3/4 inch apart over filling. Fold every other strip halfway back.

STEP 2
Starting in the center, add pastry strips widthwise, lifting every other long strip as the strips are placed. Continue to add strips, positioning and lifting until the entire pie is covered with a woven top.

STEP 3
Trim lattice strips even with the pastry edge. Fold bottom pastry over strips; press edges with a fork to seal.

BEEF TURNOVERS
(Pictured above)

My husband and I developed this recipe for the restaurant we own and operate. We make a limited number each day and never have a problem selling out.
—Judie Sadighi
Twain Harte, California

2 pounds ground beef
1/2 teaspoon salt
1/4 teaspoon pepper
1 can (4 ounces) mushroom stems and pieces, drained
1/3 cup chopped green onions
1/4 cup minced fresh parsley
2 tablespoons butter *or* margarine
2 medium tomatoes, diced
1 can (2-1/4 ounces) sliced ripe olives, drained
1/4 cup grated Parmesan cheese

DOUGH:
4 cups all-purpose flour
4 teaspoons baking powder
1 teaspoon baking soda
1/2 teaspoon salt
1/2 cup shortening
1-1/2 cups milk
Spaghetti sauce, warmed
Shredded mozzarella cheese and additional Parmesan cheese, optional

In a skillet, cook beef over medium heat until no longer pink; drain. Add salt and pepper; remove and set aside. In the same skillet, saute mushrooms, onions and parsley in butter until tender. Add tomatoes; simmer for 5 minutes. Add the olives, Parmesan cheese and beef; mix well. Cool. In a large bowl, combine flour, baking powder, baking soda and salt. Cut in shortening until mixture resembles coarse crumbs. Stir in milk. Turn onto a floured surface; knead 10 times. Divide dough into eight portions. Roll each into an 8-in. circle. Place on greased baking sheets. Mound about 1/2 cup filling on half of each circle. Fold dough over filling and press edges with a fork to seal. Bake at 375° for 30 minutes or until golden brown. Top with spaghetti sauce and cheese if desired. **Yield:** 8 servings.

CHEESY LASAGNA PIZZA

1 pound ground beef
1 can (8 ounces) tomato
  sauce
1/4 cup water
1 envelope spaghetti sauce
  mix, *divided*
1 loaf (1 pound) frozen bread
  dough, thawed
1-1/2 cups (12 ounces) small-curd
  cottage cheese
1/4 cup grated Parmesan
  cheese
1 cup (4 ounces) shredded
  mozzarella cheese

In a skillet, cook beef over medium heat until no longer pink; drain. Stir in tomato sauce, water and 3 tablespoons spaghetti sauce mix. Cover and simmer for 30 minutes. Meanwhile, knead remaining spaghetti sauce mix into the bread dough. Press onto the bottom and up the sides of a greased 12-in. pizza pan. Spread with cottage cheese. Spoon meat mixture over top. Sprinkle with Parmesan cheese. Bake at 400° for 25 minutes. Sprinkle with mozzarella cheese. Bake 5 minutes longer or until the crust is golden and cheese is melted. Let stand 5 minutes before serving. **Yield:** 4-6 servings.

PERFECT PARTNERS:

Serve Cheesy Lasagna Pizza with a store-bought salad mix that includes greens and dressing. Toss in cucumber slices, tomato wedges and packaged croutons.

TATER BEEF PIE

Pastry for double-crust pie
  (9 inches)
1/2 cup milk
1 envelope onion soup mix
Dash *each* pepper and ground
  allspice
1 pound lean ground beef
1 package (12 ounces) frozen
  cubed hash brown
  potatoes, thawed

Line a 9-in. pie plate with bottom pastry. In a bowl, combine milk, soup mix, pepper and allspice. Crumble beef over mixture and mix well. Spoon into crust. Top with hash browns. Roll out remaining pastry to fit top of pie. Place over filling; trim, seal and flute edges. Cut slits in top. Bake at 350° for 1 hour or until crust is golden brown. Let stand 15 minutes before cutting. **Yield:** 4-6 servings.

TIMELY TIP:

To quickly thaw frozen hash browns, place them in a microwave-safe dish. Cover and microwave at 50% power for 5 to 8 minutes, stirring once or twice until thawed.

My children never seem to tire of pizza, but I get bored making it the same old way. This recipe from a co-worker features a crust seasoned with spaghetti sauce mix for tasty results.
—Connie Denmark
Macon, Illinois

Leftovers of this meaty pie reheat nicely, so my husband and I can enjoy savory slices for a few days. Onion soup mix gives great flavor.
—Dorothy Presse
Montrose, Colorado

RESTAURANT-STYLE PIZZA

4 teaspoons sugar
1 package (1/4 ounce) active dry yeast
1-1/3 cups warm water (110° to 115°)
1 tablespoon butter *or* margarine, softened
1 tablespoon shortening
3/4 teaspoon salt
3-1/2 to 4 cups all-purpose flour
Cornmeal
Olive *or* vegetable oil
1 jar (14 ounces) spaghetti sauce
1 pound ground beef, cooked and drained
1 cup (4 ounces) shredded mozzarella cheese

In a mixing bowl, dissolve sugar and yeast in water. Add butter, shortening, salt and 2 cups flour; mix until smooth. Stir in enough remaining flour to form a soft dough. Turn onto a floured surface; knead until smooth and elastic, about 6-8 minutes. Place in a greased bowl, turning once to grease top. Cover and let rise in a warm place until doubled, about 1 hour. Punch dough down. Sprinkle cornmeal into a greased 14-in. pizza pan. Press dough onto the bottom and up the sides of the pan. Brush with oil. Bake at 350° for 18-20 minutes. Spread spaghetti sauce over crust. Top with beef and cheese. Bake 10-15 minutes longer or until the crust is golden and the cheese is melted. **Yield:** 4-6 servings.

HELPFUL HINT:

For a crispy pizza crust, sprinkle a thin layer of shredded cheese under the sauce and toppings. The bottom layer of cheese serves as a buffer between the crust and moist toppings.

BISCUIT PIZZAS

1 pound ground beef
1 small onion, chopped
1/2 teaspoon garlic salt
2 tubes (7-1/2 ounces *each*) refrigerated biscuits
1 can (15 ounces) pizza sauce
1/4 cup grated Parmesan cheese, *divided*
1 can (4 ounces) mushroom stems and pieces, drained
1 cup (4 ounces) shredded mozzarella cheese

In a skillet, cook beef, onion and garlic salt over medium heat until meat is no longer pink; drain. Separate biscuits. Place 3 in. apart on greased baking sheets; flatten into 3-in. circles. Spread each with pizza sauce. Sprinkle with half of the Parmesan cheese. Top with meat mixture and mushrooms. Sprinkle with mozzarella and remaining Parmesan cheese. Bake at 400° for 10-12 minutes or until cheese is melted. **Yield:** 4-6 servings.

BEEF 'N' VEGGIE CHEDDAR PIE

2 tablespoons all-purpose
  flour
1 can (10-3/4 ounces)
  condensed tomato soup,
  undiluted
1/4 cup water
1-1/2 pounds ground beef,
  cooked and drained
3 medium potatoes, peeled,
  cubed and cooked
2 cups frozen diced carrots,
  thawed
1 medium onion, chopped
CRUST:
1 cup all-purpose flour
1/2 teaspoon salt
1/3 cup shortening
1/2 cup shredded cheddar
  cheese
2 to 3 tablespoons cold
  water

In a bowl, combine flour, soup and water until smooth. Stir in the beef, potatoes, carrots and onion. Spoon into an ungreased 13-in. x 9-in. x 2-in. baking dish. For crust, combine flour and salt in a bowl. Cut in shortening until mixture resembles coarse crumbs. Add cheese and mix well. Gradually add water, tossing with a fork until a ball forms. On a lightly floured surface, roll dough to fit top of baking dish. Place over filling; seal and flute edges. Cut slits in top. Bake at 425° for 35 minutes or until golden brown. Let stand 10 minutes before cutting. **Yield:** 6-8 servings.

I usually save leftover vegetables in the freezer specifically to use in this pie. My husband and son really like the hearty filling and cheesy crust.
—Lonna Hocker
Olympia, Washington

PERFECT PARTNERS:

A simple dessert is the fitting finale to a meal of Beef 'n' Veggie Cheddar Pie. Saute apple slices in butter and brown sugar until tender. Spoon into small bowls; sprinkle with chopped nuts and a dash of nutmeg.

NUTTY BEEF TURNOVERS

1 pound ground beef
1-1/2 cups chopped nuts
1 medium onion, chopped
2 garlic cloves, minced
1 tablespoon Worcestershire
  sauce
2 teaspoons sugar
1/4 teaspoon ground cinnamon
2 loaves (1 pound *each*)
  frozen bread dough,
  thawed

In a skillet, cook beef, nuts, onion and garlic over medium heat until meat is no longer pink; drain. Remove from the heat. Stir in the Worcestershire sauce, sugar and cinnamon. On a floured surface, roll each portion of dough into a 12-in. square. Cut each into four squares. Place about 1/4 cup meat mixture in center of each square. Moisten edges of pastry with water; fold over filling, forming a triangle. Press edges with a fork to seal. Place on ungreased baking sheets. Bake at 350° for 20 minutes or until golden brown. **Yield:** 8 servings.

With crunchy nuts and a touch of cinnamon, these turnovers tantalize taste buds. I make them for appetizers as well as for lunch and dinner.
—Jim McLean
Roseau, Minnesota

My family devours this crusty pan pizza with delicious toppings. Use a combination of green, red and yellow peppers for added color.
—Patricia Howson
Carstairs, Alberta

DEEP-DISH PIZZA
(Pictured at right)

1 package (1/4 ounce) active dry yeast
1 cup warm water (110° to 115°)
1 teaspoon sugar
1 teaspoon salt
2 tablespoons vegetable oil
2-1/2 cups all-purpose flour
1 pound ground beef, cooked and drained
1 can (10-3/4 ounces) condensed tomato soup, undiluted
1 teaspoon *each* dried basil, oregano and thyme
1 teaspoon dried rosemary, crushed
1/4 teaspoon garlic powder
1 small green pepper, julienned
1 can (8 ounces) mushroom stems and pieces, drained
1 cup (4 ounces) shredded mozzarella cheese

In a bowl, dissolve yeast in water. Stir in sugar, salt, oil and flour. Beat vigorously 20 strokes. Cover and let rest for 20 minutes. On a floured surface, roll into a 13-in. x 9-in. rectangle. Transfer to a greased 13-in. x 9-in. x 2-in. baking pan. Sprinkle with beef. Combine soup and seasonings; spoon over beef. Top with green pepper, mushrooms and cheese. Bake at 425° for 20-25 minutes or until crust and cheese are lightly browned. **Yield:** 8 servings.

Instead of using a pastry crust, this recipe creates a savory crust with mashed potatoes. The bacon flavor in the filling is fabulous! I think you and your family will love this pleasing pie.
—Chris Eschweiler
Dallas, Texas

SHEPHERD'S PIE
(Pictured at right)

1 pound ground beef
3 bacon strips, diced
1 small onion, chopped
2 garlic cloves, minced
1/4 teaspoon dried oregano
1/2 cup tomato sauce
1 can (2-1/4 ounces) chopped ripe olives, drained
5-1/2 cups hot mashed potatoes (prepared without milk and butter)
2 eggs, beaten
2 tablespoons butter *or* margarine, softened
1 tablespoon minced fresh cilantro *or* parsley
1/4 teaspoon salt
Additional butter *or* margarine, melted

In a skillet, cook beef over medium heat until no longer pink; drain and set aside. In the same skillet, cook bacon, onion, garlic and oregano until bacon is crisp. Stir in tomato sauce, olives and beef. Simmer for 10 minutes. Meanwhile, combine mashed potatoes, eggs, butter, cilantro and salt; mix well. Spread half of the potato mixture onto the bottom and up the sides of a greased 9-in. pie plate. Top with beef mixture and remaining potato mixture. Bake at 375° for 20 minutes. Brush with melted butter. Bake 10 minutes longer or until golden brown. **Yield:** 6-8 servings.

DEEP-DISH PIZZA
SHEPHERD'S PIE

The ingredients for this recipe can always be found in my kitchen for last-minute meals or snacks. Our two young boys like to personalize their own pizzas with different toppings.
—Rachel DeVault
Grove City, Ohio

KID-SIZE PIZZAS
(Pictured below)

1 package (12 ounces) English muffins, split and toasted
1 jar (14 ounces) pizza sauce
1 pound ground beef, cooked and drained
2 cups (8 ounces) shredded mozzarella cheese

Place muffins on an ungreased baking sheet. Spread with pizza sauce. Sprinkle with the beef and cheese. Bake at 425° for 5 minutes or until cheese is melted. **Yield:** 12 servings.

TIMELY TIP:

Since Kid-Size Pizzas can be microwaved instead of baked to melt the cheese, it's easy for older children to make these quick and easy treats by themselves.

GREEN BEAN BURGER PIE

1 pound ground beef, cooked
  and drained
2 cups fresh *or* frozen cut
  green beans, thawed
1 can (10-3/4 ounces)
  condensed tomato soup,
  undiluted
1 tablespoon sugar
1 teaspoon salt
1/2 teaspoon onion powder
1/4 teaspoon pepper
Dash dried oregano
Pastry for double-crust pie
  (9 inches)

In a bowl, combine the first eight ingredients; mix well. Line a 9-in. pie plate with bottom pastry; add filling. Roll out remaining pastry to fit top of pie. Place over filling; seal and flute edges. Cut slits in top. Bake at 400° for 25 minutes or until crust is golden brown. **Yield:** 4-6 servings.

HELPFUL HINT:
When selecting fresh green beans, look for those that are brightly colored, unblemished and firm. Store unwashed beans in a sealed plastic bag in the refrigerator for up to 3 days. Before using, snap off the stem end and rinse in cold water.

SAVORY TRIANGLES

1 pound ground beef
1 large tomato, seeded and
  chopped
1/2 cup thinly sliced green
  onions
1 garlic clove, minced
1/2 teaspoon salt
1/2 teaspoon crushed red
  pepper flakes
1/2 teaspoon dried thyme
2 teaspoons cornstarch
2/3 cup beef broth
Pastry for double-crust pie
  (9 inches)
1 egg, beaten

In a skillet, cook beef, tomato, onions and garlic over medium heat until meat is no longer pink; drain. Stir in salt, red pepper flakes and thyme. In a small bowl, combine cornstarch and broth until smooth. Add to meat mixture. Bring to a boil; cook and stir for 2 minutes or until thickened. Remove from the heat. On a floured surface, roll pastry into two 12-in. squares. Cut each into four squares. Spoon about 1/4 cup meat mixture in the center of each square. Moisten edges of pastry with egg; fold over filling, forming a triangle. Press edges with a fork to seal. Place on ungreased baking sheets; prick tops with a fork. Bake at 425° for 10-15 minutes or until golden brown. **Yield:** 8 servings.

SERVING SUGGESTION:
If you're making homemade pie pastry for Savory Triangles, stir in a little curry powder for added flavor.

I've depended on this recipe since my college roommate shared it with me more than 25 years ago. People are always pleasantly surprised by the unusual combination of ingredients.
—Elizabeth Andrews
Mt. Laurel, New Jersey

I learned to cook by watching my mom and helping when I could. She still teaches me by sharing tried-and-true recipes like this.
—Holly Massie
Pearce, Arizona

YORKSHIRE PIE

3/4 pound ground beef
1 small onion, thinly sliced
1/2 cup canned mixed vegetables, drained
1 can (10-1/4 ounces) beef gravy, *divided*
1 tablespoon butter *or* margarine
1 cup milk
2 eggs
1 cup all-purpose flour
1/4 teaspoon salt
1/8 teaspoon pepper
1/2 cup water
1 tablespoon Worcestershire sauce

In a skillet, cook beef and onion over medium heat until meat is no longer pink; drain. Add vegetables and 1/4 cup of gravy; set aside. Place butter in a 10-in. pie plate and place in a 425° oven until melted. In a mixing bowl, beat milk and eggs. Add flour, salt and pepper; mix until smooth. Pour into prepared pie plate. Spoon meat mixture to within 1 in. of edge. Bake for 30-35 minutes or until edges are puffed and a knife inserted near the center comes out clean. Meanwhile, in a saucepan, heat water, Worcestershire sauce and remaining gravy. Serve with the pie. **Yield:** 4 servings.

HELPFUL HINT:

To easily slice an onion thinly, leave the root intact to serve as a "handle". Cut a thin slice off the bottom of the onion so it sits flat on a cutting board and doesn't roll around.

COTTAGE POTPIE

1 large onion, chopped
2 medium carrots, chopped
2 garlic cloves, minced
1 can (14-1/2 ounces) beef broth
1-1/2 pounds ground beef
1 can (8 ounces) tomato sauce
1 teaspoon salt
1/2 teaspoon pepper
1/2 teaspoon *each* dried oregano, thyme and parsley flakes
1/2 teaspoon dried rosemary, crushed
1/2 teaspoon rubbed sage
2 cups hot mashed potatoes (prepared with milk and butter)

In a saucepan, combine onion, carrots, garlic and broth. Bring to a boil. Reduce heat; cover and simmer for 20 minutes or until vegetables are tender. Drain, reserving liquid to make gravy if desired. In a skillet, cook beef over medium heat until no longer pink; drain. Add tomato sauce and seasonings; bring to a boil. Reduce heat; cover and simmer for 15 minutes. Add reserved vegetables and mix well. Transfer to a greased 2-qt. baking dish. Top with mashed potatoes. Bake, uncovered, at 350° for 30 minutes or until potatoes are lightly browned. If desired, make gravy with reserved vegetable liquid; serve with potpie. **Yield:** 6 servings.

SPAGHETTI PIZZA

(Pictured above)

2 eggs
1 cup milk
1 package (16 ounces) spaghetti, cooked and drained
1 pound ground beef, cooked and drained
1 jar (28 ounces) spaghetti sauce
1 package (3-1/2 ounces) sliced pepperoni
1 can (4 ounces) mushroom stems and pieces, drained
1/4 cup chopped onion
Garlic salt to taste
2 cups (8 ounces) shredded mozzarella cheese
1 cup (4 ounces) shredded cheddar cheese

In a large bowl, beat the eggs and milk. Add spaghetti; toss to coat. Transfer to a greased 13-in. x 9-in. x 2-in. baking dish. Top with beef, spaghetti sauce, pepperoni, mushrooms and onion. Sprinkle with garlic salt. Bake, uncovered, at 350° for 20 minutes. Sprinkle with cheeses. Bake 10 minutes longer or until cheese is melted. Let stand 15 minutes before cutting. **Yield:** 8 servings.

I got this recipe from a local radio cooking program. It's easy to assemble and features traditional pizza ingredients over a unique noodle "crust". Get ready to dish out the recipe!
—Shelly Ryun
Malvern, Iowa

SERVING SUGGESTIONS:

For added flavor and color, add some sweet red pepper strips and sliced ripe olives to Spaghetti Pizza.

HASH BROWN PIZZA

1 package (26 ounces) frozen shredded hash brown potatoes, thawed
1 can (10-3/4 ounces) condensed cheddar cheese soup, undiluted
1 egg
1 teaspoon salt
1/2 teaspoon pepper
TOPPING:
1 pound ground beef
1 medium onion, chopped
2 tablespoons all-purpose flour
1 can (10-3/4 ounces) condensed tomato soup, undiluted
1/2 teaspoon salt
1/4 teaspoon garlic powder
1/8 teaspoon pepper
2 cups (8 ounces) shredded cheddar cheese, *divided*

In a large bowl, combine the first five ingredients; mix well. Press firmly into a greased 12-in. pizza pan. Bake at 450° for 20-25 minutes. Meanwhile, in a skillet, cook beef and onion over medium heat until the meat is no longer pink; drain. Stir in flour until blended. Add soup, salt, garlic powder and pepper. Bring to a boil; cook and stir for 2 minutes. Sprinkle crust with 1 cup cheese. Top with beef mixture and remaining cheese. Bake 5 minutes longer or until cheese is melted. Let stand 5-10 minutes before slicing. **Yield:** 4-6 servings.

SERVING SUGGESTIONS:

For a boost of color and flavor, add 1 cup chopped tomatoes or green pepper (or a combination of the two) to the filling for Hash Brown Pizza.

BEEFY BROCCOLI PIE

1 pound ground beef
1/4 cup chopped onion
1 package (10 ounces) frozen cut broccoli, cooked and drained
1 can (10-3/4 ounces) condensed cream of mushroom soup, undiluted
2 tubes (8 ounces *each*) refrigerated crescent rolls, *divided*
2 cups (8 ounces) shredded cheddar cheese

In a skillet, cook beef and onion over medium heat until meat is no longer pink; drain. Add broccoli and soup; mix well. Unroll one tube of crescent rolls. Press into a greased 13-in. x 9-in. x 2-in. baking pan. Seal seams and perforations. Top with meat mixture. Sprinkle with cheese. Unroll remaining crescent dough and place over meat mixture; seal seams and perforations. Bake, uncovered, at 350° for 25 minutes or until golden brown. **Yield:** 6-8 servings.

CAULIFLOWER BEEF QUICHE

**Pastry for single-crust pie
(10 inches)**
  1 **cup (4 ounces) shredded
    cheddar cheese,** *divided*
  1 **pound ground beef**
  1 **celery rib, chopped**
  1 **medium onion, chopped**
  2 **cups fresh** *or* **frozen
    cauliflowerets, cooked and
    drained**
  4 **eggs**
1-1/2 **cups evaporated milk**
  1 **tablespoon butter** *or*
    margarine, melted
Dash *each* **paprika and pepper**
Grated Parmesan cheese

On a floured surface, roll out pastry to fit a 10-in. pie plate. Line pie plate with pastry; flute edges. Line unpricked pastry shell with a double thickness of heavy duty foil. Bake at 375° for 5-8 minutes or until light golden brown. Remove foil. Sprinkle 1/2 cup cheese over crust. In a skillet, cook the beef, celery and onion over medium heat until meat is no longer pink and vegetables are tender; drain. Spoon half of the meat mixture into the crust; top with cauliflower and the remaining meat mixture and cheddar cheese. In a bowl, beat eggs, milk, butter, paprika and pepper. Pour over the filling. Sprinkle with Parmesan cheese. Bake at 375° for 15 minutes. Cover edges with foil. Bake 30-40 minutes longer or until a knife inserted near the center comes out clean. Let stand 15 minutes before cutting. **Yield:** 8 servings.

TESTING BAKED EGG DISHES FOR DONENESS

Egg dishes are tested for doneness by inserting a knife near the center of the dish. If the knife comes out clean, the eggs are cooked.

HELPFUL HINT:
A 1-1/2-pound head of cauliflower yields about 3 cups florets.

HAMBURGER PIE

1/2 **pound ground beef, cooked
    and drained**
3/4 **cup chopped celery**
3/4 **cup chopped onion**
2/3 **cup condensed tomato
    soup, undiluted**
1/4 **cup chopped green pepper**
1/2 **teaspoon salt**
  2 **cups biscuit/baking mix**
2/3 **cup milk**

In a bowl, combine the first six ingredients; mix well and set aside. In another bowl, toss baking mix and milk until a soft dough forms. On a floured surface, roll out the dough to fit a 9-in. pie plate. Line ungreased pie plate with pastry. Fill with meat mixture; trim and flute edges. Bake at 375° for 15 minutes or until crust is golden brown. **Yield:** 4-6 servings.

MEAT AND POTATO PIE
(Pictured above and on page 256)

When I was working full-time, this hearty pie was a favorite of my family. Now that I'm retired, I still rely on this sure-to-please recipe.
—Helen Ellingson
Swan River, Manitoba

2 tablespoons shortening
1-1/2 cups biscuit/baking mix
3 to 4 tablespoons cold water
FILLING:
1-1/2 pounds ground beef
1 medium onion, chopped
1 can (10-3/4 ounces) condensed cream of mushroom soup, undiluted
1/2 teaspoon salt
1/2 teaspoon dried rosemary, crushed
1/2 teaspoon dried thyme
1 can (15 ounces) sliced carrots, drained
1 can (8 ounces) mushroom stems and pieces, drained
2 cups hot mashed potatoes (prepared with milk and butter)
1/2 cup sour cream
1/2 cup shredded cheddar cheese

In a bowl, cut shortening into biscuit mix until the mixture resembles coarse crumbs. Add water, 1 tablespoon at a time, tossing lightly with a fork until dough forms a ball. On a lightly floured surface, roll out pastry to fit a 9-in. pie plate. Line ungreased pie plate with pastry; trim and flute edges or make a decorative edge. Set aside. In a skillet, cook beef and onion over medium heat until meat is no longer pink; drain. Stir in soup and seasonings; bring to a boil. Reduce heat; simmer, uncovered, for 5 minutes. Pour into pie shell. Top with carrots and mushrooms. Combine potatoes and sour cream; spread over pie. Bake, uncovered, at 425° for 15 minutes. Reduce heat to 350°. Bake 15 minutes longer or until golden brown. Sprinkle with cheese; let stand for 5-10 minutes. **Yield:** 6 servings.

MAKING A DECORATIVE PIE EDGE

With kitchen shears or a knife, trim pastry even with edge of pie plate. Use a "C" alphabet cookie cutter, small biscuit cutter or open end of pastry tip to make a decorative edge.

PERFECT PRONTO PIZZA

1 loaf (1 pound) frozen bread dough, thawed
1 can (6 ounces) tomato paste
1/4 cup water
1/4 teaspoon garlic powder
1/4 teaspoon dried oregano
1/4 teaspoon dried rosemary, crushed
1 pound ground beef, cooked and drained
1 cup (4 ounces) shredded cheddar cheese
1/2 cup shredded mozzarella cheese

Roll dough into a 13-in. circle. Press onto the bottom and up the sides of a greased 12-in. pizza pan. Bake at 350° for 5-10 minutes. In a bowl, combine the tomato paste, water, garlic powder, oregano and rosemary. Spread over crust. Top with beef and cheeses. Bake 10-15 minutes longer or until the crust is golden and cheese is melted. **Yield:** 4-6 servings.

This traditional pizza is just the right size for our family of five. The combination of cheddar and mozzarella cheeses and blend of herbs are terrific.
—Deb Virgl
Mead, Nebraska

COUNTRY OVEN OMELET

1 large onion, chopped, *divided*
3 tablespoons vegetable oil
3-1/2 cups frozen shredded hash brown potatoes
1-1/2 teaspoons salt, *divided*
1/2 teaspoon pepper, *divided*
1 pound ground beef
1/4 cup chopped green pepper
1/4 cup chopped sweet red pepper
1 tablespoon dried parsley flakes
1 cup (4 ounces) shredded Swiss *or* mozzarella cheese
4 eggs
1-1/4 cups milk
1/4 teaspoon paprika

In a skillet, saute 1/2 cup onion in oil. Add hash browns, 3/4 teaspoon salt and 1/4 teaspoon pepper. Cook over medium heat for 5 minutes or until hash browns are thawed. Press mixture into an ungreased 10-in. pie plate, forming a shell. Bake at 400° for 20 minutes. Meanwhile, in a skillet, cook the beef, peppers and remaining onion over medium heat until meat is no longer pink; drain. Stir in parsley. Spoon into the potato shell. Sprinkle with cheese. In a bowl, beat eggs, milk, paprika and remaining salt and pepper; pour over meat mixture. Bake at 400° for 30 minutes or until a knife inserted near the center comes out clean. Let stand 5 minutes before cutting. **Yield:** 4-6 servings.

I love to make this scrumptious pie on weekends when my husband and I have time to enjoy every savory bite. Green and red peppers add color and flavor.
—Kim Pettipas
Halifax, Nova Scotia

HELPFUL HINT:

When making Country Oven Omelet, transfer the hash browns from the skillet to the pie plate with a large spoon. Then use the back of the spoon to press the hash browns onto the bottom and up the sides of the plate.

SALSA TORTILLA PIZZAS

1 pound ground beef
1 small green pepper, thinly sliced
1 cup salsa
4 green onions, thinly sliced
1/4 cup minced fresh cilantro *or* parsley
1 teaspoon ground cumin
4 flour tortillas (10 inches)
1 cup (4 ounces) shredded Monterey Jack cheese
2/3 cup shredded cheddar cheese
2 tablespoons grated Parmesan cheese

In a skillet, cook beef and green pepper over medium heat until meat is no longer pink; drain. Stir in the salsa, onions, cilantro and cumin. Remove from the heat. Place tortillas on greased baking sheets. Combine Monterey Jack and cheddar cheeses; sprinkle 1/4 cup over tortillas. Top with beef mixture, remaining cheese mixture and the Parmesan cheese. Bake at 400° for 8-10 minutes or until golden brown. **Yield:** 4 servings.

SIMPLE SUBSTITUTION:

Cilantro gives a distinctive flavor to dishes. If you don't care for the taste, reduce the amount called for in a recipe or use more mild parsley instead.

ASPARAGUS PIE

1 pound ground beef
1 cup cut fresh asparagus (1/2-inch pieces)
1 medium onion, chopped
1 cup (4 ounces) shredded cheddar cheese
1 teaspoon salt
1/4 teaspoon pepper
2 eggs
1 cup milk
1/2 cup biscuit/baking mix

In a skillet, cook beef, asparagus and onion over medium heat until meat is no longer pink and asparagus is tender; drain. Remove from the heat; stir in cheese. Transfer to a greased 10-in. pie plate. Sprinkle with salt and pepper. In a mixing bowl, beat eggs, milk and biscuit mix until smooth. Pour over meat mixture. Bake at 400° for 35-40 minutes or until a knife inserted near the center comes out clean. Let stand 5 minutes before cutting. **Yield:** 4-6 servings.

HELPFUL HINT:

Purchase asparagus with slender light green stalks and tightly closed buds. Peak months are April and May. One pound (about 14 spears) yields about 2 cups cut asparagus.

REFRIED BEAN PIZZA

(Pictured below)

1-1/2 cups biscuit/baking mix
1/2 cup cornmeal
1/2 cup cold water
1 pound ground beef
3/4 cup water
1 can (4 ounces) chopped green chilies
1 envelope taco seasoning
1 can (16 ounces) refried beans
1-1/2 cups (6 ounces) shredded cheddar cheese
1 cup shredded lettuce
2 medium tomatoes, chopped
1 medium onion, chopped

In a bowl, combine biscuit mix and cornmeal. Add water and mix well. Press onto the bottom and up the sides of a greased 12-in. pizza pan. Bake at 400° for 10 minutes or until edges are lightly browned. Cool. Meanwhile, in a skillet, cook beef over medium heat until no longer pink; drain. Stir in the water, chilies and taco seasoning; bring to a boil. Simmer, uncovered, for 5 minutes. Spread beans over crust. Top with beef mixture. Sprinkle with cheese. Bake at 400° for 10 minutes or until the crust is golden and cheese is melted. Top with lettuce, tomato and onion. **Yield:** 4-6 servings.

HELPFUL HINT:

Store cornmeal in an airtight container in a cool dry place for up to 6 months. To keep cornmeal for up to 1 year, store it in the refrigerator or freezer.

Instead of a tomato sauce, refried beans serve as the base for this Southwestern-style pizza. The cool vegetable toppings complement each oven-fresh bite.
—Lydia Ann Lantz
Christiana,
Pennsylvania

SOUTHWESTERN DEEP-DISH PIZZA

2-1/2 cups biscuit/baking mix
1/2 cup cornmeal
3/4 cup water
1 pound ground beef
1 medium onion, diced
1 can (8 ounces) tomato sauce
2 teaspoons chili powder
1 teaspoon ground cinnamon
1 can (16 ounces) refried beans
Hot pepper sauce to taste
2 cups (8 ounces) shredded Monterey Jack *or* cheddar cheese
Salsa and sliced ripe olives, optional

In a bowl, combine biscuit mix and cornmeal. Stir in water until mixture forms a soft dough. Press onto the bottom and up the sides of a lightly greased 15-in. x 10-in. x 1-in. baking pan. Bake at 425° for 10 minutes or until lightly browned. Meanwhile, in a skillet, cook beef and onion over medium heat until meat is no longer pink; drain. Add the tomato sauce, chili powder and cinnamon. Bring to a boil. Reduce heat; simmer, uncovered, for 5 minutes. Remove from the heat. Combine refried beans and hot pepper sauce; spread over crust. Top with meat mixture; sprinkle with cheese. Bake at 425° for 10 minutes or until cheese is melted. Let stand 10 minutes before cutting. Serve with salsa and olives if desired. **Yield:** 16 servings.

HERBED PASTIES

1-1/2 pounds ground beef
1 medium onion, chopped
2 beef bouillon cubes
1/4 cup boiling water
1-1/2 cups (6 ounces) shredded cheddar cheese
1 cup sliced fresh mushrooms
1 celery rib, diced
1/4 cup grated Parmesan cheese
3/4 teaspoon dill weed
3/4 teaspoon dried thyme
1/2 teaspoon dried rosemary, crushed
Salt and pepper to taste
2 packages (11 ounces *each*) pie crust mix
1 egg
1 tablespoon water

In a skillet, cook beef and onion until meat is no longer pink; drain well. Dissolve bouillon in water; stir into meat mixture. Add the cheddar cheese, mushrooms, celery, Parmesan cheese and seasonings; mix well. Prepare pie crusts according to package directions. Divide dough into four portions. On a floured surface, roll each into a 14-in. square. Cut each into four 7-in. squares. Place a scant 1/2 cup meat mixture in the center of each square. Moisten edges of pastry with water and fold over filling, forming a triangle. Press edges with a fork to seal. Make a 1-in. slit in the top of each triangle. Place on two ungreased baking sheets. Beat egg and water; brush over pastry. Bake at 375° for 30-35 minutes or until golden brown. **Yield:** 16 servings.

TACO TWISTS

1 pound ground beef
1 large onion, chopped
2 cups (8 ounces) shredded
  cheddar cheese
1 jar (8 ounces) salsa
1 can (4 ounces) chopped
  green chilies
1 teaspoon garlic powder
1/2 teaspoon hot pepper sauce
1/4 teaspoon salt
1/4 teaspoon ground cumin
3 tubes (8 ounces *each*)
  refrigerated crescent rolls

In a skillet, cook beef and onion over medium heat until the meat is no longer pink; drain. Add the cheese, salsa, chilies, garlic powder, hot pepper sauce, salt and cumin; mix well. Unroll crescent roll dough and separate into 12 rectangles. Place on ungreased baking sheets; press perforations to seal. Place 1/2 cup meat mixture in the center of each rectangle. Bring four corners to the center and twist; pinch to seal. Bake at 350° for 25-30 minutes or until golden brown. **Yield:** 12 servings.

FORMING TACO TWISTS

Place meat mixture in center of rectangle. Bring all four corners of pastry over filling to the center and twist together. Pinch to seal.

TIMELY TIP:

You can freeze baked Taco Twists for up to 3 months in a heavy-duty resealable plastic bag. Reheat frozen twists on a baking sheet at 350° for 20 to 25 minutes or until heated through.

CRESCENT BEEF BAKE

2 pounds ground beef
1 small onion, chopped
1 jar (14 ounces) spaghetti
  sauce
2 cups (8 ounces) shredded
  cheddar cheese
2 cups (8 ounces) shredded
  mozzarella cheese
2 tubes (8 ounces *each*)
  refrigerated crescent rolls
1 cup (8 ounces) sour cream

In a skillet, cook beef and onion over medium heat until meat is no longer pink; drain. Stir in spaghetti sauce. Transfer to a greased 13-in. x 9-in. x 2-in. baking dish. Sprinkle with cheeses. Unroll crescent rolls and separate into triangles; spread with sour cream. Roll into crescents. Place in two rows over cheese. Bake, uncovered, at 350° for 35 minutes or until golden brown. **Yield:** 8 servings.

SPEEDY BEEF PASTIES

1 pound ground beef
1/4 cup chopped onion
1 can (8 ounces) diced carrots, drained
1 medium potato, peeled and shredded
1 cup (4 ounces) shredded cheddar cheese
1/4 cup ketchup
1 tablespoon prepared mustard
1/2 teaspoon garlic salt
1/4 teaspoon pepper
2 packages (11 ounces *each*) pie crust mix

In a skillet, cook beef and onion over medium heat until meat is no longer pink; drain. Remove from the heat. Stir in carrots, potato, cheese, ketchup, mustard, garlic salt and pepper. Prepare pie crusts according to package directions. On a floured surface, roll each portion into a 12-in. square. Cut each into four squares. Place about 1/2 cup meat mixture in the center of each square. Moisten edges of pastry with water and fold over filling, forming a triangle. Press edges with a fork to seal; prick tops with a fork. Place on ungreased baking sheets. Bake at 375° for 30 minutes or until golden brown. **Yield:** 8 servings.

SAUCY SCALLOPED PIE

1 package (5-1/4 ounces) cheesy scalloped potatoes
1 bottle (12 ounces) chili sauce
1 tablespoon Italian seasoning
1/2 cup dry bread crumbs
1/4 cup chopped onion
1 garlic clove, minced
1 pound ground beef
1 can (8 ounces) mushroom stems and pieces, drained
2 tablespoons grated Parmesan cheese

Prepare the scalloped potatoes according to package directions. Meanwhile, in a bowl, combine chili sauce and Italian seasoning. In another bowl, combine bread crumbs, onion, garlic and 1 cup chili sauce mixture. Crumble beef over mixture and mix well. Press onto the bottom and up the sides of an ungreased 9-in. pie plate. Bake at 350° for 15 minutes; drain. Add mushrooms and Parmesan cheese to scalloped potatoes; mix well. Spoon into meat shell. Bake for 10 minutes or until potatoes are golden brown. Heat the remaining chili sauce mixture; spoon over individual servings. **Yield:** 4 servings.

SIMPLE SUBSTITUTION:

Out of chili sauce? Combine 1-1/2 cups tomato sauce, 1/2 to 3/4 cup sugar and 3 tablespoons vinegar, and use in place of a 12-ounce bottle.

VEGETABLE BEEF PIE

(Pictured above)

**Pastry for double-crust pie
  (9 inches)**
  **1 pound ground beef, cooked
    and drained**
  **1 can (16 ounces) mixed
    vegetables, drained
    or 1-1/2 cups frozen mixed
    vegetables**
  **1 can (10-3/4 ounces)
    condensed cream of onion
    soup, undiluted**
  1/2 teaspoon pepper

Line a 9-in. pie plate with bottom pastry. In a bowl, combine beef, vegetables, soup and pepper; mix well. Spoon into crust. Roll out the remaining pastry to fit top of pie. Place over filling; trim, seal and flute edges. Cut slits in top. Bake at 400° for 30-35 minutes or until crust is golden brown. **Yield:** 4-6 servings.

TIMELY TIP:

Prepare two Vegetable Beef Pies. Bake and enjoy one now and freeze the other unbaked pie for later. When ready to use, thaw in the refrigerator overnight and bake as directed.

*Like most country folks, I have busy days, so I depend on easy recipes that also taste great. This simple meat pie originally called for homemade crust, but I use purchased pastry to save time.
—Valorie Hall Walker Bradley, South Carolina*

MEXICAN MAIN DISHES

Family and friends won't give you any heat for trying new recipes when mouth-watering Mexican dishes are the featured fare. Add a little spice to your dinner table with tacos, burritos, enchiladas and more!

BEEF AND BEAN CHIMICHANGAS (P. 303)

BURRITO BAKE (P. 288)
GREEN CHILI FLAUTAS (P. 288)
TEXAS-STYLE SKILLET (P. 289)

BURRITO BAKE
(Pictured on page 287)

1 pound ground beef
1 can (16 ounces) refried beans
1/4 cup chopped onion
1 envelope taco seasoning
1 tube (8 ounces) refrigerated crescent rolls
2 cups (8 ounces) shredded cheddar cheese
2 cups (8 ounces) shredded mozzarella cheese
Toppings: chopped green pepper, shredded lettuce, chopped tomatoes, sliced ripe olives

In a skillet, cook beef over medium heat until no longer pink; drain. Add the beans, onion and taco seasoning. Unroll crescent roll dough. Press onto the bottom and up the sides of a greased 13-in. x 9-in. x 2-in. baking dish; seal seams and perforations. Spread beef mixture over crust; sprinkle with cheeses. Bake, uncovered, at 350° for 30 minutes or until golden brown. Sprinkle with toppings of your choice. **Yield:** 6 servings.

GREEN CHILI FLAUTAS
(Pictured on page 287)

1-1/2 pounds ground beef
1 cup (4 ounces) shredded cheddar cheese
1 can (4 ounces) chopped green chilies, drained
1/2 teaspoon ground cumin
10 flour tortillas (7 inches)
1/3 cup butter *or* margarine, melted, *divided*
Toppings: shredded lettuce, guacamole, salsa, sour cream

In a skillet, cook beef over medium heat until no longer pink; drain. Add the cheese, chilies and cumin; set aside. Warm the tortillas; brush both sides with some of the butter. Spoon about 1/3 cup beef mixture down the center of each tortilla. Roll up tightly; place seam side down in a greased 13-in. x 9-in. x 2-in. baking pan. Bake, uncovered, at 500° for 5-7 minutes or until golden brown, brushing once with remaining butter. Serve with toppings of your choice. **Yield:** 10 flautas.

TIMELY TIP:

To quickly warm flour tortillas, place unwrapped tortillas on a microwave-safe plate and cover with a paper towel. Microwave on high for 30 to 60 seconds or until warm.

CORNY TACOS

2 pounds ground beef
1 can (8-1/2 ounces) cream-
　style corn
1 can (8 ounces) tomato
　sauce
1 cup milk
1 can (6 ounces) ripe olives,
　drained and chopped
1/3 cup cornmeal
1/4 teaspoon salt
Chili powder to taste
　20 taco shells
Toppings: shredded cheddar
　cheese, shredded lettuce,
　chopped tomatoes

In a skillet, cook beef over medium heat until no longer pink; drain. Add the corn, tomato sauce, milk, olives, cornmeal, salt and chili powder. Transfer to a greased 11-in. x 7-in. x 2-in. baking dish. Bake, uncovered, at 350° for 30 minutes or until heated through. Spoon about 1/4 cupful into each taco shell. Serve with toppings of your choice. **Yield:** 20 tacos.

My mother received this recipe from a friend in Texas. Unlike ordinary taco fillings, this one-of-a-kind version is baked and includes corn and olives.
—Mary Lannen
Milan, Illinois

TEXAS-STYLE SKILLET

(Pictured on page 287)

1 pound ground beef
1 medium onion, diced
4 garlic cloves, minced
1 can (15 ounces) pinto
　beans, undrained
1 can (14-1/2 ounces) diced
　tomatoes, undrained
2 cans (4 ounces *each*)
　chopped green chilies
1/2 cup uncooked long grain
　rice
1/2 cup water
1 to 2 tablespoons chili
　powder
2 teaspoons dried cilantro *or*
　parsley flakes
1 teaspoon salt
1 teaspoon ground cumin

Toppings: shredded cheddar
　cheese, salsa, minced fresh
　cilantro
Tortilla chips

In a skillet, cook beef, onion and garlic over medium heat until the meat is no longer pink; drain. Add the beans, tomatoes, chilies, rice, water and seasonings; mix well. Bring to a boil. Reduce heat; cover and simmer for 25 minutes, stirring occasionally. Serve in the skillet or transfer to a shallow serving dish. Sprinkle with toppings of your choice. Serve with tortilla chips. **Yield:** 6 servings.

I grew up in Phoenix, and my husband is from Texas. When we lived in New York, we really missed Southwest-style food, so I created this recipe. It's been a staple through the years.
—Barbara Westbrook
Gainesville, Texas

SERVING SUGGESTION:

To make homemade tortilla chips, cut flour tortillas into wedges and place on a baking sheet. Spritz with nonstick cooking spray; sprinkle with chili powder and cayenne pepper. Bake at 375° for 7 to 10 minutes or until crisp and lightly browned. Cool; store in an airtight container.

Corn bread and cream-style corn add a touch of sweetness to this hearty casserole. I sometimes sprinkle crushed tortilla chips on top before baking.
—Kelley Enyeart
Marceline, Missouri

SOMBRERO CASSEROLE

1 pound ground beef
1 small onion, chopped
1 small green pepper, chopped
2 packages (8-1/2 ounces *each*) corn bread/muffin mix
1 can (14-3/4 ounces) cream-style corn
2 eggs
4 cups (16 ounces) shredded cheddar cheese, *divided*
1 cup picante sauce

In a skillet, cook beef, onion and green pepper over medium heat until meat is no longer pink; drain and set aside. In a bowl, combine corn bread mixes, corn and eggs; mix well. Spread half into a greased 13-in. x 9-in. x 2-in. baking dish. Top with the meat mixture, 3 cups of cheese and the picante sauce. Spread with remaining corn bread mixture; sprinkle with remaining cheese. Bake, uncovered, at 350° for 35-40 minutes or until a knife inserted near the center comes out clean. Let stand 5 minutes before serving. **Yield:** 6 servings.

HELPFUL HINT:

Although they're made with basically the same ingredients, picante sauce usually has a smoother texture and milder flavor than salsa.

Whenever I need a last-minute meal, this is the recipe I most often turn to. It calls for convenient frozen hash browns, so I don't have to spend my time peeling and dicing potatoes.
—Pauline Piggott
Northville, Michigan

SALSA HASH

1 pound ground beef
1 small onion, chopped
3 cups frozen O'Brien hash brown potatoes
1/2 teaspoon salt
1/4 teaspoon pepper
1 cup salsa
Sliced green onions and ripe olives, optional

In a skillet, cook beef and onion over medium heat until meat is no longer pink; drain. Add the potatoes, salt and pepper. Cook on high for 5 minutes, stirring occasionally. Stir in salsa. Cook 8-10 minutes longer or until potatoes are lightly browned, stirring occasionally. Garnish with onions and olives if desired. **Yield:** 4 servings.

PERFECT PARTNERS:

Drizzle fresh cubed melon with lime juice and honey. Serve as an easy, refreshing dessert with Salsa Hash.

CRISPY FRIED TACOS

(Pictured above)

SALSA:
- 1 can (28 ounces) diced tomatoes, undrained
- 1 can (8 ounces) tomato sauce
- 1 can (4 ounces) sliced jalapeno peppers
- 1 small onion, quartered
- 1 teaspoon garlic salt

TACOS:
- 1 pound ground beef
- 1/2 teaspoon salt
- 1/2 cup vegetable oil
- 12 corn tortillas (6 inches)
- 1 cup (4 ounces) shredded cheddar cheese
- 4 cups shredded lettuce

In a blender or food processor, combine the salsa ingredients; cover and pulse until salsa reaches desired consistency. Transfer to a bowl; cover and refrigerate. In a skillet, cook beef over medium heat until no longer pink; drain. Sprinkle with salt. In another skillet, heat oil. Fry tortillas just until softened; drain on paper towels. Fill tortillas with beef; sprinkle with cheese. Fold in half. In an ungreased skillet, fry tortillas on both sides until crisp. Serve with lettuce and salsa. **Yield:** 12 tacos.

My mother has been making these for more than 30 years. Frying the filled tacos makes them extra crispy and delicious. Our five grown sons request these whenever they visit.
—Catherine Gibbs
Gambrills, Maryland

CHEESY CHIMICHANGAS

1-1/2 pounds ground beef
   2 large onions, chopped
   2 teaspoons garlic salt
 1/2 teaspoon pepper
  12 flour tortillas (6 inches)
Vegetable oil
   1 jar (16 ounces) salsa, *divided*
   2 cups (8 ounces) shredded cheddar cheese, *divided*
   2 cups (8 ounces) shredded Monterey Jack cheese, *divided*
Shredded lettuce and chopped tomatoes
Sour cream and guacamole, optional

In a skillet, cook beef and onions over medium heat until meat is no longer pink; drain. Stir in garlic salt and pepper. Warm the tortillas; brush one side with oil. Spoon 1/4 cup beef mixture off-center on oiled side of tortillas. Top with 1 tablespoon each of salsa, cheddar cheese and Monterey Jack cheese. Fold up edge nearest filling; fold in both sides and roll up. Secure with toothpicks; place in a greased 13-in. x 9-in. x 2-in. baking dish. Brush with oil. Bake, uncovered, at 450° for 10-15 minutes or until lightly browned. Sprinkle with remaining cheeses. Bake 2-3 minutes longer or until cheese is melted. To serve, place chimichangas on a bed of lettuce and tomato. Top with remaining salsa and sour cream and guacamole if desired. **Yield:** 12 chimichangas.

TIMELY TIP:

Keep a batch of Cheesy Chimichangas in the freezer. Assemble as directed and freeze in an airtight container up to 3 months. Thaw in the refrigerator, brush with oil and bake as directed.

COLORFUL TACOS

   1 pound lean ground beef
  10 flour tortillas (8 inches)
Seasoned salt
   4 cups (16 ounces) shredded process American cheese
   1 cup shredded radishes
   1 large onion, finely chopped
   1 can (15 ounces) peas, drained and mashed
   1 can (14-1/2 ounces) diced tomatoes, drained
Hot pepper sauce to taste

Spread beef over half of each tortilla; sprinkle with seasoned salt. Fold tortillas over meat; press to seal. In a greased 10-in. skillet, brown tortillas in batches for 2-3 minutes on each side or until meat is no longer pink. Unfold tortillas. Top with cheese, radishes, onion, peas and tomatoes; fold up. Serve with hot pepper sauce. **Yield:** 10 tacos.

CHILI RELLENOS

2 cans (4 ounces *each*)
  chopped green chilies
1 pound ground beef, cooked
  and drained
4 cups (16 ounces) shredded
  cheddar cheese
1/2 cup all-purpose flour
1 teaspoon salt
2 eggs
2 cups milk

Sprinkle green chilies in a greased 13-in. x 9-in. x 2-in. baking dish. Top with beef. In a bowl, combine the cheese, flour and salt. Beat eggs and milk; stir into cheese mixture until blended. Pour over beef. Bake, uncovered, at 350° for 40 minutes or until a knife inserted near the center comes out clean. **Yield:** 10-12 servings.

PERFECT PARTNERS:

Make a tossed salad with avocado slices and tomato wedges; drizzle with creamy ranch dressing. Serve with Chili Rellenos.

I really don't recall where I first came across this recipe. I've had it in my files for years and fix it for my family quite often.
—Carolyn Gorrell
Portales, New Mexico

VEGETABLE BEEF TOSTADAS

3/4 pound ground beef
1 medium onion, thinly sliced
1 medium zucchini, thinly
  sliced
1 can (4 ounces) mushroom
  stems and pieces,
  undrained
1/4 cup chopped celery
2 tablespoons chopped green
  pepper
1/4 teaspoon salt
4 corn tortillas (6 inches)
2 tablespoons vegetable oil
1 cup (4 ounces) shredded
  cheddar cheese
1 medium tomato, chopped
1/2 cup sour cream *or* ranch
  salad dressing
Hot pepper sauce to taste

In a skillet, cook beef over medium heat until no longer pink; drain. Add the onion, zucchini, mushrooms, celery, green pepper and salt. Simmer, uncovered, for 8-10 minutes or until vegetables are tender. Meanwhile, in another skillet, fry tortillas in oil; drain on paper towels. Place the tortillas on a greased baking sheet. Spoon meat mixture onto the center of each. Sprinkle with cheese. Bake at 350° for 3-5 minutes or until cheese is melted. Top with tomato, sour cream and hot pepper sauce. **Yield:** 4 tostadas.

I got this recipe from my mother. In summer, we both prepare this dish often with vegetables from our gardens. Ranch dressing is a tasty topping twist.
—JoNee Koehn
Buhl, Idaho

HELPFUL HINT:

Unless the label states otherwise, store hot pepper sauce at room temperature for up to 1 year. Although the color may change over time, it'll still pack a punch.

SPANISH RICE ENCHILADAS
(Pictured above)

My husband and son love ground beef in every way. It's versatile and delicious in so many recipes. With an assortment of toppings, these enchiladas are a meal by themselves.
—Corine Kirscher
Auburn, Washington

1 **pound ground beef**
1 **envelope taco seasoning,** *divided*
2-1/2 **cups water,** *divided*
1 **package (6.8 ounces) Spanish rice and vermicelli mix**
2 **tablespoons butter** *or* **margarine**
1 **can (14-1/2 ounces) diced tomatoes, undrained**
6 **flour tortillas (10 inches)**
2 **cups (8 ounces) shredded cheddar cheese,** *divided*
1 **can (8 ounces) tomato sauce**
Toppings: diced avocado, sliced ripe olives, shredded lettuce, sour cream, taco sauce

In a skillet, cook beef over medium heat until no longer pink; drain. Set aside 1 tablespoon of taco seasoning; add remaining seasoning to beef. Stir in 3/4 cup water; cover and simmer for 15 minutes. Meanwhile, in a saucepan, saute rice mix in butter over medium heat until golden brown. Add the tomatoes, contents of rice seasoning packet and remaining water. Bring to a boil. Reduce heat; cover and simmer for 15 minutes or until rice is tender. Stir in beef mixture. Spread over tortillas to within 1/2 in. of edge. Sprinkle with 1 cup cheese. Roll up and place seam side down in a greased 13-in. x 9-in. x 2-in. baking dish. Combine tomato sauce and reserved taco seasoning; pour over the enchiladas. Sprinkle with remaining cheese. Cover and bake at 350° for 30 minutes or until heated through. Serve with toppings of your choice. **Yield:** 6 enchiladas.

SEASONED TACO MEAT

1-1/4 pounds ground beef
    2 small onions, finely
      chopped
    1 cup water
    2 tablespoons chili powder
1-1/4 teaspoons salt
  1/4 teaspoon garlic powder
  1/4 teaspoon crushed red
      pepper flakes
  1/4 teaspoon ground cumin

In a skillet, cook beef and onion over medium heat until meat is no longer pink; drain. Add water and seasonings. Bring to a boil. Reduce heat; simmer, uncovered, for 15 minutes or until the water is absorbed. **Yield:** 2-1/2 cups.

SERVING SUGGESTION:

*You can serve Seasoned Taco Meat in a variety of ways.
Use it as a filling for tacos or enchiladas,
or as a topping for pizza or baked potatoes.*

I got this recipe from the restaurant where I work. Everyone in town loves the blend of different seasonings ...and now the secret is out!
—Denise Mumm
Dixon, Iowa

BURRITO STACK

    4 flour tortillas (8 inches)
  1/4 cup vegetable oil
  1/2 pound ground beef
    1 medium onion, chopped
    1 garlic clove, minced
    1 can (16 ounces) refried
      beans
    1 can (4 ounces) chopped
      green chilies, drained
  1/3 cup salsa
  1/4 teaspoon salt
    2 cups (8 ounces) shredded
      Monterey Jack cheese
Toppings: shredded lettuce, diced
  tomato, sour cream

In a large skillet over medium heat, cook tortillas, one at a time, in oil until lightly browned and puffed, about 30 seconds on each side. Drain on paper towels. In the same skillet, cook beef, onion and garlic over medium heat until meat is no longer pink; drain. Stir in beans, chilies, salsa and salt. Place one tortilla in an ungreased 9-in. pie plate. Top with a fourth of the bean mixture. Sprinkle with 1/2 cup cheese. Repeat layers three times. Bake, uncovered, at 350° for 30 minutes or until heated through. Let stand for 5 minutes. Cut into wedges. Garnish with toppings of your choice. **Yield:** 4-6 servings.

SIMPLE SUBSTITUTION:

*Instead of using refried beans in Burrito Stack, use a
15-ounce can of black beans that has been rinsed and drained.
Mash lightly with a fork before adding to the ground beef mixture.*

Folks love the beefy bean and cheese layers in this main dish. I sometimes cut it into smaller wedges to serve as appetizers.
—Catherine Allan
Twin Falls, Idaho

TOMATO CORN BREAD BAKE

1-1/2	**pounds ground beef**
3/4	**cup chopped onion**
2-1/2	**cups canned diced tomatoes, drained**
1-1/2	**cups fresh *or* frozen corn**
1	**teaspoon salt**
1/8	**teaspoon pepper**
1	**package (8-1/2 ounces) corn bread/muffin mix**
1	**egg**
1/3	**cup milk**

In a skillet, cook beef and onion over medium heat until meat is no longer pink; drain. Add tomatoes, corn, salt and pepper; bring to a boil. Transfer to a greased 11-in. x 7-in. x 2-in. baking dish. Combine corn bread mix, egg and milk just until moistened. Spoon over meat mixture. Bake, uncovered, at 400° for 25-30 minutes or until golden brown. **Yield:** 6 servings.

PERFECT PARTNERS:

Combine any leftover tomatoes from Tomato Corn Bread Bake with your favorite salsa and serve with tortilla chips while the casserole bakes.

TAHOE CASSEROLE

2	**pounds ground beef**
1	**large onion, chopped**
1/2	**teaspoon salt**
1/4	**teaspoon pepper**
2	**cans (8 ounces *each*) tomato sauce**
1	**can (15-1/4 ounces) whole kernel corn**
1	**can (14-1/2 ounces) stewed tomatoes**
1	**can (6 ounces) ripe olives, drained and chopped, *divided***
1/2	**teaspoon chili powder**
4	**cups (16 ounces) shredded cheddar cheese**
1	**package (7 ounces) corn tortillas**

In a skillet, cook beef, onion, salt and pepper over medium heat until meat is no longer pink; drain. Add tomato sauce, corn, tomatoes, half of the olives and the chili powder. Bring to a boil. Reduce heat; cover and simmer for 30 minutes. In a greased 13-in. x 9-in. x 2-in. baking dish, layer half of the meat mixture, cheese and tortillas. Repeat layers. Sprinkle with remaining olives. Cover and bake at 350° for 30 minutes. Uncover and bake 15 minutes longer or until heated through. **Yield:** 8 servings.

ENCHILADA PANCAKES

(Pictured above)

1 pound ground beef
1 garlic clove, minced
1 can (10 ounces) diced
    tomatoes and green chilies,
    undrained
1 can (8 ounces) tomato
    sauce
Salt to taste
4 cups biscuit/baking mix
1-1/3 cups all-purpose flour
1-1/3 cups cornmeal
4 cups milk
12 eggs
1-1/2 cups (6 ounces) shredded
    cheddar cheese
1 cup sliced green onions

In a saucepan, cook beef and garlic over medium heat until meat is no longer pink; drain. Add tomatoes, tomato sauce and salt. Bring to a boil. Reduce heat; simmer, uncovered, for 30 minutes. Meanwhile, in a bowl, combine the biscuit mix, flour and cornmeal. Stir in milk just until moistened. Pour batter by 1/2 cupfuls onto a greased hot griddle; spread to 6-in. diameter. Turn when bubbles form on top of pancakes. Cook until the second side is golden brown. Meanwhile, in a skillet, fry eggs until center is completely set. Place two eggs on two pancakes. Top with meat mixture, cheese and onions. **Yield:** 6 servings.

It's customary in the Southwest to serve fried eggs on top of enchiladas. In this recipe, fried eggs and a meaty enchilada sauce top golden pancakes for a tasty twist.
—Marilyn Olander
Tucson, Arizona

ZIPPY BEEF FIESTA

1-1/2 pounds ground beef
1 large onion, chopped
2 tablespoons all-purpose flour
2 tablespoons chili powder
1 teaspoon salt
1/4 teaspoon ground cumin
2 cups water
2 cans (8 ounces *each*) tomato sauce
2 tablespoons vinegar
12 corn tortillas (8 inches)
2 cups (8 ounces) shredded process American cheese
1 can (2-1/4 ounces) sliced ripe olives, drained

In a skillet, cook beef and onion over medium heat until meat is no longer pink; drain. Stir in flour and seasonings until blended. Add the water, tomato sauce and vinegar; cook for 10 minutes or until heated through. Cut each tortilla into six wedges. In a greased 13-in. x 9-in. x 2-in. baking dish, layer half of the tortillas, meat mixture, cheese and olives; repeat layers. Bake, uncovered, at 350° for 35 minutes or until heated through. **Yield:** 8 servings.

TIMELY TIP:

It's quick and easy to cut corn tortillas for Zippy Beef Fiesta if you use a kitchen shears or pizza cutter instead of a knife.

TACO IN A BOWL

1 pound ground beef
1 can (14-1/2 ounces) stewed tomatoes
1 envelope taco seasoning
3/4 cup water
1 can (16 ounces) pork and beans
Corn chips
Toppings: shredded lettuce, chopped tomatoes, chopped onions, sliced ripe olives, shredded cheddar cheese, taco sauce

In a skillet, cook beef over medium heat until no longer pink; drain. Add the tomatoes, taco seasoning and water; mix well. Add pork and beans. Bring to a boil. Reduce heat; cover and simmer for 15 minutes. To serve, place corn chips in four soup bowls. Top with beef mixture and toppings of your choice. **Yield:** 4 servings.

SIMPLE SUBSTITUTIONS:

To make Taco in a Bowl more spicy, use Mexican-style stewed tomatoes and stir in a can of chopped green chilies.

SAN ANTONIO SPECIAL

2 **pounds ground beef**
Salt and pepper
1 **jar (16 ounces) salsa**
1 **can (15 ounces) pinto**
   beans, undrained
1 **can (15 ounces) chili**
   without beans
1 **medium onion, chopped**
1 **block (8 ounces) cheddar**
   cheese, cut into 8 slices

Shape the beef into eight patties. Sprinkle with salt and pepper. In a skillet, cook patties over medium heat until no longer pink. Transfer to a greased 13-in. x 9-in. x 2-in. baking dish; set aside. In a saucepan, combine salsa, beans, chili and onion. Bring to a boil. Reduce heat; simmer, uncovered, for 15 minutes. Pour over patties. Top each patty with a cheese slice. Bake, uncovered, at 350° for 10 minutes or until cheese is melted. **Yield:** 8 servings.

PERFECT PARTNERS:

For a quick side dish to serve with San Antonio Special, cook a 10-ounce package of frozen corn according to package directions, adding 1/4 cup chopped green pepper and 1/4 chopped sweet red pepper. Serve in seeded green or red pepper halves.

I brought this recipe back with me after ordering it a San Antonio restaurant a number of years ago. Everyone enjoys the beef patties topped with salsa and chili.
—Lila Schneider
Wichita, Kansas

TORTILLA TORTE

1 **pound ground beef**
1 **medium onion, chopped**
1 **can (14-1/2 ounces) stewed**
   tomatoes
1 **can (8 ounces) tomato**
   sauce
1 **can (4 ounces) chopped**
   green chilies
1 **envelope taco seasoning**
6 **flour tortillas (10 inches)**
4 **cups (16 ounces) shredded**
   cheddar cheese
Toppings: salsa, guacamole,
   sour cream

In a skillet, cook beef and onion over medium heat until meat is no longer pink; drain. Add the tomatoes, tomato sauce, chilies and taco seasoning; mix well. Layer one tortilla, 1 cup meat sauce and 2/3 cup cheese on a 10-in. microwave-safe pie plate. Repeat layers four times. Top with the remaining tortilla and cheese. Microwave, uncovered, on high for 5-10 minutes or until cheese is melted. Cut into wedges. Serve with toppings of your choice. **Yield:** 4 servings. **Editor's Note:** This recipe was tested in a 700-watt microwave.

HELPFUL HINT:

To seed an avocado, cut lengthwise through the fruit around the pit. Twist the halves in opposite directions to separate them. Remove the pit. Slice the halves and carefully pull the skin away.

This family favorite was given to me by a friend, who received it from her friend in Southern California. I like to serve it with refried beans and Spanish rice.
—JoAnne Radosevich
Ottumwa, Iowa

I came across this recipe while spending a winter in Arizona. Now as soon as we return home each spring, our grandchildren are waiting for me to make these refreshing salads. To save time, bake the salad shells in the morning. Cool; store in an airtight container.
—Betty Johnson
Olympia, Washington

Taco Salad

(Pictured below and on front cover)

2 packages (5.6 ounces *each*) refrigerated taco salad shells*
3 bacon strips, diced
1 pound lean ground beef
2 large onions, chopped
2 garlic cloves, minced
3 tablespoons chili powder
1 teaspoon salt
1 teaspoon ground cumin, optional
1 can (14-1/2 ounces) diced tomatoes, undrained
1 can (16 ounces) refried beans
Toppings: shredded lettuce, chopped tomatoes, salsa, sour cream, guacamole

Prepare taco salad shells according to package directions; set aside. In a skillet, cook bacon until crisp; remove with a slotted spoon to paper towels to drain. In the drippings, cook beef, onions, garlic and seasonings over medium heat until meat is no longer pink. Stir in tomatoes. Bring to a boil. Reduce heat; cover and simmer for 10 minutes. Stir in beans; heat through, about 5 minutes. Spoon about 1/3 cup meat mixture into each salad shell. Top with lettuce, about 1/4 cup meat mixture, tomatoes, salsa, sour cream, guacamole and bacon. **Yield:** 8 servings. ***Editor's Note:** 10 taco shells can be substituted for the salad shells. Fill each with 1/2 cup meat mixture and bacon. Add toppings of your choice.

BLACK BEAN BURRITOS

1 pound ground beef
1/4 cup chopped onion
1 can (15 ounces) black
  beans, rinsed and drained
1 cup salsa
16 corn *or* flour tortillas
  (6 to 8 inches)
2 cups (8 ounces) shredded
  cheddar *or* Monterey Jack
  cheese
Sour cream and sliced ripe olives,
  optional

In a skillet, cook beef and onion over medium heat until meat is no longer pink; drain. Add beans and salsa; mix well. Bring to a boil. Reduce heat; simmer, uncovered, for 5 minutes. Warm the tortillas; spoon 1/4 cup of the beef mixture off-center on each. Sprinkle with cheese. Top with sour cream and olives if desired. Fold the sides and ends over filling and roll up. Serve immediately. **Yield:** 16 burritos.

PERFECT PARTNERS:

Try this easy fried ice cream—scoop 1/2-cup balls of vanilla ice cream into muffin cups; freeze for 15 minutes. Roll in crushed cinnamon-toast-flavored sweetened cereal. Cover and freeze. When ready to serve, place each ice cream ball in a serving dish; drizzle with warmed honey.

BAKED NACHOS

2 pounds ground beef
3 cups (12 ounces) shredded
  Co-Jack cheese, *divided*
3 cups salsa
1 package (10 ounces) frozen
  corn, thawed
1 cup (8 ounces) sour cream
1 to 2 tablespoons chili
  powder
1 teaspoon ground cumin
6 cups tortilla chips

In a skillet, cook beef over medium heat until no longer pink; drain. Stir in 2 cups cheese, salsa, corn, sour cream, chili powder and cumin; mix well. Pour half into a greased 13-in. x 9-in. x 2-in. baking dish. Top with half of the chips; repeat layers. Bake, uncovered, at 350° for 25 minutes or until heated though. Sprinkle with the remaining cheese. Bake 5 minutes longer or until cheese is melted. **Yield:** 8 servings.

My husband and I took a batch of these burritos to friends of ours who moved into a new home. It's a quick and easy recipe everyone enjoys.
—Emily Miller
Massillon, Ohio

My family loves any type of Mexican food, so I'm always in search of something different. In this recipe, nachos become a main-dish casserole.
—Janice Lyhane
Marysville, Kansas

Sweet 'n' Savory Enchiladas

1 can (14-1/2 ounces) whole tomatoes, undrained
2 medium onions, cut into wedges
2 garlic cloves
1-1/2 teaspoons dried oregano
1-1/4 teaspoons salt
1 teaspoon pepper
1/2 teaspoon ground cumin
4-1/2 teaspoons vegetable oil
1 cup whipping cream
2 pounds ground beef
1 pound bulk pork sausage
12 flour tortillas (8 inches)
3/4 cup shredded Colby cheese
1/2 cup shredded Monterey Jack cheese
1/2 cup thinly sliced green onions

In a blender or food processor, combine tomatoes, onions, garlic and seasonings. Cover and process until smooth; transfer to a saucepan. Add oil; bring to a boil. Cook and stir for 3 minutes or until thickened. Remove from the heat. Gradually add a small amount of hot tomato mixture to cream, stirring constantly. Return all to pan; set aside. In a skillet, cook beef and sausage over medium heat until no longer pink; drain. Stir in 2/3 cup of the tomato cream sauce. Spoon meat mixture onto tortillas. Roll up and place seam side down in a greased 13-in. x 9-in. x 2-in. baking dish. Pour remaining sauce over enchiladas. Bake, uncovered, at 350° for 20 minutes or until heated though. Sprinkle with cheeses. Bake 10 minutes longer or until cheese is melted. Sprinkle with onions. **Yield:** 12 enchiladas.

Helpful Hint:

*Purchase green onions with fresh-looking tops and clean white ends.
Store them wrapped in the refrigerator for up to 5 days.
For longer storage, freeze sliced or chopped green onions for
up to 1 year. One green onion equals about 2 tablespoons sliced.*

Picadillo

1 pound ground beef
1 medium onion, chopped
2 garlic cloves, minced
1 can (14-1/2 ounces) diced tomatoes, undrained
1 medium tart apple, peeled and chopped
1/3 cup raisins
1 tablespoon chili powder
3/4 teaspoon salt
1/2 teaspoon ground cumin
1/4 teaspoon ground allspice
1/4 teaspoon pepper

In a large skillet, cook beef, onion and garlic over medium heat until meat is no longer pink; drain. Add the tomatoes, apple, raisins and seasonings; mix well. Cover and simmer for 10 minutes. **Yield:** 4 servings.

BEEF AND BEAN CHIMICHANGAS
(Pictured above and on page 286)

1-1/2 **pounds ground beef**
   1 **medium onion, chopped**
   1 **medium green pepper, chopped**
   1 **garlic clove, minced**
   2 **cans (16 ounces *each*) refried beans**
1/2 **cup shredded cheddar cheese**
1/2 **cup taco sauce**
  16 **flour tortillas (10 inches)**
Vegetable oil
Toppings: shredded lettuce, sour cream, chopped ripe olives, chopped tomatoes, additional cheddar cheese

In a large skillet, cook beef, onion, green pepper and garlic over medium heat until the meat is no longer pink; drain. Add the beans, cheese and taco sauce. Cook and stir until cheese is melted, about 5 minutes. Remove from the heat. Spoon about 1/3 cup off-center on each tortilla. Fold up edge nearest filling; fold in both sides and roll up. Secure with a toothpick. In a large skillet, fry tortillas, folded side down, in oil for 2-3 minutes or until lightly browned. Turn; cook 2-3 minutes longer. Drain on paper towels. Serve with toppings of your choice. **Yield:** 16 chimichangas.

SHAPING CHIMICHANGAS

Spoon filling off-center on tortilla. Starting with the edge closest to the filling, fold over to cover filling. Fold in sides and roll up. Secure with a toothpick.

My family never gets bored with what I serve for dinner, because I'm always trying new recipes. These chimichangas, though, are often requested, especially by our teenage daughter.
—Janice Lyons
Eagle River, Wisconsin

This slightly spicy casserole was always a hit at our potlucks at work, so I finally asked the co-worker who brought it for the recipe. Now I make it for my family with the same success.
—LeeAnn McCue
West Springfield,
Massachusetts

CREAMY LAYERED CASSEROLE

1 pound ground beef
1 tablespoon finely chopped onion
2 cans (8 ounces *each*) tomato sauce
1 can (2-1/4 ounces) sliced ripe olives, drained
1/2 teaspoon garlic salt
1 cup small-curd cottage cheese
1 cup (8 ounces) sour cream
1 can (4 ounces) chopped green chilies
4 cups crushed tortilla chips
2 cups (8 ounces) shredded Monterey Jack cheese
Additional tortilla chips

In a skillet, cook beef and onion over medium heat until meat is no longer pink; drain. Add tomato sauce, olives and garlic salt; set aside. In a bowl, combine cottage cheese, sour cream and chilies; mix well. In a greased 11-in. x 7-in. x 2-in. baking dish, layer half of the tortilla chips, meat mixture, cottage cheese mixture and Monterey Jack cheese. Repeat layers. Top with additional tortilla chips. Bake, uncovered, at 350° for 40 minutes or until heated though. **Yield:** 6 servings.

Living near the Mexican border, we've developed a love of spicy cuisine. I came up with this recipe by mixing and matching different foods.
—Marilyn Long
Spring Valley, California

PICANTE EGG ROLLS

2 pounds ground beef
2 cups (8 ounces) shredded cheddar cheese
1/2 cup picante sauce
1 envelope chili seasoning
1 teaspoon garlic powder
2 packages (16 ounces *each*) egg roll wrappers*
1 egg, beaten
Vegetable oil for frying
SAUCE:
1 cup picante sauce
1/2 cup sour cream

In a skillet, cook beef over medium heat until no longer pink; drain. Remove from the heat. Stir in cheese, picante sauce, chili seasoning and garlic powder. Place an egg roll wrapper on work surface with one point facing you. Place 1/4 cup filling in center. Fold bottom third of wrapper over filling. Fold in sides. Brush top point with egg. Roll up to seal. Repeat with remaining wrappers and filling. In a large saucepan, heat 1 in. of oil to 375°. Fry egg rolls, three at a time, for 3-4 minutes or until golden brown. Drain on paper towels. Combine sauce ingredients; serve with egg rolls. **Yield:** 2-1/2 dozen, (1-1/2 cups of sauce). ***Editor's Note:** Fill egg roll wrappers one at a time, keeping the others covered until ready to use. Egg rolls may be reheated in a microwave for 2-1/2 to 3 minutes.

TIMELY TIP:

Instead of frying Picante Egg Rolls, brush them with oil, place on a baking sheet and bake at 375° until golden brown.

PITA TACOS

1 pound ground beef
Salt and pepper to taste
Vegetable oil for frying
    4 whole pita breads (6 inches)
    4 cups shredded lettuce
    2 medium tomatoes, diced
    1 medium onion, chopped
Ranch salad dressing

In a skillet, cook beef over medium heat until no longer pink; drain. Sprinkle with salt and pepper; set aside. In another skillet, heat 1/4 in. of oil. Fry the pita breads until puffed and golden brown. Drain on paper towels. Cut each bread in half. Fill with beef mixture, lettuce, tomatoes and onion. Drizzle with salad dressing. **Yield:** 4 tacos.

ZESTY CORN CAKES

1 pound ground beef
1 medium onion, chopped
1 small green pepper, chopped
1 celery rib, chopped
1 can (6 ounces) tomato paste
1/3 cup water
2 garlic cloves, minced
1 teaspoon chili powder
1 teaspoon salt
1/4 teaspoon pepper
CHEESE SAUCE:
    8 ounces process American cheese, cubed
2/3 cup evaporated milk
1/2 teaspoon chili powder
CORN CAKES:
    1 package (8-1/2 ounces) corn bread/muffin mix
1/2 cup evaporated milk
1/4 cup water
    1 egg, beaten
    2 tablespoons butter *or* margarine, melted

In a skillet, cook beef over medium heat until no longer pink; drain. Add the next nine ingredients; mix well. Bring to a boil. Reduce heat; simmer, uncovered, for 2 minutes or until thickened. In a saucepan, combine sauce ingredients. Cook and stir over low heat until cheese is melted. In a bowl, combine corn cake ingredients just until moistened. Pour 1/4 cupfuls of batter onto a hot greased griddle. Turn when bubbles form on top of cakes. Cook until the second side is golden brown. Place a corn cake on four serving plates. Top each with 1/4 cup of filling. Repeat layers once. Serve with cheese sauce. **Yield:** 4 servings.

SAVORY SAUCES & GRAVIES

Is your family enthusiastic about savory sauces and crazy about down-home gravies? They'll relish these meaty selections that deliciously top off pasta, potatoes, rice, hot dogs and more. You'll love their fast-to-fix convenience!

GROUND BEEF GRAVY (P. 311)

BACHELOR'S SPAGHETTI SAUCE (P. 309)
CHILI DOG SAUCE (P. 309)

TOMATO HAMBURGER TOPPING

(Pictured above)

I created this recipe a few years ago, and it earned me a prize in a local cooking contest. You can also serve the topping over hot cooked noodles.
—Irene Smith
Lidgerwood,
North Dakota

1 **pound ground beef**
1 **medium onion, chopped**
1 **medium green pepper, chopped**
1 **medium tomato, seeded and chopped**
1 **cup water**
1 **can (6 ounces) tomato paste**
1/2 **teaspoon garlic powder**
1/2 **teaspoon salt**
1/4 **teaspoon pepper**
Hot cooked wild and long grain rice

In a large skillet, cook the beef and onion over medium heat until meat is no longer pink; drain. Add the green pepper, tomato, water, tomato paste, garlic powder, salt and pepper. Simmer, uncovered, for 15 minutes or until heated through. Serve over rice. **Yield:** 3 cups.

SEEDING A TOMATO

Cut tomato in half widthwise. Gently squeeze each half over a bowl to remove seeds and excess juice.

TIMELY TIP:

Tomato Hamburger Topping would keep well in the freezer in an airtight container for up to 3 months.

BACHELOR'S SPAGHETTI SAUCE

(Pictured on page 307)

1 pound ground beef
1/2 pound fresh mushrooms, chopped
1 large onion, chopped
2 garlic cloves, minced
4 medium tomatoes, chopped
2 cans (6 ounces *each*) tomato paste
1 cup water
2 tablespoons soy sauce
3 bay leaves
2 teaspoons *each* dried basil, oregano and parsley flakes
1 teaspoon salt
1 teaspoon honey
1/2 teaspoon *each* dried marjoram, thyme and rosemary, crushed
Dash pepper
Hot cooked spaghetti

In a large skillet, cook beef, mushrooms, onion and garlic over medium heat until meat is no longer pink; drain. Add the tomatoes, tomato paste, water, soy sauce and seasonings. Cover and simmer for 20 minutes or until heated through. Discard bay leaves. Serve over spaghetti. **Yield:** 7 cups.

TIMELY TIP:

Buy a pair of tweezers and keep it in your kitchen drawer. Use it to easily remove bay leaves from sauces and soups.

My husband, Eric, perfected this sauce when he was still single. He shared the recipe with me after we got married. Now everyone in the family loves it, no matter what their marital status!
—Rhandi Tyssen
Calgary, Alberta

CHILI DOG SAUCE

(Pictured on page 307)

2-1/2 pounds ground beef
3 medium onions, chopped
1 medium green pepper, chopped
1 garlic clove, minced
1 bottle (28 ounces) ketchup
1/4 cup chili powder
Hot dogs, heated
Hot dog buns, split
Shredded cheddar cheese

In a large saucepan, cook beef, onions, green pepper and garlic over medium heat until meat is no longer pink; drain. Stir in ketchup and chili powder. Simmer, uncovered, for 2-1/2 hours or until thick and bubbly, stirring occasionally. Serve over hot dogs in buns; sprinkle with cheese. **Yield:** 6 cups.

HELPFUL HINT:

To easily turn hot dogs on a grill, thread them end to end onto metal skewers.

This big batch of sauce disappears quickly. Why not put some sauce into pretty jars and take it to your next cookout? You're sure to be the hit of the barbecue.
—Karen Ann Bland
Gove, Kansas

CONEY ISLAND SAUCE

4 cups water
1-1/2 pounds ground beef
1 medium onion, chopped
1 can (28 ounces) tomato
sauce
2 tablespoons brown sugar
1-1/2 teaspoons chili powder
1/2 teaspoon salt
1/4 teaspoon pepper
Hot dogs, heated
Hot dog buns, split

In a large saucepan, bring water to a boil. Carefully crumble beef into water. Add onion. Boil until meat is no longer pink; drain. Add the tomato sauce, brown sugar, chili powder, salt and pepper. Simmer, uncovered, for 15 minutes or until heated through. Serve over hot dogs in buns. **Yield:** 4 cups.

BEEFY TACO SAUCE

1 pound ground beef
1 large onion, chopped
1/2 cup chopped green pepper
1 garlic clove, minced
2 cans (15 ounces *each*)
tomato sauce
1 tablespoon chili powder
1/4 teaspoon pepper
1/4 teaspoon hot pepper sauce

In a large saucepan, cook the beef, onion, green pepper and garlic over medium heat until meat is no longer pink; drain. Stir in the remaining ingredients. Simmer, uncovered, for 15 minutes or until thick and bubbly, stirring occasionally. **Yield:** 5 cups.

THICK 'N' HEARTY PASTA SAUCE

1 pound ground beef
1 jar (28 ounces) spaghetti
sauce
1 can (8 ounces) mushroom
stems and pieces, drained
25 slices pepperoni (about
1-1/2 ounces)
1 small onion, chopped,
optional
Hot cooked pasta

In a large saucepan, cook the beef over medium heat until no longer pink; drain. Add spaghetti sauce, mushrooms, pepperoni and onion if desired. Cover and simmer for 1 hour or until thickened. Serve over pasta. **Yield:** 5 cups.

SIMPLE SUBSTITUTION:

*Thick 'n' Hearty Pasta Sauce can also be made with 1/2 pound
Italian sausage instead of the pepperoni. Brown it along with the beef.*

GROUND BEEF GRAVY

(Pictured below and on page 306)

1 pound ground beef
1 can (14-1/2 ounces) beef broth, *divided*
1 small onion, chopped
2 tablespoons dried parsley flakes
1 tablespoon dried basil
1 teaspoon garlic powder
1 teaspoon seasoned salt
1/4 to 1/2 teaspoon pepper
2 tablespoons cornstarch
Hot mashed potatoes *or* cooked pasta

In a large skillet, cook beef over medium heat until no longer pink; drain. Add 1-1/2 cups beef broth, onion, parsley, basil, garlic powder, seasoned salt and pepper. Simmer, uncovered, for 5-10 minutes or until onion is tender. In a small bowl, combine the cornstarch and remaining broth until smooth. Stir into beef mixture. Bring to a boil; cook and stir for 2 minutes or until thickened. Serve over mashed potatoes or pasta. **Yield:** 3 cups.

HELPFUL HINT:

To prevent lumps when thickening with cornstarch, don't mix cornstarch with a hot liquid. Combine it with a cold or room temperature liquid and gradually add it to the hot mixture in a skillet or saucepan.

While I was growing up, this is the dinner Mom let me make once a week. Now when I prepare it for my family, I'm reminded of happy times with Mom in the kitchen.
—Diane Krasley
Graterford,
Pennsylvania

❖ GENERAL RECIPE INDEX ❖

This handy index lists every recipe by food category and/or major ingredient.

APPETIZERS & SNACKS
Barbecue Meatballs, 19
Beef 'n' Egg Pockets, 21
Cheese Meatballs, 17
Cheesy Pizza Fondue, 13
Easy Egg Rolls, 17
Hawaiian Roll-Ups, 20
Hearty Cheese Dip, 20
Kid-Size Pizzas, 272
Mexican Fiesta Platter, 18
Mini Crescent Burgers, 12
Mushroom Burger Cups, 15
Party Meatballs, 12
Picante Egg Rolls, 304
Poppy Seed Squares, 14
Ranch Mushroom Dip, 16
Slow Cooker Cheese Dip, 66
Southwestern Bean Dip, 19
Spaghetti Meatballs, 27
Veggie Nachos, 15
Zucchini Pizza Bites, 16

APPLES
Apple Meatballs, 34
Autumn Meatballs, 47
Picadillo, 302
Stuffed Acorn Squash, 174

APRICOTS
Apricot Meatballs, 29
Curry Meat Loaf, 31

BACON
Bacon Burger Puffs, 95
Bacon Nut Meatballs, 31
Bacon-Wrapped Hamburgers, 108
Hawaiian Roll-Ups, 20

BARLEY *(see Rice & Barley)*

BEANS
Appetizers and Snacks
  Mexican Fiesta Platter, 18
  Southwestern Bean Dip, 19
Main Dishes
  Beef and Baked Beans, 214
  Beef and Bean
    Chimichangas, 303
  Beef Potato Supper, 183
  Biscuit-Topped Beef 'n'
    Beans, 201
  Biscuits and Beans, 206
  Black Bean Burritos, 301

Burrito Bake, 288
Burrito Stack, 295
Chili Mac, 61
Chili-Topped Taters, 191
Classic Red Beans 'n' Rice, 218
Corn Bread Beef Bake, 203
Cowboy Baked Beans, 196
Green Bean Beef Bake, 184
Green Bean Burger Pie, 273
Hungry Man's Dinner, 208
Kidney Beans and Rice, 212
Lima Bean Bake, 217
Mexican Lasagna, 228
One-Pot Casserole, 208
Pork 'n' Beans Bake, 220
Quick Tamale Casserole, 223
Ranch Beans, 203
Refried Bean Pizza, 281
San Antonio Special, 299
Snowcapped Casserole, 178
Southwest Skillet, 219
Southwestern Deep-Dish
    Pizza, 282
Stovetop Pinto Beans, 222
Taco in a Bowl, 298
Tasty Green Bean Bake, 253
Texas-Style Skillet, 289
Three-Bean Bake, 213
Tropical Beans, 204
Two-Pot Dinner, 60
Salads and Sandwiches
  Corn Bread Salad, 79
  Layered Chalupa Salad, 89
  Taco Salad, 300
  Western Range Sandwiches, 105
Soup, Stews and Chili
  Black Bean Potato Chili, 151
  Cabbage Patch Stew, 154
  Green Bean Chili, 122
  Mixed Bean Soup, 133
  Nacho Chili, 143
  Pinto Pepperoni Chili, 132
  Pork and Beans Stew, 152
  Steak and Bean Chili, 130

BREADS *(also see Corn Bread; Sandwiches)*
Breakfast Rolls, 77
Cheeseburger Loaf, 89
Chili in Biscuit Bowls, 84
Enchilada Pancakes, 297
Fiesta Biscuit Squares, 79
Mushroom Burger Stromboli, 83
Pinwheels with Vegetable Cream
    Sauce, 80
Rustic Beef Bread, 85
Sauerkraut Beef Buns, 76

Stuffed Bread Boat, 78
Taco Muffins, 82
Zesty Burger Puffs, 86

BROCCOLI
Beefy Broccoli Pie, 276
Broccoli Beef Lo Mein, 238
Broccoli Beef Supper, 162
Broccoli Biscuit Squares, 176
Broccoli Meat Roll, 24
Cheesy Broccoli Rice, 213
Golden Broccoli Bake, 181

BURRITOS & CHIMICHANGAS
(also see Enchiladas; Tacos & Tostadas)
Beef and Bean Chimichangas, 303
Black Bean Burritos, 301
Cheesy Chimichangas, 292
Green Chili Flautas, 288

CABBAGE & SAUERKRAUT
Cabbage Casserole, 168
Cabbage Patch Stew, 154
Country Cabbage Soup, 139
Cranberry Meat Loaf, 47
Easy Egg Rolls, 17
German Skillet, 199
Meatball Cabbage Rolls, 68
Reuben Burgers, 100
Reuben Loaf, 51
Sauerkraut Beef Buns, 76

CASSEROLES *(also see Lasagna; Meat Pies & Quiches; Microwave Recipes; Slow Cooker Recipes)*
Beans and Rice
  Baked Beef and Brown
    Rice, 210
  Baked Black-Eyed Peas, 207
  Beefy Spanish Rice, 197
  Biscuit-Topped Beef 'n'
    Beans, 201
  Biscuits and Beans, 206
  Cajun Rice Dish, 196
  Cheesy Broccoli Rice, 213
  Corn Bread Beef Bake, 203
  Covered Dish Dinner, 200
  Cowboy Baked Beans, 196
  Creamy Vegetable Rice, 221
  Crunchy Rice Casserole, 198
  Lima Bean Bake, 217
  Mushroom Wild Rice, 211
  One-Pot Casserole, 208

❖ ALPHABETICAL INDEX ❖

Refer to this index for a complete alphabetical listing of all the recipes in this book.

Family-Favorite Soup, 125
Farmhouse Dinner, 173
Fast Beef and Rice, 221
Fast Minestrone, 153
Fiesta Biscuit Squares, 79
Finnish Meat Pie, 259
Firemen's Meat Loaf, 38
Five-Vegetable Delight, 183
Four-Star Chili, 128
Frankburgers, 117
French Onion Meat Loaf, 50

G

Garden Skillet, 176
Garden's Plenty Meatballs, 40
German Skillet, 199
Glazed Beef Loaf, 28
Golden Broccoli Bake, 181
Grandma's Corn Stew, 144
Grandma's Potpie, 260
Grandma's Sloppy Joes, 96
Grandmother's Chowder, 141
Green Bean Beef Bake, 184
Green Bean Burger Pie, 273
Green Bean Chili, 122
Green Chili Flautas, 288
Green Chili Stew, 146
Green Onion Burgers, 110
Ground Beef Gravy, 311
Ground Beef Stew, 59
Ground Beef Vermicelli, 240
Gumbo Joes, 93

H

Hamburger 'n' Fries Dinner, 179
Hamburger Garden Soup, 145
Hamburger Hash Browns, 190
Hamburger Hash, 197
Hamburger Hoagie, 92
Hamburger Noodle Bake, 237
Hamburger Pie, 277
Hamburger Rice Soup, 129
Hamburger Supper, 57
Harvest Stir-Fry, 186
Hash Brown Pizza, 276
Hash Brown Quiche, 261
Hawaiian Roll-Ups, 20
Heartwarming Chili, 148
Hearty Baked Stew, 123
Hearty Cheese Dip, 20
Hearty Mushroom Loaf, 42
Hearty Skillet Supper, 216
Hearty Spinach Salad, 76
Hearty Wild Rice, 63
Herb Garden Pasta, 233
Herbed Pasties, 282
Herbed Vegetable Medley, 169
Hobo Stew, 66
Homemade Pinwheel Noodles, 255

Hungry Man's Dinner, 208
Hunter's Stew, 125
Hurry-Up Casserole, 190

I

Italian Burgers, 114
Italian Pasta Supper, 251
Italian Tortellini Salad, 85
Italian Wedding Soup, 136

J

Jalapeno Swiss Burgers, 119

K

Kid-Pleasing Spaghetti, 244
Kid-Size Pizzas, 272
Kidney Beans and Rice, 212

L

Lasagna in a Bun, 108
Lasagna Loaf, 45
Layered Beef Casserole, 167
Layered Chalupa Salad, 89
Lazy Lasagna, 231
Lemon-Herb Gyros, 109
Lima Bean Bake, 217

M

Macaroni Royale, 246
Make-Ahead Meatball Salad, 86
Mandarin Beef Skillet, 204
Mashed Potato Soup, 152
Meal in a Packet, 172
Meat and Potato Pie, 278
Meat 'n' Potato Stew, 153
Meat Loaf Dinner, 25
Meat Loaf Gyros, 102
Meat Loaf Stew, 43
Meat Loaf with Sweet Potatoes, 41
Meatball Cabbage Rolls, 68
Meatball Noodle Soup, 158
Meatball Party Sub, 97
Meatball Sausage Dinner, 180
Meatballs with Mushroom
   Sauce, 46
Meatballs with Pepper Sauce, 25
Meatballs with Spaetzle, 39
Meaty Garden Salad, 82
Meaty Macaroni, 229
Meaty Pita Pockets, 99
Meaty Tomato Soup, 59
Meaty Vegetable Chili, 147

Mexicali Meat Loaf, 27
Mexican Fiesta Platter, 18
Mexican Lasagna, 228
Microwave Classic Chili, 144
Microwave Meat Loaf, 51
Mini Beef Rolls, 117
Mini Crescent Burgers, 12
Mini Italian Meat Loaves, 26
Minted Meatballs, 44
Mixed Bean Soup, 133
Mixed Veggie Casserole, 182
Mock Pot Roast, 36
Mock Ravioli, 237
Mom's Mostaccioli, 238
Monterey Jack Meatballs, 32
Mushroom Burger Cups, 15
Mushroom Burger Pockets, 264
Mushroom Burger Stew, 158
Mushroom Burger Stromboli, 83
Mushroom Wild Rice, 211

N

Nacho Chili, 143
Nacho Meatballs, 36
No-Bean Chili, 73
Nutty Beef Turnovers, 269

O

Olive Beef Pasta, 240
Olive Raisin Rice, 214
One-Pot Casserole, 208
Onion Beef Fettuccine, 254
Onion Loose-Meat
   Sandwiches, 109
Open-Faced Pizza Burgers, 107
Oriental Chili, 138
Oriental Patties, 103
Oriental Rice, 223
Oven Meatball Stew, 127
Oven Spaghetti, 249

P

Parmesan Penne, 229
Party Meatballs, 12
Pepper Beef with Cashews, 187
Pepper Cheese Patties, 94
Pepper Soup, 147
Pepperoni Pasta, 242
Pepperoni Stromboli, 112
Peppy Meatball Subs, 100
Perfect Pronto Pizza, 279
Personal Pizzas, 258
Picadillo, 302
Picante Egg Rolls, 304
Pinto Pepperoni Chili, 132
Pinwheels with Vegetable Cream
   Sauce, 80

❖ REFERENCE INDEX ❖

Use this index as a guide to the many helpful hints, step-by-step instructions and timely tips throughout the book.